98285

D0489251

658.7

Purchasing and Supply Management

Purchasing and Supply Management

P. J. H. Baily

BSc(Econ), ACIS, FInst PS

FIFTH EDITION

INTERNATIONAL THOMSON BUSINESS PRESS

I ⓣ P An International Thomson Publishing Company

London • Bonn • Boston • Johannesburg • Madrid • Melbourne • Mexico City • New York • Paris
Singapore • Tokyo • Toronto • Albany, NY • Belmont, CA • Cincinnati, OH • Detroit, MI

Purchasing and Supply Management

Copyright ©1963, 1987 P.J.H. Baily

 A division of International Thomson Publishing Inc.
The ITP logo is a trademark under licence

All rights reserved. No part of this work which is copyright may be reproduced or used in any form or by any means – graphic, electronic, or mechanical, including photocopying, recording, taping or information storage and retrieval systems – without the written permission of the Publisher, except in accordance with the provisions of the Copyright Designs and Patents Act 1988.

Whilst the Publisher has taken all reasonable care in the preparation of this book the Publisher makes no representation, express or implied, with regard to the accuracy of the information contained in this book and cannot accept any legal responsibility or liability for any errors or omissions from the book or the consequences thereof.

Products and services that are referred to in this book may be either trademarks and/or registered trademarks of their respective owners. The Publisher/s and Author/s make no claim to these trademarks.

British Library Cataloguing-in-Publication Data
A catalogue record for this book is available from the British Library

**First edition published by Chapman & Hall 1963, Second edition 1969, Third edition 19
reprinted 1976, Fourth edition 1978, Fifth edition 1987, reprinted 1990, 1991, 1992.
Reprinted by International Thomson Business Press 1997**

Typeset by Scarborough Typesetting Services
Printed in the UK by TJ International, Padstow, Cornwall

ISBN 0-412-28940-7

International Thomson Business Press
Berkshire House
168–173 High Holborn
London WC1V 7AA
UK

International Thomson Business Press
20 Park Plaza
13th Floor
Boston MA 02116
USA

http://www.itbp.com

Contents

vi   Contents

Preface

This is virtually a new book, although launched under an old title. The new improved version of *Purchasing and Supply Management* includes new chapters on quality assurance, buying abroad, constructional contracts, supplying merchandise for resale, supplying the public sector, and cost reduction in purchasing and supply. The coverage of the legal aspects of purchasing has been updated and extended, and in fact the whole work has been revised and reconstructed. To avoid making the book too long, case studies have been dropped. They are not so hard to find as they used to be.

The book is intended to provide a general introduction to purchasing and supply management both for students and for practitioners. Those who are studying purchasing, stores or stock control for BTEC diplomas and certificates, or for the Association of Supervisors in Purchasing and Supply (ASPS) qualifications, or who are starting on professional studies for the Institute of Purchasing & Supply (IPS) should find it useful.

The first edition of this book was written many years ago, in the dark ages before the Institute of Purchasing and Supply existed, and before Farmer, Compton, Stevens, Jessop and others had published their learned works. I had been asked by institutions, now called Leeds Polytechnic and the University of Bradford, to lecture part-time on purchasing to large and articulate classes of people studying management. This taught me a lot about what I did not know about purchasing. Teaching is an educational process, for the teacher. Everyone wanted a textbook to refer to, and there wasn't one. I complained about this to a publisher I chanced to meet, who said 'Well, why not write one?'

So I did. The first edition became the first book published in Britain to cover the field of purchasing and supply; and partly as a consequence, its author became the first full time lecturer in this subject in Britain.

Since then, a number of books have appeared which cover purchasing, stock control and stores management in more depth and detail. But there is still a need for a general introduction, which this book aims to provide.

I also wanted to give the person actually working in purchasing and supply something to refer to: the sort of book I wished I had been able to find in my early days in purchasing along the Scotswood Road. So many changes are occurring in purchasing and supply management that it is hard to keep up. I hope this new edition will help.

Peter Baily
Cardiff, 1987

PART ONE

Fundamentals of purchasing and supply

Purchasing, supply and materials management

The winds of change are blowing in purchasing and supply. Continued upgrading of conformance quality standards, just-in-time approaches to material availability, long-term relationships with fewer suppliers and a win–win approach to negotiations instead of the more traditional adversarial or win–lose approach, are just some of the changes in the way procurement is managed. These changes are helping organizations to survive and succeed in a very competitive world.

Purchasing and supply is a necessary function in almost every organization, from the private household to the national government. This book is mainly about larger organizations which have purchasing and supply departments, but purchasing and supply is just as important in small organizations which do not employ full-time people to do the work, and it is hoped that the latter may also find the book useful.

SMALLER ORGANIZATIONS

Paul Bocuse, a world-famous French cook, employs about 50 people at his main restaurant; not enough to have a purchase department. But every day when he is in residence he shops personally at the Lyon market. According to him, 'a good cook is someone who knows how to buy produce'. Franco Taruschio, who runs what is perhaps the best restaurant in Wales, also gets to the market in Abergavenny early to buy the best on offer.

As we read in the *Good Food Guide 1985*, 'nearly all the restaurants in this book take as much care over their ingredients as they do in the cooking. They have supported local producers, cajoled people back to

the land, created new jobs by providing a market for small-scale operations that would otherwise be unable to compete with big factory
farms.' This close attention to buying, and to developing new supply
sources if existing sources do not meet requirements, are just the sort of
policies adopted by large supply departments.

THE PROCESS DEFINED

Organizational purchasing is the process by which organizations define
their needs for goods and services; identify and compare the supplies
and suppliers available to them; negotiate with sources of supply or in
some other way arrive at agreed terms of trading; make contracts and
place orders; and finally receive, accept and pay for the goods and
services required.

Purchasing is closely associated with other organizational functions,
such as inventory management, stores operation, and transport. Production planning and control, in manufacturing organizations, and
merchandizing, in distributive organizations, have to work closely with
buying. Often some or all of these functions are combined with the
purchasing function under a single head, the materials manager or
supply manager.

Traditionally, purchasing objectives were defined as: to obtain the
right quality of goods, in the right quantity, at the right time, from the
right supplier, at the right price. These five 'rights' were often thought
of in the context of a static environment, so that by a series of successive
approximations it would eventually be possible to arrive at the final
right answer for each one.

But in highly competitive world markets the environment is not static
but dynamic, tending not towards equilibrium but always towards
something new. Purchasing objectives continually need to be updated
and revised. Arriving at the final right answer for some old product just
as it is discontinued does nothing for the competitive position of an
organization.

Proactive, rather than reactive; dynamic, rather than static, is the way
in which the purchasing role is now conceived. Better quality, in more
suitable quantities, just in time for requirements, from better suppliers,
at prices which continue to improve, are the sort of aims set by the
dynamic purchasing function today.

A GLANCE BACKWARDS

Long before the large organization appeared with its functionally
specialized departments, people bought and sold. Buying, that is

acquiring goods and services in return for a price, dates back before the invention of written records. So also does selling, the disposal of goods and services in return for a price. It is likely that human communities have always bought and sold and that culturally and materially they have benefited from these transactions.

Archaeological evidence shows that trade occurred between the pre-historic tribes of Britain's stone age. The distinctive products of a flint axe factory at Langdale in the Lake District have been found hundreds of miles away in South Wales. Did Langdale send out travelling sales-men, or did South Wales have tribal buyers searching the land for better buys in stone age weaponry? We do not know. But what *is* known is that among the earliest things to be written down were stock records and accounts of commercial transactions. In days when literature and history were still being recited from memory, the pioneer develop-ments in written record, whether incised on baked clay in cuneiform or carved or painted in pictographs, dealt with purchases, stocks and sales.

When books were invented, they dealt at first with higher matters than trade. Yet in the Bible itself, the oldest of all best-sellers, we read: 'It is naught, it is naught, saith the buyer; but when he is gone his way then he rejoiceth' (*Proverbs* 20.14). In Chaucer's *Canterbury Tales*, one of the oldest works in the canon of English literature, several of the horse-back pilgrims are described as 'purchasours' or (since the ruling classes had previously spoken a kind of French) 'achatours'. No salesmen made the pilgrimage.

Many of Chaucer's pilgrims have occupational titles which with the passage of time have come to sound more like surnames. There was a 'manciple', for instance, described as an expert catering buyer. There was a 'reeve', who could 'better than his lord purchase', and no auditor could catch him out. The merchant was stately in bargaining, and as for the sergeant of law,

So great a purchasour was nowhere none . . .
Nowhere so busy a man as he there was,
And yet he seemed busier than he was.

There are buyers today who have never made a pilgrimage and would not know a reeve from a manciple of whom the same could be said.

THE GROWTH OF THE FIRM

Most firms start off as very small organizations, growing in size as they become more successful. The small firm consists of the entrepreneur who runs it and who usually started it, plus a number of other people to whom work is assigned which the entrepreneur either does not wish to do himself (such as perhaps packaging and despatch), or cannot do himself because he does not know how (such as, perhaps, preparation of final accounts), or else because there are not enough hours in the day to do everything. In such a small firm, major purchasing decisions are usually made by the head of the organization and minor purchasing decisions together with the detailed purchasing work fall to those in charge of any departments that exist. When a purchasing officer is appointed, his job may at first be seen as to do the legwork and the paperwork associated with purchasing, rather than to take the basic purchasing decisions.

Eventually, if the firm continues to increase in size, proper departments are set up for all major functions, and it is at this stage that management needs to delegate to purchasing the authority and responsibility to identify and evaluate purchasing problems, and to initiate, recommend and implement effective solutions.

A COMPLEX PROCESS

Organizational purchasing can be a complex process. Many people may take part, at various levels in the management hierarchy and in several functional departments. It can be a lengthy process: major 'one-off' decisions may take years to finalize. Even routine repeat orders that are placed immediately without consultation may be placed in accordance with policies previously laid down after much consultation and experiment over a lengthy period of time.

It is made more complex by its detailed involvement with other decision and control processes such as:

(1) stock control policies and procedures which determine, control and replenish the range of items stocked;
(2) the physical supply cycle which goods pass through as they are despatched, transported, received, stored and either issued or sold;
(3) production planning and control which determines and controls the quantities of parts and materials required to meet production commitments;
(4) merchandizing which decides which goods will be offered for resale and at what price.

It is when some or all of these other processes are combined in one department or under one head that the term *materials management* is used. The term *purchasing and supply* also suggests a joint consideration of purchasing with stock control and stores management, without necessarily implying that all those concerned with carrying out the relevant activities report to a single manager.

Purchasing works for every department in the business, and may be particularly involved with:

(1) the specification and design of the end-product;
(2) the quality control policies and procedures which set standards, assess capability, and control performance;

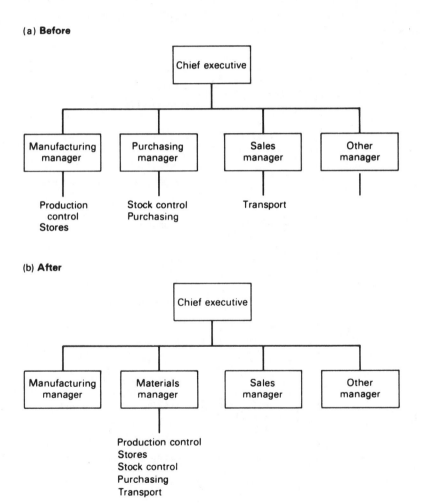

Fig. 1.1 Materials management reorganization.
(Source: Baily and Farmer, 1982)

(3) the finance function that pays bills and is also particularly concerned with capital expenditure, terms of credit, budgets, and stock investment.

ORGANIZATION STRUCTURES

The way purchasing and other supply activities are organized into departments, how tasks and activities are allocated to supply personnel, and the extent to which authority is delegated to the department head to decide matters in the supply area on his own responsibility, are all subject to considerable variation in practice.

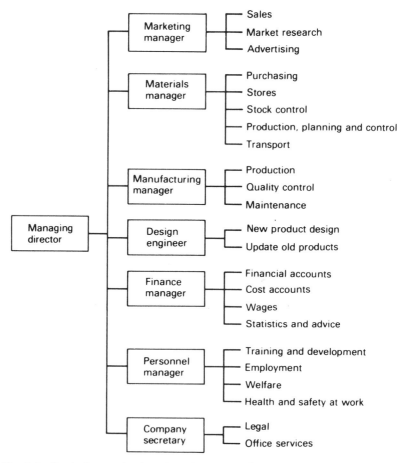

Fig. 1.2 Typical organization chart for a manufacturer.

For instance Fig. 1.1 shows two alternative ways of grouping together people working on materials-related activities. In part A, the purchasing manager is responsible for stock control as well as purchasing; in part B, purchasing, stock control, and also transport, stores, production control come under the same manager, now known as the materials manager.

Such organizational questions are considered in more detail in Chapter 22. But an important point needs to be made in this first chapter, which is that the management of materials contributes most effectively to general management and to the success of the organization if it is seen as a single process, from definition of requirements to delivery to customer.

It is not usually feasible to group all the activities involved into one department. Only the smallest firm can operate as a single department, and once more than one department has to be set up, alternative departmental groupings have to be considered, each with its own set of advantages and disadvantages.

A typical organization structure for a medium size manufacturing business which has adopted a materials management approach is shown in Fig. 1.2. This represents one particular organization, and others would be different. Some would not have a product design department, for instance, perhaps because they sub-contract design, or perhaps because they make only to customer design.

THE RESPONSIBILITIES OF PURCHASING

Some organizations issue an internal charter or purchasing manual which incorporates a formal statement signed by management of what services the purchasing department is expected to provide and what its responsibilities are. Croell (1977) suggests the following:

(1) Provide all materials and services that the company elects not to provide internally. In accomplishing this, purchasing must perform the following basic tasks.

    (a) Select and develop as required, vendors capable of meeting company needs.

    (b) Prepare and sign all purchase orders/contracts, so that the needs of the company and all pertinent terms and conditions related to the purchase are clearly understood by the supplier and documented accordingly.

    (c) Monitor supplier performance and related company activities during the course of the contract to assure that performance is accomplished by both parties in accordance with that originally intended.

   (d) Renegotiate or terminate purchase orders/contracts as required when changes occur, or as other conditions develop that warrant such action.

(2) Provide information to and participate in management planning sessions on subjects related to purchased materials services.

(3) Review purchase specifications and assist operating departments in selection of required materials and services for standardization purposes, and to assure their availability from competent suppliers at reasonable prices.

(4) Protect the company from all unnecessary or unauthorized commitments which may result from inappropriate contacts or discussions with suppliers.

(5) Dispose of all obsolete materials, equipment, or scrap that is no longer required for company operations.

MARKETING AND PURCHASING

The buying department and the selling department are the two departments mainly concerned with external relations, with reaching out into the supply markets and the sales markets outside the firm. To what extent does it make sense to say that both are engaged in marketing? This question is partly semantic (what words mean and how they are used) and partly about what departments do and how their work is perceived.

Definitions and discussions of marketing have certainly been dominated by selling considerations in recent years, although not in earlier periods. Consumer product manufacturers in the West which were competing for discretionary spending by consumers took to the marketing concept in a big way. The marketing concept, so called, could be described as the realization that firms need to find out what their customers want and take steps to provide it if they are to prosper; rather than producing the goods they were interested in producing, they needed to provide the goods the consumer was interested in purchasing. The marketing concept was less prevalent in industrial marketing, where many firms remained firmly and indeed proudly product-oriented rather than customer-oriented.

Industrial marketing differs from consumer marketing in several ways. Firstly, it usually sells different products. It deals in heavy equipment, such as tractors and machine tools; light equipment, such as photocopiers and hand power tools; construction, for example, of factories, docks and housing estates. It sells raw materials, such as iron ore and coal; processed materials, such as steel bar, chemicals and plywood; components, such as ball bearings and electric motors and semiconductors; consumable supplies, such as cleaning materials and cutting oils; and a variety of services, such as those of the forwarding agent, the contract painter, or machine maintenance.

Secondly, it usually sells to different customers. Consumer marketing aims at households and individuals. Industrial marketing aims at organizations, and these have different and often much more complex buying processes. Consequently, when products such as motor cars or typewriters are sold to both consumers and to organizations the marketing approach tends to be very different for the two.

As Webster and Wind (1972) point out,

industrial and institutional marketers have often been urged to base their strategies on careful appraisal of buying behaviour within key accounts and in principal market segments. When they search the available literature on buyer behaviour, however, they find virtually exclusive emphasis on consumers, not industrial buyers. Research findings and theoretical discussions about consumer behaviour often have little relevance for the industrial marketer.

Yet the total value of interfirm purchases of raw materials, components and semi-finished parts, finished parts, tools and supplies, is considerably greater than the total of sales to retail consumers. Rowe and Alexander (1968) quote an estimate to the effect that interfirm sales are worth about 2.5 times as much as sales to individual consumers – 3.5 times as much if sales to the government are included. They conclude that:

resource allocation, in effect the sorting or matching of needs to supplying ability, is what marketing and selling is all about when looked at from the economist's viewpoint, and nowhere is this function more in need of being expertly carried out than in the area of interfirm transactions where industries are becoming interlocked in increasing interdependence.

This remains at least equally true if the words 'purchasing and supply' are substituted for the words 'marketing and selling'. It could indeed be said that the sorting or matching of needs to supplying ability is what purchasing is all about, and that in the area of interfirm transactions this often calls for marketing initiatives on the buying side.

This is sometimes described as 'marketing in reverse'. But one definition of 'to market', in the most popular dictionary in the United Kingdom, is 'to buy or sell in market', and the very word 'market' derives from a Latin word which means 'to buy' (*mercari*). In earlier days the merchant venturers set forth through unknown seas and distant countries in search, not so much of customers although they had to have something to trade, but more of new suppliers of new products – spices, furs, carpets, turkeys, tomatoes, oranges – as well as of new sources of known materials such as gold, diamonds and tin. Sourcing, and buying generally, was the venturesome and creative part of their marketing effort.

In the distributive industries, the selection and pricing of merchandise to sell is fundamental to marketing plans, and buying is therefore an important part of marketing for the retailer. In the manufacturing industries on the other hand, it is the selection and pricing of products to make which corresponds to this, and the procurement of parts and material to make them tends to be seen as part of the production process rather than part of the marketing process.

Even here, some buying activities call for creative and entrepreneurial skills, for commercial innovation and persuasion. It is widely feared that shortages of materials and certain products will be increasingly common as the twentieth century draws to a close. And Kotler (Kotler and Levy, 1973; Kotler and Balachandrian, 1975) for instance argues that in times of shortage the marketing problem shifts its location from selling to buying. The development of new suppliers is another example of purchasing firms marketing their buying requirements to the supply markets. And in the negotiation of major contracts (for the design and development of equipment at the frontier of the art) to meet customer requirements, the term marketing may well be equally appropriate to the proposals and arguments coming from each side (if indeed it is appropriate at all in this situation).

The increasing concentration of markets has been a noticeable feature of recent years and accounts for part of the difference between industrial marketing and consumer marketing. For example, if three detergent manufacturers sell to tens of millions of households, scientific studies can be made of the market and how it can be segmented, of marketing methods and how best to apply them. But if an industrial manufacturer sells to six major industrial customers plus a number of minor customers, the scope for science is less, and it is more a matter of art. The shotgun communications of mass media advertising are used in the first case; the sharpshooter methods of field salesmen and low budget advertising in specialist trade journals are used in the second case.

In many industries a small number of manufacturers produce most of the output; and in quite a high proportion of cases, a small number of customers take most of the output. Buying and selling are both affected by the situation; after all, every purchase is someone's sale, purchasing and marketing are the two sides of one coin. Purchase cost analysis, negotiated prices based on mutually agreed figures for cost, larger and more expert departments both for buying and for selling, are typical features.

When two or three large firms supply equivalent or interchangeable products to the same market, at prices which each is reluctant to change because of the risk of retaliation by the others, two obvious ways to increase security as well as profits are: firstly by product differentiation, and secondly by cost reduction. Product differentiation makes the products seem less equivalent or interchangeable to the customer. Cost reduction enables a manufacturer to increase profits without starting a price war.

Cost reduction initially concentrated on manufacturing costs, with much success in many firms. But as one managing director said:

we have over the years by dint of research, engineering development and good management, reduced operating costs to such an extent that now nearly 80% of total cost consists of purchased materials. Obviously it is important that buyers have an eye for more than the cheap price. Purchasing and supply have a major part to play in reducing cost and increasing profit.

2

Make or
buy?

Retailers and wholesalers normally buy the merchandise they sell rather than manufacturing it themselves. This applies not only to small distributors, but also to the large chain stores which often not only select merchandise from what is available, but also draw up specifications themselves. While doing this they are talking to suppliers and finding firms which can supply goods to their specifications.

There are exceptions. Some retailers use backward integration into products or packaging to improve their competitive position, and some manufacturers aim to strengthen their competitive position by forward integration into distribution. Breweries, which are beer manufacturers, often own most of their retail outlets, and many filling stations are owned by the petrol manufacturers. Inhouse bakeries have become common in the superstores, an exception to the normal policy which is for shops to buy rather than make.

Manufacturers on the other hand normally make the products they sell, although a few products may be bought in to complete a range. They manufacture them from parts and material which are either produced internally or bought out, so that make-or-buy decisions have to be made at each stage in formulating manufacturing strategy. Outside processing may be used in addition to or instead of internal processing. Subcontracting also requires make-or-buy decisions.

TACTICAL AND STRATEGIC

Every time an organization issues a purchase order or an internal make order, somebody must have decided whether the item is to be bought or made. Deciding whether to make or buy is, in principle, a top management decision. Yet, in practice, decisions of this kind seem to be taken routinely without reference to higher authority or to any written policy guide.

The fact is that every organization has a definite policy about what it makes and what it buys. Make-or-buy decisions taken at departmental level are those which simply apply the existing policy. It is only when there are reasons to change the policy that the decision needs to be made at higher levels where strategy is decided.

The existing policy is expressed by the facilities actually available for making goods. Decisions to make internally goods that can be made economically on those facilities, and to buy those that cannot, are routine applications of the existing policy. However, routine does not necessarily mean simple. Comparing make costs with buy costs can be quite complex, since company custom, prejudice, costing conventions and other partly arbitrary considerations are involved.

Changes in policy, such as extensions to plant and facilities, or divesting existing manufacturing facilities, are also complex decisions.

ROUTINE MAKE-OR-BUY DECISIONS

Large organizations sometimes set up a make-or-buy committee, with representatives from design, production, buying, and costing departments. Deciding which parts can be made economically on available plant is of course simpler than deciding whether or not to invest in new plant, and the decisions have a shorter time-span – they can often be reversed the next time the item is required. The economics of particular cases can be complicated, especially when capacity is underemployed. Another difficult problem occurs when capacity is fully employed and the question is which parts to subcontract. As new suppliers appear or new processes are introduced, the make-or-buy cost balance may alter.

There are two main reasons why a factory buys out parts which it is equipped to make in: the first is that it can often buy cheaper than it can make; and the second is that it may not be able to make all it needs of the sort of part for which its plant is suitable because it has not got enough plant. This capacity shortage may result from a rush of orders, or from an expansion in sales which is outrunning the expansion in manufacturing facilities; or it may result from a deliberate policy of gearing capacity to *average* output and subcontracting exceptionally high output in order to run the factory at a stable base load.

How can a factory buy parts cheaper than it can make them, if it is equipped with suitable plant, when the buy price must include the seller's selling expenses, distribution expenses, and profit?

The short answer is through specialization. This enables the specialist supplier to get long runs and use special tackle. Any machine shop can turn black steel bar into bright bar, but it is less expensive to buy bright bar in the first place if that is what is wanted. Any machine shop can make a white metal bearing, but costs will be reduced substantially if one of the wide range of commercially available standard designs can be adopted. Many parts can be made in any machine shop in short runs on general purpose plant. But making them in long runs on special purpose equipment enables the specialist supplier to take his profit and deliver the product to the buyer's door, often through distributors who also have costs to cover and profits to take, at a selling price that may actually be lower than the buyer's bare direct cost for making in.

But specialization extends beyond tooling up for long runs. The motor car industry buys in quantities which give long runs on a single order, and has never been slow to equip itself with special plant; yet it supports a host of specialist suppliers employing between them four times as many people as the motor car firms themselves. Some of these suppliers are large firms, but many are tiny concerns in the backstreets of Birmingham and the Black Country. How can a gasket supplier employing a hundred or so people sell successfully to a motor car manufacturer whose qualified design staff alone heavily outnumbers the whole payroll of the gasket manufacturer? Why does the motor manufacturer not buy out the gasket firm?

The fact is that specialization does not stop at the plant, the process and the product; it extends to research and management too. In buying out components such as gaskets and lamps and brakes vehicle manufacturers are buying research and development as well as components. This enables them to benefit from a supplier's specialist design talent and trade knowledge based on experience in the service of the whole industry.

In general therefore most factories concentrate their research facilities, talents, and development on the main product, and buy from, rather than compete with, suppliers who have specialized in the accessories and subsidiary parts they require. But there are plenty of exceptions to this rule. Make-or-buy decisions are based on facts which may alter, when buyers and others concerned should request a reappraisal in the light of changes and developments both in their own plant and outside.

MAKE-OR-BUY QUESTIONS INVOLVING CAPITAL INVESTMENT

Serious problems in *quality*, *delivery* or *price*, or in guaranteeing *continuity* of supplies, sometimes justify the purchasing manager in making a recommendation that consideration should be given to investing in new manufacturing facilities in order to switch items from purchase to production. Such a recommendation will usually be made with reluctance, because it could be construed as an easy way out of a purchasing problem, because it does involve some loss of flexibility, and because of course it builds up someone else's empire, at the expense of one's own.

Ensuring that very tight quality specifications are met by making the parts within the organization is a traditional approach to quality problems. For instance, spool Axminster carpets with floral patterns may use 60 or 70 different hues. Getting these colours right requires great and repeatable accuracy in the dyeing of the yarn. It is quite easy for two shades of green to diverge slightly from the standards and become indistinguishable. Consequently many firms which weave spool Axminster operate their own dyehouses despite the facts that dyeing is a specialist trade and a very different one from weaving, and that there are many textile dyeing and finishing firms producing high quality work. Supplier development to meet difficult quality standards is an alternative approach.

Delivery problems have prompted firms to take over their suppliers in seller's market conditions, in order to ensure supplies of sufficient quantities at the time required.

Price problems can sometimes be solved by threatening to make the part internally instead of purchasing it. The threat is often implied. The buyer insists on cost breakdowns from the supplier. He then compares these with internally prepared cost estimates. His cost estimator, who usually sits in on the negotiation, adopts the position that these are the costs which apply in *your* (the supplier's) industry. Nobody has to spell out that these are the costs which *we* (the purchaser) estimate we should incur if we decide to make it ourselves. There has to be a serious possibility that the purchaser will embark on manufacture if necessary, for this tactic to be effective.

Continuity of supplies can be a problem in bilateral oligopoly markets. The motor car industry is rich in examples of situations where two or three firms supply some specialist item to the whole trade. If one or other of the vehicle manufacturers decides to increase its security by taking over one of the supplier firms, the result is a sharp decrease in the security of the other vehicle manufacturers. Many years ago there were two or three specialist suppliers of steel pressings who made car bodies for the whole British motor car industry. A long strike at the firm which supplied car bodies to Jowett Cars forced this estimable little manufacturer to close down. Ford Motor pondered this situation, and decided to take over their main body supplier – not, as the chairman explicitly stated in his annual report, because of any dissatisfaction with their quality, delivery or price:

> For many years Briggs supplied us with almost all our body requirements. A car body today costs about 40% of the total cost of a car. . . . We are greatly indebted to Briggs Motor Bodies Ltd for their unfailing cooperation in meeting so success-fully all demands we have made on them, sometimes under conditions of considerable difficulty. Nevertheless our great dependence on their supplies has been of increasing concern to us.

Before making a recommendation to solve problems in quality, delivery, price or continuity by embarking on substantial capital expenditure so that the items can be manufactured, it would be prudent to ask some searching questions, for instance: what have we done already to solve the problem? What else could we try apart from making in? Is it really a permanent difficulty or might it clear itself up in, say, a year? What would it cost to give effect to the proposal? What sort of problems might it involve? Could we absorb all the output ourselves? If we could make it pay only by selling part of the output, is this the sort of business we want to go into? Should we aim at making the whole of our requirements, or at making part and buying part? Would this harm or help our relations with suppliers?

SUPPLIERS WITHIN THE GROUP

Top management must decide what plant will be provided and hence what goods can be made, and what plant will not be provided and hence what things must be bought out. This is because there is no general rule; policy depends largely on what skills and talents the management has and where its interests lie, as well as on what funds are available and on the strict economics of the situation.

Policy may also be affected by the nature of the industry. In old and declining industries there may sometimes be a tendency for successful firms to acquire their suppliers in order to eke out a slim profit margin by vertical integration. In expanding industries horizontal integration, broadening the end-product, may provide a better return on investment. But the difference between firms in a single industry is far greater than the difference between industries. In every industry there are firms that have succeeded by specializing – and others, equally success-ful, that have diversified. There are also firms that have not been saved from failure by specialization, and firms that have diversified and still failed. There is one firm making nothing but aperients for parrots, a specialization so extreme as to strike awe in the beholder; at the other extreme great combines like Imperial Chemical Industries produce paint, plastics, wallpaper, dyestuffs, metals: a score or more of specialist product groups.

Diversification on this scale brings purchasing problems of its own. When one division buys the product of another division in the group, the operation is intermediate between making in and buying out. In the short term the price paid may not matter much, since it is like transferring money from one of your suits to another; the money stays in the group. But in the long term interdivisional pricing does matter and does affect group profitability; because of its effect on relative profitability of divisions it affects the allocation of resources between divisions. Price bargaining between the divisions of a great corporation is consequently often as keen as price bargaining between the company and its outside suppliers. In theory at least the buying division is often free to place its orders with an outside source if the supplier within the group cannot match market price. But in practice this freedom is far from absolute.

Research into the policies of 193 companies in the United Kingdom revealed that large firms, and firms with a decentralized management style, gave considerably more freedom to buyers in this respect than others did (Rook, 1972).

TRANSFER PRICES

Large concerns have to find some way to set transfer prices – the prices at which goods manufactured by one division are transferred as supplies to another division. In highly centralized firms these prices are set centrally in three-quarters of cases (Rook, 1972). This is said to be because only central staff have enough information to set prices properly. In multinational companies, transfer prices between divisions in different countries involve exchange rates and different tax laws, and may be set with the main object of reducing the total tax liability of the company.

Prices *negotiated* between selling division and buying division are not always a happy solution. If the seller is compelled to sell internally his negotiating position is poor. If the buyer is not allowed to buy externally, his position is poor. Personalities and positions in corporate hierarchies complicate matters. A great deal of time can be taken up by these internal negotiations. Yet some negotiation is necessary, and purchasing managers may try to negotiate a discount off market price where this is the basis chosen for transfer pricing on the grounds that market price includes selling overheads such as advertising and salesmen which an internal supplier does not need to incur.

Market price, and full cost of production, emerge as the two most widely used methods of setting transfer prices. Market price is preferred when firms are interested in divisional profitability, and production cost when they are more interested in the profitability of the product (Rook, 1972). Setting up product divisions as profit centres is the standard method of running large manufacturing businesses. The authority and the accountability of the division chief cannot be quite as untrammelled as that of the managing director of an independent business. If it were, the whole firm would degenerate into a collection of separate units gaining nothing by association. But within defined limits, and subject to central or corporate management's reservation of certain matters such as sources of finance and major capital expenditure, division chiefs have a good deal of autonomy so long as they earn acceptable returns on the assets they employ.

This is why it matters to them how prices are fixed for goods or services supplied by one division of the company to another division. If Division A supplies goods to Division B at an excessively high price, then Division A is profitable and its return on assets is high. It gets all the finance it wants. Corporate headquarters backs the winner. Meanwhile Division B cannot get approval for sorely needed development. But the figures are misleading; A's good results, and B's poor results, are due to an unfair transfer price.

In principle the fairest approach is to charge opportunity costs: that is, what the seller division could charge an outside customer, or what the buyer division would have to pay an outside supplier – market price, in fact; but this is not easy to establish unless the item is a standard price-list part. With made-to-order castings, forgings, fabrications, the price may be determined by selling some of the output, and buying some of the input, externally.

The *stated* policy may then be to buy from the best source, inside or outside the company. Buying departments get dispirited when they find what seems a better source outside the company only to see their decision to switch to an outside supplier overruled. But the *real* policy may in fact be to sell the output of the supplier division at opportunity cost. This is equal to outside supplier price when the internal supplier division is fully employed, but it would change downwards if the division had unused capacity.

Market price can hardly be used as the basis for transfer pricing when there is no real opportunity to buy outside. Production cost (full cost or standard cost rather than marginal cost) is then the usual basis for transfer prices.

Psychological complications make thoroughly rational policies on transfer pricing difficult to implement. As Edwards and Townsend (1958) stated:

the material suppliers within a group may be supported even beyond the point that a cool appreciation of the economics of the situation would justify. Pride is at stake; the investment has been made and its results must be bolstered. Loyalty is also at stake; once an undertaking has been acquired, those who run it are in the family and therefore to be supported in bad times as well as good.

Cyert and March (1963) describe the real-world firm as a 'coalition of participants in which conflict is only partly resolved'. When divisional results depend partly on how well a division has coped with external circumstances and partly on the transfer payments they have managed to arrange with other divisions, prices result in practice from a permanent bargaining process, rather than from the solution of a theoretical problem in 'resource allocation, performance disaggregation, or cost distribution', and divisions whose results are poor will bargain hard for better results. 'In general we should find that transfer payments are made on the basis of a few simple rules that (1) have some crude face validity and (2) have shown some historical viability. We should find that they are the focus of conflict between sub-units in the same way as other allocative devices.'

SUBCONTRACTING AND OUTSIDE PROCESSING

In the construction industries, the normal practice is for a single main contract to be signed with one firm, often after a competitive tendering procedure. The main contractor then places subcontracts with a number of specialist firms to carry out parts of the work. Subcontractors may be nominated by the customer (or client, or purchaser, as the organization placing the contract is sometimes called), or decided on by the main contractor, possibly subject to the approval of the customer. Many terms of the main contract may be passed on to subcontractors by incorporating them in the contracts made with them by the main contractor, and additional special terms may also be inserted in subcontracts.

In other industries, the term subcontracting is used for outside processing. This means arranging for work to be done or parts to be made by outside suppliers which could in principle be done internally on the organization's own facilities. It may be work normally undertaken by the buyer which has, when order books are full, to be farmed out if delivery dates are to be met. Or it may be work which could in principle be undertaken by the purchaser, but which as a matter of policy is given to outside contractors. Security, and running the canteen, are two common examples.

Subcontracting of this kind involves the purchase department because it is a kind of purchasing: goods are supplied or work done in accordance with a contract and payment has to be made. Nearly always it is a combined operation in which other departments are also involved. Production planning and control will naturally be involved if what is purchased is capacity rather than components as such, a short-term extension of the manufacturing facilities. Much of the detailed planning and progressing may be undertaken by production control as an extension of their normal work. Quality control will also be involved since the subcontracted work may be inspected just as if the work had been done inhouse.

Choosing and dealing with subcontractors involves the same considerations as choosing and dealing with suppliers generally. But there are also special considerations. In most cases, for instance, much more time has to be spent talking to people both inside and outside the organization. A special section in the purchase department, or a specialist buyer, may be nominated to deal with subcontracting. One buyer who was put in charge of subcontracting found that he spent only about one day in four at his desk; half his time was spent on visiting subcontractors, and a quarter in other departments within the organization. When there is not enough subcontracting to assign someone to it fulltime, close and thorough cooperation between departments affected may be harder to achieve, but it is just as important.

Purchase requirements and supplier selection

Purchase transactions are made to supply various types of requirement, and several methods of purchasing are used. Types of requirement include:

(1) merchandise for resale;
(2) parts and material for production;
(3) maintenance, repair and operating supplies;
(4) capital plant and equipment;
(5) services such as maintenance of equipment, cleaning, catering.

Some of these requirements are normally bought for stock, for instance merchandise. Parts and material for production are bought either for stock or else to arrive just in time to meet manufacturing schedules. Maintenance, repair and operating supplies may be bought to meet immediate needs, or else put into stock for future needs.

Purchasing methods include word-of-mouth contracts, such as purchases at auction sales, the use of standard purchase order forms, simplified order forms, purchase for cash and many others. The choice of ordering method can be affected by the type of requirement and by other things such as the type of market in which the purchase is made.

AUCTION SALES

Second-hand plant and machinery is often bought at auction. Fleet car buyers can trade in their old vehicles in part exchange for new ones; but instead they may prefer to go for the best deal they can get on new vehicles without part exchange, selling the old vehicles at car auctions, which are run by well-established firms.

An auction is a public sale in which articles are sold to the highest bidder. Usually the auctioneer starts with a low price, obtaining successively higher bids until the article is knocked down to the last or highest bidder. An unusual version is the Dutch auction in which the auctioneer starts with a high price, reducing it until a bidder is found. The article still goes to the highest bidder, but this is the one who bids first, not last.

Auctioneers usually post up a short clear statement of their conditions of sale in the auction room. These may include such terms as:

(1) The auctioneers are not responsible for any loss or damage to lots after the fall of the hammer, the goods being then at the risk of the purchaser.
(2) The auctioneers are not responsible for correct description or condition of lots offered for sale.
(3) Goods are to be paid for and taken away within 48 hours of the date of sale with all faults and errors of any kind at the purchaser's expense.

Auction sales are also used for some primary commodities, such as newly landed fish and fresh farm products.

OTHER PURCHASING METHODS

Spot contracts (for immediate delivery) and futures contracts (for delivery at a stipulated future date) are in common use in the commodity markets, as considered in Chapter 6.

Blanket orders, period contracts, call-off orders, and a variety of other ordering methods may be used where appropriate, and many different payment methods are used to settle the bill, including: cash-with-order; part payment when the contract is made; stage payments during the course of the contract; payment on completion or within a month of completion; retention of part of the amount due until the work or product has been proved satisfactory; lease, hire, and rent.

TYPICAL TRANSACTION STAGES

A typical purchase transaction in an organization goes through at least the four stages shown in Fig. 3.1: originating, selecting, ordering, and completing. Other models of the purchasing transaction have been developed with more than these four stages. Which model is preferred depends partly on what the model is to be used for.

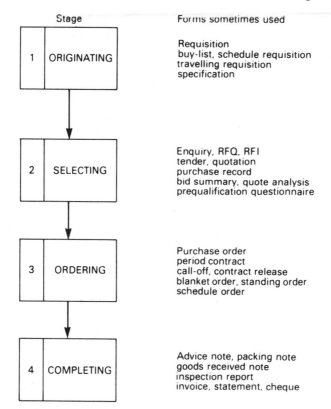

Fig. 3.1 Stages in typical purchase transaction.

This chapter deals with the first two stages in the four-stage model: originating and selecting. The third and fourth stages are considered in Chapter 4.

ORIGINATING THE PURCHASE

For specific individual needs such as purchases for immediate use, the person requiring the item writes out a purchase requisition for it. A typical general purpose requisition form is shown in Fig. 3.2. This document notifies purchasing of the requirement, authorizes the expenditure, and after processing is filed for audit and reference purposes. Anyone can make out a requisition, but no action will be taken unless it is signed by one of the few senior people who can authorize the expenditure. A list of authorized signatories is kept by purchasing, and states

PURCHASE REQUISITION		Department _____	
To Purchase Department Please obtain the undermentioned		Date _____ Number _____	
Suggested supplier	Quantity and description	Price	Required for
	Requisitioned by	Authorised by	

Fig. 3.2 Typical purchase requisition; handwritten, one copy to the purchasing department, and second copy retained by originator.

what sort of purchases the person concerned can authorize and any cash limit which applies; for instance, it may state that J. Brown, toolroom foreman, can authorize expenditure on toolroom requirements up to £500 in value, and above that value the works manager must sign the requisition.

The requisition is date-stamped when received by the purchasing department and allocated to a buyer. The buyer checks the authorizing signature, and the description of the goods (which may need to be corrected or amplified), before taking action to obtain the goods required.

Capital expenditure

Capital goods include additions to or replacements of plant and machinery, such as machine tools, computers, company cars, and buildings.

Capital expenditure is treated differently from revenue expenditure in the accounts and for taxation purposes. Typically it comprises longterm investments such as new machine tools with an expected life of at least five years rather than short-term investments such as materials for immediate processing. At the bottom end of the range of capital goods, where price is not high or expected life is not long, the borderline between capital goods and revenue goods may be a bit vague, and it is for the accountants to say where it lies, with the approval of the auditors. In principle, a £5 pocket calculator expected to last for a year or two is capital expenditure, but in practice it will be written off to revenue, with no effect on the overall results as stated in final accounts. Principle and practice converge further up the range. Most firms do not regard a purchase as capital expenditure if it is below a certain figure, such as £30, or £300, or even £3000.

Special authorization rules are often used for capital expenditure. The requisition may have to be signed by a director, or approved by a sub-committee of the board of directors, with the board approval number stated on the requisition. In large organizations it may not be feasible for all capital expenditure to be approved at board level, so authority is delegated to local directors or division managers to authorize capital expenditure up to a stated cash limit. Above this limit capital expenditure proposals still go to the main board.

Capital goods are often acquired by a normal purchase transaction, but other methods are used. These include hire-purchase, leasing through a finance house or bank, and renting. Hire purchase is a system in which goods are hired or rented for a certain period of time after which they become the property of the hirer on payment of the final instalment. Leasing and renting are alternative ways of purchasing the use of capital equipment without actually buying it. Leasing is a form of rental; property is transferred by one party to another for a specified time in consideration of rent. Rent is a periodical payment to the owner for the use of goods or premises.

The main advantage of hiring, renting or leasing equipment, as compared to buying it outright, is that there is no capital outlay. Payment is made monthly or weekly in relatively small amounts instead of in one large sum at the date of acquisition. Some arrangements enable you to make the most of rapidly advancing technology by exchanging your equipment periodically for something newer.

These methods are often used for vehicles, and for electronic equipment such as computers, or facsimile transmitters which send printed, written, drawn or photographed material to anywhere in the world where there is a receiver. Rental usually includes sales and service support and maintenance.

Hiring or renting is much used in the construction industry. This is a very large industry in which at least half the capital equipment used is obtained on rental from plant hire firms, of which about 2000 exist. The equipment, often highly specialized, is usually supplied with trained operators.

Vehicle hire on the other hand is often on a self-drive basis, because the operating skills are commonly available. It is of course possible to arrange for drivers to be supplied, in customized vehicles. Contract hire usually includes provision for relief vehicles, renewal of batteries and tyres, and arrangements for servicing and maintenance.

Purchases for stock

In order to replenish stock as it is used up, or (a much better way to think of the process) in order to provide for expected future demands after allowing for stock on hand, stock control will originate purchases by issuing requisitions. These may be general purpose requisitions as described earlier, but much use is also made of travelling requisitions and buy-lists or schedule requisitions.

Travelling requisitions are documents which travel from the originating department to purchasing in order to initiate a purchase, and then after transaction details have been recorded on them travel back to the originating department where they are filed for future reference and for use again the next time the item is required. They have nothing to do with travelling expenses or with requests to visit an overseas supplier. Alternative names for travelling requisitions are permanent order cards and perpetual requisitions.

An example of a travelling requisition is shown in Fig. 3.3. This form is printed on heavyweight card for repeated use, unlike the general purpose requisition which is on flimsy paper for once-only use. Purchase description and other permanent data such as supplier name and address are written in. Space is provided to enter date, quantity on hand, quantity required, initials of originator and authorizer, and order number. The same card is used for years without rewriting.

Buy-lists (also known as blanket or schedule requisitions) are used when a large number of items need to be ordered at one time. This happens with some stock control systems and also with some production planning systems. No special form is used for these schedules of requirements. Often they are retained in the computer system as planned orders and not printed out as hard copy until action needs to be taken by purchasing.

In smaller organizations, the same person may be responsible for deciding what is to be ordered for stock as well as for actually ordering it – such as the buyer/first sales in a department store, the manager of a small retailer, the purchaser/stock controller in a small manufacturing firm.

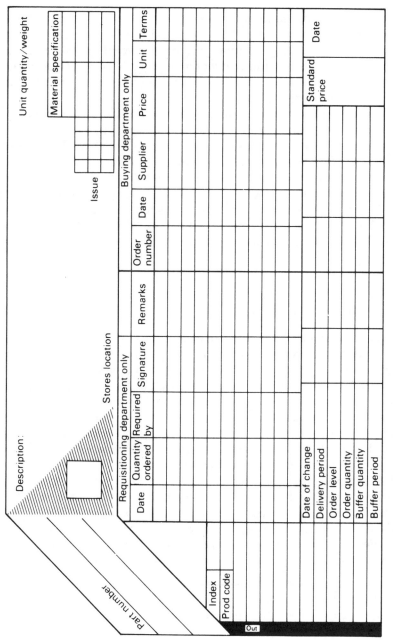

Fig. 3.3 Travelling requisition, or permanent order card.

Purchases for production

Parts and material required to make products to meet manufacturing schedules are normally supplied from stock, in the case of both common use and inexpensive items. For expensive or bulky items, and those used in large quantities, material requirements are planned week by week, or even day by day, and deliveries are timed so as to meet needs with little or no stock.

Material requirements for manufacturing schedules are notified to purchasing in the same way as stock requirements, by general purpose requisitions, travelling requisitions, or buy-lists, which may be retained in the computer system until they need to be actioned.

In some small organizations the purchasing and stock control department is given a master production schedule showing what end-products are due out week by week, plus parts lists for the end-products. They calculate materials requirements, adjust for stock, and place orders accordingly. This is now usually done on a computer, using MRP software.

THE SELECTION STAGE

The next stage, once the purchase department is aware that a requirement exists, is to select a supplier, and perhaps to select a brand or specification of goods. It is at this stage that the purchase department can make a major contribution to success. In most cases the specification will already have been decided and will not need to be reviewed every time a purchase transaction occurs. In many cases this will also be true of the supplier, as is shown in Fig. 3.4. Reference to purchase records will show where previous orders were placed and whether supplier performance was satisfactory.

Existing purchase contracts may cover the requirement. In this case the selection stage has already been carried out. The order or call-off goes to the agreed supplier, mentioning the existing contract.

Even if there is no period contract, there may be an established supplier. Competent buyers do not change from an established supplier without good reason. As research has shown (Buckner, 1967):

(1) Approximately half the persons involved in purchasing would not change from their best supplier to buy an identical product from a new supplier for a price reduction of less than 5%, that is, on average 27% increase in profitability; approximately one-fifth would not change for less than 10% reduction in price.

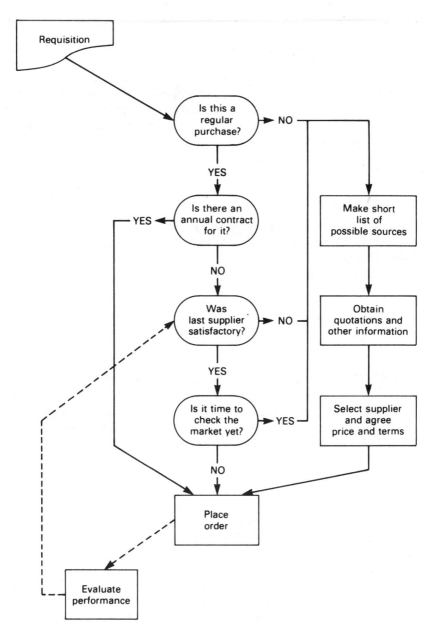

Fig. 3.4 Supplier selection.
(Source: Baily, 1983)

(2) Even if an existing supplier is regarded as satisfactory, it is prudent to check the market periodically and see what any other possible sources have to offer. Research indicates that buyers in fact do check the market when the existing supplier requests a price increase or when a new supplier knocks hard at the door, but it is also desirable to check the market periodically even if trigger events of this kind have not occurred. How often? It could be three months after the last check, or three years: experience and market knowledge are the best guide.

Identifying potential suppliers

If there is no established supplier, or if the previous supplier proved unsatisfactory, or if it is considered to be time to check the market to see what alternative suppliers have to offer, then as shown in Fig. 3.4 the standard procedure is:

(1) Draw up a short list of potential sources.
(2) Send them details of the requirement and ask for quotations.
(3) Compare the quotations, obtain additional information as required, and decide.

In drawing up a short list of possible sources of supply, buyers rely on their own trade knowledge. They learn of potential suppliers from trade magazines, exhibitions and trade shows, calls by company representatives, catalogues and literature delivered by post. Colleagues in other departments may have useful information. Through personal contacts and membership of professional associations buyers may be able to consult people in other firms. Competent purchase departments keep a basic reference library including such general directories as *Kelly's Manufacturers and Merchants Directory*, *Sell's*, *Kompass*, *Who Owns Whom*, and perhaps the *Directory of Directors*. (There's also a *Directory of Directories*.) For particular areas, yellow pages and local business directories are useful; and for particular trades, excellent guides are published by trade magazines, trade associations and independent publishers.

These publications are usually reprinted annually, but even so the information given may be as much as 18 months out of date. Increasingly, similar information is available on computerized databases which can in principle be updated daily. Dun and Bradstreet's well-known *Business Information Reports*, which can be used to assess the creditworthiness and financial stability of suppliers, are derived from a large database maintained by the company. This can be accessed online from a subscriber's office, using a terminal or personal computer, where the information is shown on the screen and can be printed out.

Enquiry procedures

General buyers' guides give you a long list rather than a short list of potential suppliers. This can be cut down by sending to the firms listed a preliminary enquiry giving brief details of the requirement, and asking firms, if they are able and willing to supply the requirement, to give some details about capability, performance record, financial status and other matters useful in drawing up a short list. These preliminary enquiries are usually called *requests for information* (RFI). In connection with construction contracts they are often called *prequalification question-naires*, since the aim is to 'prequalify' or make a preliminary selection of potential suppliers who appear qualified to undertake the work.

Existing commitments or future plans may make it difficult for a supplier to bid for the requirement, in which case the supplier should say so. The purchaser should be pleased by this responsible attitude and keep the firm on the list of potential suppliers.

Having prepared a short list of possible suppliers, the next step is to send out formal enquiries or *requests for quotation* (RFQ), or tender forms. If a preprinted form is used it should not look like the order form and should not need to have such messages as 'This is not an order!' printed across it in large letters. It should either be a specially designed form such as the one shown in Fig. 3.5, or else should be a version of the normal letterhead with such words as 'Your quotation is invited not later than . . . for the supply and delivery of the goods specified below, subject to the terms and conditions printed on the back of this form', preprinted to save typing. With the increasing use of word processors preprinted forms of this kind are used less than before.

One dictionary definition of 'quotation' is: 'amount stated as current price of stocks or commodities'. So a supplier could in principle reply to a request for quotation by saying 'we are currently selling this article at £p per thousand and delivery is usually about four weeks from receipt of order'. This is indeed a quotation but it is not an offer to sell so much as a statement of fact. Or a supplier could reply, as many do, by saying 'in reply to your enquiry we offer to supply you with the articles specified at a price of £p per thousand for delivery four weeks from receipt of your order'. This is an offer to sell, which can be converted into a contract by acceptance, for instance by sending an order.

Or a supplier could reply in similar words on a preprinted quotation form, with a set of terms and conditions printed on the back which are

REQUEST FOR QUOTATION

ALEXANDER CONTRACTS PLC.,
122 Baker Street,
London WC1 3RG

TELEX 32148 & 32273
TELEPHONE 01-222 666

Please quote this Reference in any correspondence
or Telephone call

Reference	Date	Contact
_ _ _ _ _		

Please quote us delivered carriage paid on the
conditions specified overleaf your lowest
fixed price for goods enumerated
below A Cash Discount of $2\frac{1}{2}$% M/A will be deducted from
Invoice (unless otherwise stated in your Quotation)

Your Quotation should reach this office by:

For and on behalf of
ALEXANDER CONTRACTS PLC.

Specification:

Delivery date required _____

Delivery of goods to be made to

Fig. 3.5 Request for quotation.

not the same as the buyer's. This is also an offer to sell, but if the buyer accepts it using a purchase order form with different terms printed on it he is not in law accepting the offer but making a counter-offer. These legal aspects are discussed in Chapter 5. They are regarded as relatively unimportant for a transaction which is one of a series between a regular supplier and a regular customer. They are important for an isolated transaction, for instance to build a new factory, where buyer and seller may never deal with each other again. For constructional work of this kind it is usual to use standard forms of contract which cover most of the things which could go wrong, and it is also usual for suppliers to quote for the work on tender forms.

A tender has been defined as 'a written offer to execute work or supply goods at a fixed price', and this offer is usually made on a form supplied by the purchaser, or the engineer or architect acting on behalf of the purchaser. This enquiry procedure is normal for building and civil engineering contracts, and is considered in more detail in Chapter 17 on that subject.

Evaluating suppliers' quotations or tenders

The usual procedure is to keep a copy of the request for quotations in a pending file until all replies are received or until the closing date, and the quotations are then compared and analysed. It is convenient both for comparison and for subsequent reference to transfer key data from suppliers' quotations to a quotation summary sheet or bid summary – either a copy of the request for quotation form or a special form. When set-up costs or tooling charges or transport costs or payment arrangements differ, it is useful to show them on a bid summary so that direct comparison is easier. The order number and the name of the selected supplier are entered on the form before filing it away. The reason why that supplier was selected may also be shown.

Any anomalies or discrepancies between the offers and the enquiry documents should be sorted out at this stage, at least for the preferred bidders. Delivery promises should be considered in the light of past experience with the bidder or reports from other customers of actual delivery performance. Escalation clauses and, in the case of foreign sources, the possible effect of currency fluctuations should be taken into account.

Quality capability may have been examined at the previous, prequalification or RFI, stage; or it may be known from past dealings. At any rate it is certainly a key factor to be considered in comparing offers

When everything is equal except price, the order goes to the firm which offers the lowest price. But it does not often happen that every-thing except price is equal, and both technical and commercial evaluation is usually required. The low bid or cheapest offer is not always the best buy.

Sometimes the low bidder turns out on investigation to be unable to meet volume requirements, or quality standards, or to be a bad risk in some other way. Buyers do not ask unsuitable suppliers to quote for major purchases. But for minor purchases they may not investigate untried suppliers unless they submit an attractive quotation. Sometimes the low bidder cannot deliver when required, and it has to be decided whether to pay another supplier more for earlier delivery.

Quoted price is only one factor in obtaining good value for money. It may be the main determinant of monetary cost, but there are other factors. Specification and design standard, delivery reliability, performance, durability and maintenance costs, and perhaps improvements in productivity are some of the factors that may affect total cost over the life of the product. Lower lifetime cost leads to better value for money even if the initial quoted price is higher.

It is a courtesy to tell unsuccessful bidders why they lost the order, with a word of thanks for their quotation and a tick against a preprinted list of reasons for failure, such as: lower quote accepted, better delivery elsewhere, other material or equipment preferred, no order placed this time, etc.

Price analysis and cost analysis

In considering quotations and tenders, some form of price analysis is used. Price may be compared with prices submitted by others, or paid in the past, or with the going rate if one exists. It may be compared with the cost of alternative materials or articles which could be used as substitutes.

When several quotations are received, it sometimes happens that one is much lower than the rest. It is wise to find out why. Perhaps the seller has made a mistake. If the low bid is 25% below the rest, the seller should be given the opportunity to correct or withdraw his offer: bankrupt suppliers and half-finished contracts are not the aim. Or perhaps the seller is short of work and is offering a price which just covers labour and materials without making full contribution to profit and overhead. This could lead to a good deal for both buyer and seller – unless the supplier is short of work because his work has been unsatisfactory. Low prices are also sometimes offered to get potential customers to give a fair trial to a new supplier. This is a legitimate ploy, since there is some risk in switching to an untried supplier. Special offers cannot be made the basis for standard prices, however.

Cost analysis is not the same as price analysis. Cost analysis is a systematic attempt to determine what a cost-based price ought to be by analysing the underlying costs of labour, materials, and overheads and adding a suitable figure for profit. This technique is particularly useful when competitive quotations do not provide a simple way to check the price.

It may be within the buyer's capability to carry out a cost analysis if it occasionally needs to be done for relatively simple articles. But the main application is in bulk regular purchases for high volume manufacturing. Here the buyer gets help from qualified estimators or cost analysts.

Suppliers are asked to submit a cost breakdown in support of their quoted price. Meanwhile qualified cost estimators in the purchase department analyse the cost of the articles. Price is settled by negotiation on a factual basis, with detailed comparison of the two price estimates, the seller's and the purchaser's. Suppliers are reluctant to do this if they have not done it before. But once one supplier agrees to it the others tend to follow. Civil engineering and building contracts based on bills of quantity are placed on a similar basis.

Breakeven analysis

Parts made on special tooling have two cost elements: the cost of the tool, and the cost of the parts made with the aid of the tool. High tool costs often give low piece costs, and vice versa. One method of assessing these two-element quotations is to decide on a write-off quantity for the tool, divide the tool cost by this quantity, and add the resultant figure to the piece cost. However it is not easy to decide on write-off quantities because of uncertainties as to tool life and future demand for the parts. So it is usually better to apply breakeven analysis.

Suppose for instance that the following quotations are received:

Supplier A: £1000 for tooling, parts at £30 per 1000
Supplier B: £2000 for tooling, parts at £20 per 1000
Supplier C: £4000 for tooling, parts at £10 per 1000

The cost position can be shown on a breakeven chart, as in Fig. 3.6. From this it can be seen that total invoice cost is lowest for supplier A until total off-take exceeds 100 000 parts, when B becomes the low-cost source, while for total off-takes greater than 200 000 parts C becomes cheaper still.

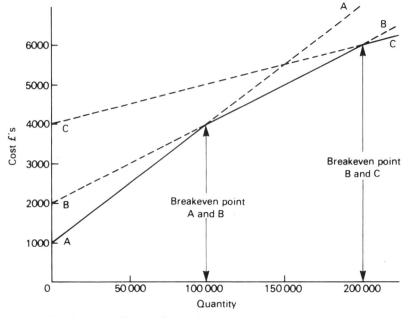

Fig. 3.6 Breakeven analyses of two-element quotations.

The breakeven points can also be derived by calculation, without drawing the graph. The difference between A's piece price per 1000 and B's piece price per 1000 is £10. The difference between A's tooling price and B's tooling price is £1000. Dividing one difference cost into the other gives the breakeven point between A and B as 100 000. In the same way the breakeven point between B and C can be calculated:

$$\frac{\text{(tool cost C minus tool cost B)}}{\text{(part price B minus part price C)}} = 200\,000$$

Sometimes suppliers quote a figure for part tool cost. This enables them to use the same tool on work for other customers – which may or may not be desirable. It prevents the customer taking the work to another source unless he pays for a new tool, which is desirable from the seller's viewpoint but not from the buyer's viewpoint.

DISCOUNTS AND REBATES

A discount is normally a deduction from the list price, quoted price or usual price, or from the invoice total, which is given for a variety of reasons and is usually expressed as a percentage. However, chain discounts sometimes incorporate pluses as well as minuses. Chain discount is the term used when nominal price is subject to a series or chain of percentage adjustments, such as: £75 less 7½% plus 5% less 12½%. Consequently a discount is sometimes defined as a percentage *variation* to the nominal price rather than as a deduction.

A rebate has been defined as 'deduction from the sum to be paid, discount', and thus appears to be just another word for discount. Perhaps the term rebate is used most commonly in connection with cumulative discounts or annual rebates.

The three main kinds of discount are: settlement discounts, trade discounts, and quantity discounts, but some other kinds are encountered.

Settlement discounts are given for payment earlier than is usual. They are often called cash discounts, a term which is correctly used for discounts given for immediate payment in cash rather than on credit. They were formerly very common, typical terms being 3¾% for payment in seven days, or 2½% for payment in 30 days. This is substantial; to lose 2½% of the invoice total for taking an extra month's credit is roughly equivalent to borrowing money at about 30% interest. Rather than lose the discount, every solvent business paid on time. Some suppliers saw little point in giving a discount for standard practice, so they altered their terms of payment to net monthly account. Unfortunately, some customers saw that taking an extra month's credit without change to the invoice total was equivalent to borrowing money at zero interest; or from the supplier's viewpoint, lending money at zero interest.

Trade credit is a legitimate source of finance provided that it is taken with the supplier's consent. Cases have been reported, however, in which large purchasers have abused their position by taking up to 12 months credit despite objections from the victim. Unpaid suppliers can take their customer to court or even arrange for a liquidator to take over their affairs, but are usually reluctant to take such drastic action. The better suppliers are unlikely to look with favour on customer organizations which fail to honour agreed terms of payment. They may demand cash with order, payment in full of all previous debts before accepting further orders, 4% surcharge on bills not paid when due, or Romalpa-type contract clauses under which goods supplied remain the property of the supplier until paid for.

Unless an organization has explicit terms of payment which it applies rigorously, the buyer should be authorized to negotiate terms and times of payment along with other aspects of the contract and to commit the organization to them.

Terms of payment are significant issues in major contracts likely to take several years to complete, which may provide for initial payments to finance development work, progress payments to cover work packages as they are completed month by month, contract price adjustments to cover increases in the costs of labour and materials, and retention amounts if a trial period is required to ensure that the work or equipment meets the specification. They are also important in international contracts where rate of exchange or availability of foreign currency may present problems.

Trade discount no doubt originally meant discounts given to tradesmen such as plumbers, builders and decorators, or to 'the trade' in the sense of the distribution channels used by manufacturers – wholesalers, retailers, and many others. Now it seems to mean a discount given to any special class of customer: educational discounts, OEM (original equipment manufacturer) discounts, major user discounts, etc. 'List price is the notional price, but I don't know who pays it,' one sales manager is quoted as saying. 'Everyone seems to qualify for a trade discount of some kind.'

Discount structures are often laid down formally in the case of price list goods – x% for the wholesaler, y% for the retailer for instance – but discretionary discounts are usually available in addition to these: that is, discounts available at the discretion of the sales manager or his representative. 'I always ask for a discount,' said one buyer. 'Sometimes I can think of a reason for it, sometimes not. Usually I get it.'

Price lists are applicable to standard articles sold to many customers, but not to special goods to the specification of one customer. Most of the more important purchases in most organizations are not charged by price list.

Special discounts are sometimes available to buyers who take seasonable goods out of season: road salt, antifreeze or coal in summer for instance. The advantage to the seller of these seasonal discounts is that production can be smoothed, and the cost of distribution and stockholding may be reduced. The advantage to the buyer is a lower price, but this has to be offset against the disadvantage of higher stocks.

Quantity discounts are given for large orders or to large customers. The seller benefits from big orders which often enable direct as well as indirect costs to be reduced. Sometimes quantity discounts are expressed as percentages. Sometimes a price–quantity table is drawn up, such as the one shown below.

Alternatively, the price could be quoted as 40p kg, subject to a 5% surcharge for orders below 1000 kg, and to quantity discounts on the following scale: less 5% for orders of 2250–4999 kg, less 10% for orders of 5000–9999 kg, and less 12½% for orders of 10 000 kg or more. These

Price per kg	For quantities of:
42p	Below 1000 kg
40p	1000–2249 kg
38p	2250–4999 kg
36p	5000–9999 kg
35p	10 000 kg upwards

two ways of expressing the price–quantity relationship are arithmetically equivalent. It is a matter of preference which one the seller adopts.

Small quantity extras, small order premiums, and minimum order charges are imposed by some firms; in a sense they are the reverse of quantity discounts, but they have the same effect of charging higher prices for smaller quantities.

When offered a lower price (whether in the form of a discount or not) for ordering a larger quantity for delivery at one time, the buyer needs to weigh the advantage of a lower purchase cost against the disadvantage of carrying larger stocks than would otherwise be needed. This can sometimes be quantified, as discussed in Chapter 9. Other possible disadvantages include: having to place all the business with a single source instead of dividing it between two suppliers; and undertaking to deal with a particular supplier for a longer period.

Buyers also take the initiative in looking for quantity discounts. Group contracts are an example of this: a group of establishments can often get a lower price if they all agree to deal with a single source for a particular item. Imaginative approaches can pay off: order quantities can be adjusted to make the most of price breaks, rebates can be requested on total annual volume of business, if it exceeds a certain figure.

NEGOTIATION

The four main price negotiation situations are:

(1) An established supplier wants to increase price.
(2) The buyer wants an established supplier to reduce price.
(3) A potential supplier wants to get the business and oust the established supplier.
(4) There is no regular supplier and this is a new purchase.

Negotiations about price changes usually turn on costs. Suppliers in a position to dictate price do not need to negotiate. Suppliers who do negotiate need to make out a reasonable case.

Buyers negotiate many other matters apart from price: terms and conditions of contract, tooling, transport, quality control arrangements, delivery and stockholding arrangements, in fact any aspect of the agreement which is not standard.

Negotiation should not be difficult between reasonable persons who want to reach a mutually satisfactory agreement quickly, upon a matter they understand. Lengthy and arduous negotiations occur mainly when one or more of the parties are not being reasonable, and when large numbers of people are affected by the result.

A common mistake is not preparing thoroughly enough. Inadequate preparation is sometimes attributed to lack of time, but everyone has all the time there is; no-one's day has more than 24 hours in it. Faulty allocation of time might be nearer the mark.

Another mistake is trying to score a great victory. 'Win–win' negotiations do not lead to the defeat of one side and the victory of the other, since buyer and supplier are not at war with each other. The aim in this kind of negotiation must be a mutually satisfactory solution. Trying to win every point is the result of not thinking the situation through. Most commercial negotiations occur between buyers and sellers who intend to continue trading with each other; whose objectives cannot rationally include leaving the other party stone cold dead in the market; who cannot therefore be said to have succeeded in achieving their objectives unless the other party is also reasonably satisfied with the outcome.

Preparation for negotiations

Objectives, and tactics, are the two areas where advance planning and preparation can pay off.

In considering objectives, the major issues and the minor issues should be spelled out. The other parties' needs should be considered: what are they really after? How can we satisfy some of their needs? What do *we* stand to lose or gain, and what do *they* stand to lose or gain, if settlement is not reached? What are the relevant facts and figures? Often these have to be collected and collated in consultation with colleagues in other departments – in finance, engineering, production or sales. Long-term objectives such as the future supply pattern should not be left out of account when planning a short-term negotiation such as the price to be paid or the supplier to be chosen for a particular contract.

In fixing objectives for a negotiation, some margin for manoeuvre should be left. We might for instance aim at a settlement price of £10 000, while hoping to settle for £8000 and being willing to agree at most to

£12 000. These are precise figures but do not send the negotiator into battle with his hands tied.

In considering the tactical plan, we have to consider relative bargaining strengths. How much the seller needs the business, how sure he is of getting it, and how much time there is to reach agreement; how much the buyer needs the seller's product, what alternatives are open to him, how much time he has to develop alternatives, how much business he has to give the supplier, and what cost and price data he has; these are particularly relevant. Time and location of meeting have to be settled. The home player has a small advantage. It is hardly enough to justify booking a hotel room to make sure of a neutral meeting ground.

In fixing the tactical plan, what questions to ask, and how to word them; what approaches the other side may come up with, and how to counter them; and the order in which issues will be tackled, are the main things to plan.

Conduct of negotiations

The reasonable negotiator begins on a positive friendly note, perhaps by referring to a past history of mutually satisfactory transactions. He shows clearly that he intends if at all possible to come to a mutually satisfactory settlement of the points at issue as soon as he can. He deals systematically in succession with the various points. He concludes by recapping what has been agreed, and he confirms this in writing the following day. He does not attempt to put one over on the other side by smuggling into the confirmation matters that were not mentioned in the recap. His plain and evident intention is to reach agreement on terms which satisfy both sides. Provided that the other party is also reasonable, it is on the whole a pleasure to do business with him. It cannot, however, be denied that unreasonable negotiators sometimes enjoy an undeserved success.

Some practical advice is as follows:

(1) DO give plenty of thought to the other party's probable objectives, tactics, and attitude.
(2) DON'T waste time scoring debating points, proving your opponent wrong, or otherwise showing off.
(3) DON'T let emotional reactions such as rage or pride cloud your thinking.
(4) DON'T do all the talking; ask questions, listen to the answers.
(5) DON'T keep your eyes on the papers. Watch your opponent's body language: his eyes, physical attitudes, and facial expressions.

Most people signal their feelings and attitudes quite clearly, even while saying verbally something rather different.

(6) Be ready to modify your approach.

(7) If you seem to reach an impasse on one point and you do not seem to be getting anywhere, switch to another point; say 'Let's leave that one for the moment. How about . . .?' When the less controversial point has been settled, the sticky one may look less sticky. Or else suggest a break for coffee, conference, referring back.

(8) Have a list of points at issue and work through it systematically, ticking off points as they are dealt with and recapping periodically.

(9) If you gain an important concession, think of something you can concede in turn. If on the other hand you have had to yield on some major point, use this as a lever to gain some *quid pro quo*.

(10) The alternatives are not win or lose, as Gerry Nierenberg has pointed out: 'The creative negotiator is where there are no wars, no strikes, no lockouts. The old clichés of the playing field, I win, you lose, survival of the fittest, winner take all, don't apply to commercial negotiations in an advanced cultural system.'

Learning curves

Learning curves are used in negotiations about the price for complicated products made in relatively small quantities. They are based on the fact that people learn from experience. The second product should

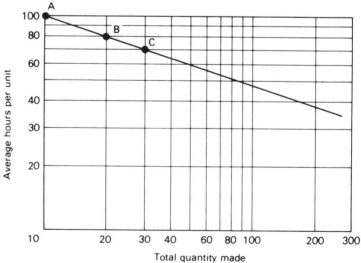

Fig. 3.7 The learning curve.

be completed in less time than the first. When we get to the 20th product, production time should be a lot less than for the first one, and further reductions should be achieved as the total quantity made increases, although at a reducing rate.

As usually drawn, learning curves are shown as straight lines on log–log graph paper, as shown in Fig. 3.7. They are based on the empirical fact that the average man-hours required to build some products decreases by a fixed percentage every time the total quantity made doubles.

The calculations are not too difficult so long as it is remembered that the reduction applies to man-hours per product averaged over the total quantity made, from product 1; and that the percentage reduction occurs when total quantity made doubles. The calculations can quite easily be done on a pocket calculator.

Figure 3.7 shows the average hours per unit as 100 for the first ten made. This falls to 80 for the first 20. Total hours for the first ten were thus 1000; total hours for the first 20 were 1600. Consequently the second lot of ten took 600 hours, with an average time per unit of 60 hours. This corresponds to an 80% learning rate.

4

Purchase orders and contracts

Most organizations use a standard purchase order form and insist that all purchases are made by use of this form. This is not to meet legal requirements, since contract law allows contracts to be made with very few exceptions by a variety of methods: by word of mouth, in writing, by telephone, using standard forms, etc. It is rather to meet organizational requirements, since an organization employing large numbers of people and processing thousands of invoices every month needs standard procedures to ensure that payment is not made for goods which have not been received, or even ordered, or have wrongly been bought for private use on the company's account.

It can also happen that non-purchasing employees who quite properly talk to suppliers' representatives about what they need and what the suppliers have to offer, get sweet-talked or pressurized into signing suppliers' order forms or giving oral assent for the supply of unwanted goods or goods at excessive prices or in excessive quantities. A simple way to avoid trouble of this kind is to stipulate that everything bought by the organization must be bought by use of the standard purchase order form, issued only against a requisition countersigned by a responsible person or authorized by some other officially approved method.

But using a single standard procedure for everything bought has drawbacks too. Special ordering procedures are often used both for regular high-volume requirements and also for the large number of small orders most organizations need to place.

STANDARD PURCHASE ORDERS

A typical purchase order form is shown in Fig. 4.1. It is a preprinted

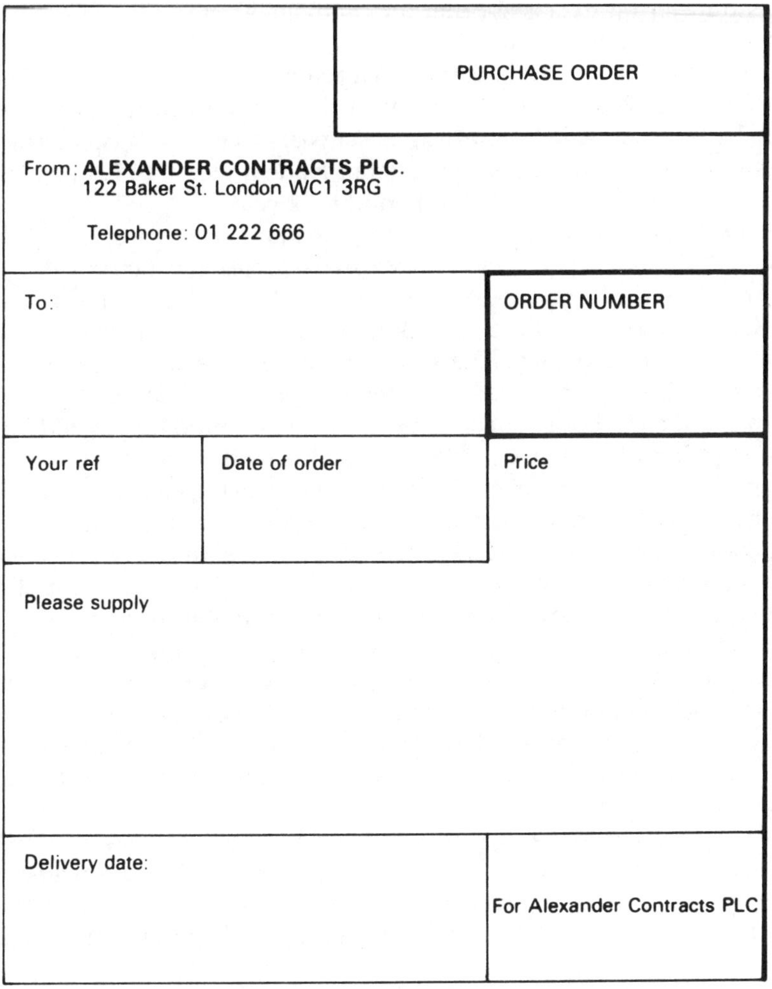

	PURCHASE ORDER
From: **ALEXANDER CONTRACTS PLC.** 122 Baker St. London WC1 3RG Telephone: 01 222 666	

To:	ORDER NUMBER

Your ref	Date of order	Price

Please supply

Delivery date:	
	For Alexander Contracts PLC

Fig. 4.1 Purchase order form.

multipart multicolour form, sequentially numbered, and is signed by an authorized buyer in the space provided. Four copies are produced of each order: one for the supplier; one for the requisitioner; one for goods receiving; and the fourth is the purchase department copy, used for progressing, invoice approval and reference. The copies are different colours to aid sorting.

The purchase department copy is filed alphabetically by supplier name in open-order (or outstanding order) files until completed, when it is transferred to closed-order (or completed order) files arranged in numerical sequence.

Closed-order files are kept for seven years and then destroyed. This is because the Limitation Act 1980 limits the period in which legal action can be taken on simple contracts to six years from the cause of action. Simple contracts here means those not made under seal. For contracts made under seal the limitation period is 12 years.

Most organizations use forms with from four to six copies. In addition to the four copies mentioned above, extra copies may be provided for acknowledgment, progressing, invoice checking, and other purposes.

Some firms send the extra acknowledgment copy to the supplier along with the top copy. The supplier is asked to sign and return it to acknowledge that the order has been received and accepted, on the terms and conditions stated therein. This may sound like a good idea, but supplier resistance or indifference makes it hard work to get enough signed acknowledgment copies back to be worth the effort. One survey found that half the purchase departments contacted did not use acknowledgment copies. Of the half who did, one-third failed to follow up suppliers and insist on getting signed copies back. Also, suppliers who returned acknowledgment copies did not always sign them, or signed them after crossing out the part about accepting conditions, or attached their own acceptance of order form with quite a different set of terms and conditions detailed on it. All this is part of the 'battle of the forms', a contest to establish who would win if a contract dispute had to be taken to court, and is one of the legal aspects of purchasing considered in Chapter 5.

An extra progressing copy may be provided if most orders need to be expedited. This is filed in due date order, so that each day reference to the file shows which orders are due to be followed up.

The accounts department also need a copy of the order if they check invoices.

Should all orders be priced?

Some firms insist that every purchase order must show the price at which the goods are ordered. Other firms show the price when it is specially quoted, or when a major occasional purchase is made, but omit the price for regular purchases, purchases against period contracts, or goods sold off the shelf on price lists.

The arguments for pricing all orders are:

(1) It proves that the buyer knows the price at which he is buying; it

encourages price-consciousness and checks that the buying job is being done.

(2) It reduces invoice checking to a clerical routine; the invoice clerk passes bills on which prices agree with those shown on the order, refers the rest to the buyer.

(3) It facilitates routine preparation of commitments reports.

On the other hand purchase departments which do not price all orders argue that:

(1) Delays in placing orders delay delivery of goods; delays in passing invoices often do not matter to a day or two. It is therefore efficient to check a known price at the invoice stage rather than at the pre-order stage.

(2) When many purchases are against period contracts or price lists, price checks at the invoice stage can be selective (every item above £50 and every tenth item below, perhaps), but price checks at the preorder stage must be exhaustive if the price is to be shown on every order; so they take longer without necessarily performing better.

(3) Insistence on pricing every order can mean a costly waste of time if buyers are obliged to phone suppliers and note down prices before they can write small-value non-repeating orders.

Many purchasing men like to see most orders, if not all, priced, as evidence of a job properly done. But departments mainly concerned with routine maintenance orders, or call-off orders against period contracts, often favour the unpriced order subject to proper safeguards.

PERIOD CONTRACTS AND BLANKET ORDERS

Period contracts and blanket orders aggregate a variety of requirements into single agreements in order to get a better deal. For instance, the head office or corporate headquarters of a multiestablishment organization may sign contracts on behalf of the whole organization against which local branches and divisions may be able to call off supplies or place orders on more advantageous terms than if they ordered individual requirements separately. The period for which the contract runs is usually one year, although both longer and shorter periods are used. It is good practice to stagger renewal dates so that each month several contracts come up for reconsideration, instead of having them all expiring at year-end.

Another version of the period contract is used when annual requirements are not known exactly. A one-year contract may then be made for a quantity which is 50% of estimated annual requirements. Actual requirements as they arise are ordered or called off against this contract. This arrangement is mutually advantageous. The advantage to the supplier is the assurance of a substantial workload and the ability to plan capacity and commitments accordingly. The advantage to the purchaser is usually a lower price and better delivery because of the advance capacity booking. In one instance, parts had been bought in lots of 1000 at 26p each. Sales forecast for the product on which the parts were used was 12 000 a year. Placing a period contract for half of this, 6000 parts, with delivery called off at 1000 a month or a lower rate if appropriate but with completion in 12 months, enabled the buyer to get the price reduced to 20p each. This is a useful technique for many production parts.

Blanket order is another name for period contract, used most often when the agreement covers many items. It is often used for an agreement, usually with a local stockholder, which covers the supply for a period of a year (or more) of a large variety of maintenance, repair and operating (MRO) items. Considerable numbers of these are required by any large establishment, but the quantity required at any time of an individual item is usually small. By consolidating the requirements into a single blanket agreement and arranging for a single monthly invoice for goods called off against the agreement, appreciable savings in time and paperwork can be made for both buyer and seller.

The term blanket order is also used for period contracts made for a single item, rather than many items, when the word blanket seems to refer to the fact that many call-off orders may be made against the agreement.

CALL-OFF ORDERS

Period contracts and blanket orders are not usually instructions to deliver goods, rather they are agreements as to total quantities, descriptions, prices and terms on which goods are to be supplied.

Instructions which tell the supplier which goods to deliver, in what quantities, and when, against a period contract or blanket order, take a variety of forms, such as:

(1) contract release form, which releases goods for delivery;
(2) call-off order, which calls off goods for delivery;
(3) the normal purchase order form, with specific reference to the date and number of the main contract against which goods are ordered;
(4) a simplified purchase order form, similar to a purchase requisition

except that it is addressed to the supplier instead of to the purchase department; this usually states that it is not valid for amounts above, say, £100, and may be signed by an authorized person outside purchasing;

(5) a 'laundry list' type of order is also used with period contracts. The user fills in weekly requirements on a preprinted order form, which the supplier collects each week, delivering the goods a week later on the next visit.

SCHEDULE ORDERS

Schedule orders are those which schedule future requirements for one or more items. The supplier may be authorized to deliver stated requirements for the current period, to manufacture but not deliver requirements for the following period, and to purchase materials but not work on them for a further period of time. This enables the supplier to make the best arrangements possible for manufacturing and material supply within the scope allowed by the purchaser's advance planning. Suppliers can place orders for materials with long lead times and can consolidate production requirements into economical batches, while the purchaser's commitment to pay for work done and materials bought is limited and defined.

ELECTRONIC MAIL FOR ORDERING

Electronic data interchange (EDI) between organizations is used by Marks and Spencer, Sainsburys, Tesco and many others to order goods, and this computer to computer method of ordering is set to increase in popularity. Agreements are negotiated person to person in the traditional way; but call-off orders against these agreements are sent by the purchaser's computer to the supplier's computer, and invoices are sent in the same way. Big savings in the cost of paperwork are expected, especially in import/export transactions where the cost of paperwork can be as much as 7% of total contract cost.

This is one example of electronic mail, defined as sending readable, rather than audible, messages from one place to another electronically rather than by sending them on pieces of paper which have to be moved physically.

Telex and fax are older examples of electronic mail. Modern telex machines are compact, easy to use and quiet in operation. The telex system is like two typewriters in different places linked by a telephone line, so that what is typed into one keyboard is printed out on the other. With over a million subscribers around the world, telex has been used for purchase enquiries and purchase orders for many years.

Fax, or facsimile, is like two photocopiers in different places linked by a telephone line, so that text and pictures input at one end appear at the other end about 15 seconds later. Unlike telex, which sends messages in capital letters, fax can send contracts complete with signature and drawings. Like telex it operates any hour of day or night, can be hired or bought outright, and communicates only with other subscribers.

SMALL ORDERS AND THE 80–20 LAW

A large number of routine requirements have to be bought in most organizations, including the numerous small requirements for factory maintenance, small tools, office supplies, and design and development work.

Individual small orders present few problems, but considered as a whole small orders do constitute a problem. They can take up too much time and cost too much money. Small-quantity extras or minimum charges per order may be imposed by suppliers, or carriage may be charged for on small orders while large orders are delivered free, thus increasing the cost of purchase. If users wanting some inexpensive article available off the shelf from local stockholders have to wait for weeks while their small purchase for immediate use grinds through the mill of an administrative system designed for large long-term requirements, they will rightly complain about the delay. Any system in which a lot of paperwork and time is used to procure a few pence worth of goods needs to be improved. Something is wrong if it costs more to process a purchase transaction than it costs to pay for the goods purchased. Many small orders can be eliminated by adopting appropriate ordering systems, but in the nature of things there will be plenty left.

A well-known rule of thumb (the 80–20 law) states that about 80% of any organization's purchase expenditure tends to go on 20% of the things purchased. At the other end of the scale, more than three-quarters of the orders placed tend to account for less than a fifth of the total expenditure.

It seems obvious that buyers should spend a lot of time on the 20% of big spend items if they aim to make a contribution to profitability.

Less obvious is the fact that administrative effort tends to be allocated to transactions in proportion to their number, rather than their value or importance. If there is little scope for cost reduction in purchasing toilet rolls, carbon paper, envelopes and miscellaneous hardware, little thought may be given to these MRO transactions that can occur in large numbers. What tends to happen is that purchasing them takes up a large part of purchasing time. By giving extra thought this tendency can be defeated.

BLANKET ORDERS AND STANDING ORDERS

Some of the ordering systems used for small orders are: blanket orders, standing orders, cash pick-up, and blank cheque enclosed with order.

Blanket orders have already been mentioned. They can appreciably reduce the amount of administrative work required to process routine transactions.

Standing orders are arrangements under which a supplier goes on delivering something until told to stop. Many households use standing orders for newspapers and milk. Most factories use standing orders for service and maintenance contracts, for instance for weighing machines or computers.

This system can be used for any regular requirement which is not subject to sales fluctuations, for instance carbon paper. Instead of placing two or three orders a month for carbon paper, and wasting hours every month saying no to enthusiastic carbon paper salesmen, the whole question is examined in depth once a year and standing orders are placed which call for delivery every four to six weeks, enabling the carbon paper issue to be considered once a year only. Lubricating oil, coolant, cleaning rags and many other MRO items can be dealt with in this way. Lower prices can be negotiated because the order is larger. Stocks are no higher because of frequent deliveries. Lots of small orders are replaced by one or two annual orders that have been properly investigated and negotiated.

SYSTEMS CONTRACTING

Systems contracting was invented by one American firm and the term subsequently came into common use. Referring to American sources for clarification, we find that according to Heinritz and Farrell (1981), headquarters staff negotiate agreements with suppliers, usually distributors, for large groups of such items as office supplies, bearings, steel. The agreements require suppliers to hold sufficient stocks and allow requisitioners in the purchaser's organization to call off goods directly from the designated supplier. Lee and Dobler (1977) define a systems contract as 'a contract that authorises designated employees of the buyer, using a predetermined release system, to place orders directly with the supplier for specified materials during a given contract period'. Newman (1985) states that a systems contract involves a joint effort by the buyer and the supplier to construct a 'parts' book with ordering and delivery procedures which enable the requisitioner to order things directly from the supplier, using a multipart requisition form with copies to purchasing and accounting. The supplier makes frequent regular deliveries, weekly or even daily.

These are useful and sensible procedures which have also been widely used in Britain. They have already been mentioned under the name of blanket order.

CASH PURCHASES

Small occasional purchases from retailers or firms which are not regular suppliers may be paid for in cash to save the trouble of opening a credit account.

Cash-on-delivery (COD) orders are sometimes used. For instance buyers call off delivery from local suppliers, who are paid out of petty cash by goods inwards department on receipt of goods.

Cash with order may seem unusual for organizations which normally buy things on 30 days credit and pay by cheque, but it is of course normal for most purchases by most people, and it can save time and money on internal paperwork, such as accounting and purchasing documentation. One person is usually authorized to visit suppliers, pick up requirements and pay for them. An imprest petty cash book may be used to record purchases and payments, supported by receipt vouchers signed by those who received the goods. An upper limit is set for cash purchases, and because this is usually quite low, purchase authorization can also be at a low organizational level.

Blank cheque with order is another version of cash purchase. A three-part set of requisition, order and cheque is used. The cheque form is valid only up to £500 and payable within 90 days of date. When the goods are delivered, the supplier completes the cheque form, deposits it at the bank, and is paid immediately.

AMENDING AND CANCELLING ORDERS

In law either both or neither parties are bound by a contract. Hence the buyer has no unilateral right to amend or cancel a contract. What was originally agreed is as binding on the buyer as on the seller. Attempting to get round this by inserting in the terms of contract a right to cancel or amend could have the legal effect of invalidating the contract.

In practice buyers do have to approach suppliers with amendments to orders or requests to cancel them. Common reasons are design changes or alterations in sales or production plans. The supplier may be legally entitled to refuse, since a contract binds both parties. The supplier is entitled to compensation for work done or materials bought in accordance with the contract up to the date of cancellation. The supplier is not entitled to refuse cancellation or make cancellation charges if the reason is his own failure to comply with conditions of contract.

ORDER PROGRESSING AND EXPEDITING

The supply task is to deliver goods and services where and when they are wanted. Simply placing orders and leaving the rest to suppliers may not be enough to achieve this. Some administrative effort is usually required to get orders delivered at the desired time.

This process may be thought of as delivery *assurance* and delivery *control*, in the same way as we refer to quality assurance and quality control. Delivery assurance means making sure that suppliers will meet very tight delivery schedules without expediting, and this has to be done if just-in-time systems are used. Delivery control means setting up systems to indicate when orders are due and taking expediting action as needed.

In both cases an essential preliminary is to devise firm and realistic plans for delivery dates. This can be difficult when suppliers quote longer lead times for material than the purchaser quotes his own customers for end-products. Purchasing must then make a positive effort to find out about and keep in touch with developments. Getting materials is the buyer's job, and colleagues in other departments can hardly be expected to know about market problems if he does not tell them. Designers, production planners and requisitioners need to know what lead times apply, and need to understand that early warning must be given to purchasing of needs which may be difficult to fill as soon as such needs take shape, even before specifications are finally settled. This enables the purchasing groundwork to be done so that orders can be placed as soon as the go-ahead is given, or a place can be booked in the queue by letter of intent, provisional order or capacity booking order.

The first step in delivery control is to decide, at the time the order is placed, whether it needs to be progressed, and if so when. Most orders do not need to be progressed unless they are late. An important minority of orders do need to be progressed, some of them almost from the day they are placed, and some on more than one occasion: for instance when design work should be completed, when tooling should be ready, when prototypes should be delivered, etc.

Having decided that a particular order needs to be followed up, and also when this should be done, the next step is to enter it in some sort of reminder system. This should be done within 24 hours of issuing the order. The simplest reminder system is a desk diary. Each day the orders placed the previous day which need to be progressed are entered under the date at which progress action may be needed. Other systems use progress cards, coloured tags attached to copy orders, wallcharts, etc. If more than a quarter of orders need progressing, an extra progress copy of the order may be made, as shown in Fig. 4.2. These are put into files numbered from 1 to 31 for days of the current month, and January to December for the next 12 months, plus a slot for orders due for progressing in more than 12 months time. Each day copy orders for that day are taken out and those which are in transit or have been received are destroyed. The rest are progressed if necessary. If open order files are computerized the reminder system can also be computerized.

Periodically it is also necessary to scan through outstanding orders to clear out dead orders that have been overlooked and to follow up orders that were not entered in the reminder system, but which have been outstanding longer than is reasonable.

Routine expediting may start with a standard letter asking for confirmation that delivery is on the way or will be made as agreed. No reply

Follow-up copy	Purchase order	Number _____	
Due for delivery			
Date urged	Delivery promised	Date urged	Delivery promised

Fig. 4.2 Progress copy of order.

or unsatisfactory reply leads to personal letters, phone calls and visits by the buyer or expediter. 'Just as both the soft sell and the hard sell have their uses,' one buyer said, 'so in progressing orders we need a whole range of approaches, from pained aggressiveness to soft soap.' In critical cases buyers start looking for alternatives to fill the gap and may consult higher management to see what extra pressure can be applied.

RECEIVING AND INSPECTING GOODS

The transaction is completed when goods are accepted and paid for.

A goods-receiving bay is usually provided for goods inwards. This is normally in the main stores building if there is one. Alternatively, goods may be delivered direct to the department which ordered them. It is important to lay down clear procedures for receiving goods so that they are available promptly to those requiring them, and also so that payment is not made for faulty goods or goods that have not come in or were not properly authorized.

Most suppliers send advice notes by post, as formal notice that goods are on the way. These go to the order progressing section for information and are passed on the same morning to the goods-receiving section in the stores. Each day also the goods-receiving section look through the advice notes they have and take appropriate action if any consignments are overdue.

When goods arrive, they are identified with the aid of the advice note received by post or enclosed with them, the packing note which is often packed with them, and the copy order provided for goods receiving. Goods are checked to see that what has arrived is what was ordered. If something is received which does not appear to have been ordered, goods receiving check with purchasing before accepting it. Visual examination of the goods or their box labels to check description, and counting or weighing to check quantity are usually required. Any discrepancy or damage in transit is reported to purchasing.

Technical inspection may be called for. This is done by qualified inspectors using test devices and measuring equipment and leads to an inspection report. This delays things and is expensive, so that the less of it that can be done the better, so long as quality can be assured. Chapter 14 goes into this matter in more detail.

When goods have been accepted this is recorded on a goods-received note with copies to interested departments. Small organizations use a goods-received book instead of separate multipart notes. Sometimes a computer terminal is provided on which details of the delivery are entered instead of using goods-received notes or books.

DISCREPANCIES AND DEFECTS

Normal procedure when goods are defective or fail to comply with specification is to advise the supplier at once how much of the consignment is rejected and why, and to offer the supplier an opportunity to inspect the goods on-site. Rejected goods can be held on-site for the supplier to collect, or with his agreement returned at his expense. Or they can be accepted at a reduced price to compensate for extra processing; or corrected by the purchaser at the supplier's expense; or sold for scrap on the supplier's account, in each case with the supplier's agreement. Goods which have been rejected remain the supplier's property. This is why the supplier's agreement should be obtained before they are worked on or disposed of. In the absence of such agreement the purchaser may be deemed to have accepted the goods by construction from his behaviour, irrespective of what the correspondence says.

One firm finds that three standard letters cover most situations. The first (known internally as 'naughty boy') states that goods have been accepted although marginally outside specification, adding that it is sincerely hoped that future consignments will comply fully with the specification. The second states that goods were defective, explains why, adds that they have been put right at the supplier's expense, and refers to an enclosed invoice for the cost of rectification. The third is a rejection letter, advising that the consignment was not acceptable and requesting that replacements be sent urgently.

Situations which cannot be handled satisfactorily in these routine ways call for skill and creative thinking, and buyers report much job satisfaction from solving the problems arising when an urgently needed article fails to pass inspection.

INVOICES AND PAYMENT

The normal terms on which organizations trade are that the supplier posts an invoice for the goods, dated the same day as they are despatched, and allows the customer a month to pay. There are also many special terms as mentioned previously. Large quantities of invoices may arrive every day. They have to be sorted, checked and approved for payment quickly so that payment can be made within the time allowed. This clerical work is usually done by the accounts department. Some firms prefer it to be done in the purchase department since the records

FOR
TERMS
POSTED TO ORDER
PRICE CORRECT
CALCULATIONS CORRECT
GOODS RECEIVED
PASSED FOR PAYMENT

Fig. 4.3 Invoice stamp.

required are available there, and since it is the purchase department which takes up any queries with sellers. Invoices are usually rubber-stamped with a block such as the one shown in Fig. 4.3 so that the persons who make the various checks can certify that they have done their part.

5

Legal aspects of purchasing

In commercial practice the word contract is sometimes used only for agreements which either involve exceptionally large sums of money or cover exceptionally long periods of time or are embodied in more formal documents than usual. In law however a contract is any legally binding agreement, breach of which can be grounds for action in the civil courts.

An order is an instruction – to make or supply goods or carry out work, for instance. A contract is an agreement between two or more parties – for instance, to make or supply goods or carry out work – which is legally binding. In this chapter we consider how an order becomes a contract.

Contracts may be subject to a variety of terms and conditions, express or implied, and are regulated to some extent by legislation. Some terms and conditions in common use are examined in this chapter, including those which may be implied by law, and also some special contract clauses and types of contract.

Standard form contracts are widely used on the selling side by travel agents, insurance companies, and many others. On the buying side they are used for major constructional and building contracts and some other types of engineering contract. The contract is the whole agreement. The ICE form of contract states: ' ''contract'' means the Conditions of Contract Specification Drawings Priced Bill of Quantities the Tender the written acceptance thereof and the Contract Agreement (if completed)'. Lawyers do not seem to like commas. Even without commas, this states clearly what is meant by a contract of this type.

TYPICAL PURCHASE TRANSACTIONS

The typical organizational purchase transaction is between honest persons representing organizations with reputations that they do not wish to lose. It is one of a series of transactions which both parties want to continue. Consequently most purchase departments do not and need not rely entirely on the letter of the law and the wording of their contracts. The real basis of their dealing with suppliers is mutual trust.

This makes for a considerable difference between the commercial view of a contract as an arrangement for goods and services to be supplied in return for a price, and the lawyer's view of it as a legally enforceable agreement. The buyer may be mainly concerned with specification, time, price, conformance and so on; the lawyer is more concerned with how the agreement would stand up in court. The last thing a purchase department wants to do is to go to law. Its job is to get the goods economically and on time, and litigation rarely if ever assists in this.

This does not mean that legal aspects are not important: far from it. Disputes may be settled by negotiation or arbitration rather than litigation. But settlement is usually based on what the parties believe to be their legal rights.

Buyers are not expected to know the whole of English law, both common law as evidenced by some 300 000 reported cases, and statute law comprising about 3000 Acts of Parliament plus delegated legislation made under the authority of those Acts. Even less can they be expected to know the law of all the other countries they buy from. But they should know when to consult a legal expert. They should also know what in the course of ordinary commercial transactions they are committing their organization to – if indeed they are committing it at all, for many orders are placed which do not bind either buyer or seller by contractual obligations which would stand up in court.

If the parties never come to an agreement, clearly there can be no contract. When one party makes an offer (whether an offer to sell, such as a tender, or an offer to buy, such as an order) which the other party accepts as made, then they have agreed and there is a contract. Offer and acceptance, with very few exceptions, need not be in writing. The statement 'verbal contracts aren't worth the paper they are written on' does not refer to their legal validity but to the difficulty of proving what was actually agreed if the parties have different views on this.

Word-of-mouth contracts are in fact very common in ordinary life and are sometimes used by purchase departments too. For instance, at an auction sale the auctioneer invites bids, and a contract comes into existence when a customer makes a bid which the auctioneer accepts and the hammer falls.

THE BATTLE OF FORMS

The legal view is that agreement exists when either party makes an offer which the other party accepts, as shown in Fig. 5.1. The offer, complicated as it may often be, and modified perhaps by much discussion and negotiation before reaching its final form, must be accepted as made if agreement is to be reached. Any variation put forward in accepting an offer converts the acceptance to what is called a counteroffer.

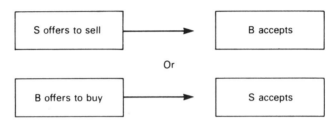

Fig. 5.1 Contracts are formed when one party accepts an offer made by the other.

But if the parties exchange a series of standard forms, each referring either to conditions of purchase or to conditions of sale that are not compatible, and which neither buyer nor seller attempts to reconcile or even read, a contract will nevertheless be assumed to have come into existence if the goods are supplied, accepted and paid for.

The question is: which set of conditions applies.

The situation shown in Fig. 5.2 occurs quite often in practice, and indeed the exchange of shots could continue beyond what is shown there, with advice notes, goods received documents and invoices being fired back and forth, each reiterating on behalf of its originator a set of conditions which are in some respects at variance with the set put forward by the other party. Lord Denning, in *Butler Machine Tool Co. Ltd v. Excello Corp (England)*, said:

In most cases when there is a battle of forms there is a contract as soon as the last of the forms is sent and received without objection being taken to it. . . . The difficulty is to decide which form, or which part of which form, is a term or condition of the contract. In some cases the battle is won by the man who fires the last shot. He is the man who puts forward the latest terms and conditions; and if they are not objected to by the other party, he may be taken to have agreed

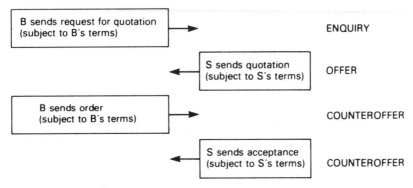

Fig. 5.2 The battle of forms.

to them. In some cases, however, the battle is won by the man who gets his blow in first. If he offers to sell at a named price on the terms and conditions stated on the back and the buyer orders the goods purporting to accept the offer on an order form with his own different terms and conditions on the back, then if the difference is so material that it would affect the price, the buyer ought not to be allowed to take advantage of the difference unless he specifically draws it to the attention of the seller. There are yet other cases where the battle depends on the shots fired on both sides. There is a concluded contract but the forms vary. The terms and conditions of both parties are to be construed together. If they can be reconciled so as to give a harmonious result, all well and good. If differences are irreconcilable, so that they are mutually contradictory, then the conflicting terms may have to be scrapped and replaced by a reasonable implication.

In an effort to tie up the loose ends of every transaction some buyers resort to terms and conditions of the kind shown in Fig. 5.3. These tell the seller that the buyer is liable only for orders (a) on the official order form, which (b) the seller has accepted by signing and returning within 14 days the acknowledgment copy of the order form. Of course in law the buyer is liable for any valid contracts however made. They also attempt to override (in section 15.1) any subsequent counteroffer by the seller. Perhaps what the buyer is really saying here is, these are the terms on which we do business, and you must agree to them if you want to do business with us in future.

IMPLIED TERMS AND CONDITIONS

In addition to any terms and conditions expressly included in contract documents, a number of terms and conditions may be implied into contracts by statute, custom of the trade, or the practice of the two parties in regular dealing with each other.

2.   ACCEPTANCE

The Buyer shall not be liable for any order unless:

(a)   it is issued or confirmed on the Buyer's official order form,

(b)   the Seller accepts it by returning the acknowledgement copy of the Buyer's order fully completed within 14 days of the date of the order.

3.   VARIATION

Neither the Buyer nor the Seller shall be bound by any variation, waiver of or addition to these conditions, except as agreed by both parties in writing and signed on their behalf.

15.   LAW AND APPLICATION

15.1 These Conditions shall have precedence over any Conditions appearing on any acceptance form, delivery form, or other documents or letter emanating from the Seller, and such conditions shall have no effect whatsoever except insofar as they confirm the terms of the order.

15.2 These Conditions shall be construed in all respect in accordance with English Law. Nothing in these Conditions shall prejudice any conditions or warranty (expressed or implied) or right or remedy to which the Buyer is entitled in relation to the material or goods ordered by virtue of statute or common law.

Fig. 5.3   Some conditions of purchase.

The main relevant statute is the Sale of Goods Act 1979, which consolidated the original Act of 1893 with subsequent amendments. This applies to contracts 'whereby the seller transfers or agrees to transfer the property in goods to the buyer for a money consideration called the price' (S.1). 'Goods' are defined in the Act in a way which includes a huge variety of things from a nail to a jet airliner, but excludes intangible goods such as patents, trademarks, copyright and designs. Barter deals or contracts of exchange are excluded if no money passes, as are hire purchase contracts and contracts for services or the performance of work. But most contracts made by most purchase departments are contracts for the sale of goods as defined in the Act.

A distinction is made between the less important terms, called warranties, and the more important terms, called conditions. Breach of a warranty usually entitles the injured party to damages, as does breach of a condition; but in addition breach of a condition entitles the injured party to repudiate the contract.

Any contract for the sale of goods includes an implied condition that the seller has the right to sell the goods (S.12). There are also two warranties implied into contracts by this section: that the buyer will have quiet possession of the goods and that the goods are free from undisclosed third party claims. For instance if S sold goods to B and a third party turned out to own the patent on the goods, S would be in breach of this warranty and B would be entitled to damages.

If the goods are sold by description, there is an implied condition that the goods will correspond to the description (S.13). If they are sold by sample as well as description, the bulk of the goods must correspond to the sample as well as to the description.

An important protection for the customer is provided by S.14. If the goods are sold in the course of business, and the buyer expressly or by implication makes known to the seller any particular purpose for which the goods are being bought, there is an implied condition that the goods supplied under the contract will be reasonably fit for that purpose, whether or not it is a purpose for which the goods are commonly supplied, unless it is clear from the circumstances that the buyer did not rely, or that it would be unreasonable of him to rely, on the skill or judgment of the seller.

There is a further implied condition that goods sold by description will be of 'merchantable' quality. This is not a word used in commerce nowadays. So the Act gives us a definition: 'as fit for the purpose or purposes for which goods of that kind are commonly bought as it is reasonable to expect having regard to any description applied to them, the price if relevant, and all the other relevant circumstances'.

These implied terms apply to all sales in the course of business to consumers. If the sale is to business customers most of them can be prevented from applying by an *exclusion clause*.

The Supply of Goods and Services Act 1982 applies similar provisions to contracts for work and materials, and to contracts of exchange. Contracts for work and materials include building contracts, and maintenance contracts where the supplier does the work of maintenance and supplies materials such as spare parts required to keep equipment in good order. Contracts of exchange are barter transactions. A common example is when new vehicles are bought and old vehicles are offered in part exchange.

A condition is implied that goods transferred by description will comply with the description, and goods transferred by sample as well as by description will comply with both sample and description even if the transferee selects them, unless there are defects specifically drawn to his attention or which he ought to have noticed in examining them. A condition is also implied that goods supplied under a contract in the course of business are merchantable in the sense described above. The expressions transferror and transferee mean the person who transfers ownership and the person who receives it: buyer and seller, as we would normally say. They are used because in this legal context the Sale of Goods Act confines the expressions buyer and seller to the sale of particular kinds of goods for 'a money consideration called the price'.

The Supply of Goods and Services Act also applies to contracts for services. These include contracts for transport, for window cleaning, for security, and for professional services such as legal advice, but not employment contracts which are contracts of service rather than contracts for service. The Act lays down that there is an implied term in such contracts that reasonable care and skill will be used in carrying out the service, that it will be done within a reasonable time if no time has been agreed, and that a reasonable charge will be payable if the consideration for the service is not stated in the contract or clear from past history. What is reasonable is stated to be a question of fact.

EXCLUSION CLAUSES

The law protects consumers more than business customers. But a business customer who has to make a contract on the seller's standard form contract is also protected against the imposition of exclusion clauses by S.3 of the Unfair Contract Terms Act 1977. This would not apply to a business customer who was free to contract with other sellers who did not try to impose such clauses. The protection does not take the form of invalidating all such clauses, but of requiring them to be reasonable. Unreasonable clauses will not be enforced by the courts unless it is considered that the two parties have equal bargaining power, and risks are normally borne by insurance, when as Lord Wilberforce said in a 1980 case 'there is everything to be said for leaving the parties free to apportion the risks as they think fit'. In other words we are quite free to make unreasonable contracts with each other if we so desire, and there is no reason why they should not be legally binding unless one of us has the power to impose clauses on the other, when the other party may ask the courts to decide if the clauses are reasonable in the circumstances.

WHEN PROPERTY PASSES

If something goes wrong, such as loss, damage or theft, before goods are actually in the buyer's possession, it is important to know who is the legal owner of the goods at the time. Generally the risk of loss or damage 'passes with the property', or goes with ownership. The buyer is responsible for insuring goods or standing the risk once they have become his property. When does property pass, or as we would normally say ownership change? This may be stated expressly in the contract, for instance by such terms as ex works or FOB or delivered our premises.

Ex works means that goods cease to be the seller's property as soon as they leave his works. Even if the seller arranges transport on behalf of the buyer, the goods cease to belong to the seller as soon as they leave his premises, and it is the buyer who has to make any claim for damage or loss in transit against the transport firm. In principle the buyer is responsible for collecting the goods from the seller's establishment.

Delivered our premises, or delivered to this address, or delivered buyer's works, mean that goods are the property of the seller until delivered to the buyer. The buyer would make any claim for damage or loss in transit against the seller, not against the transport firm.

FOB and other terms used in international trade are considered in Chapter 15.

EXPRESS TERMS AND CONDITIONS

A great deal of business is done under the law of the land without special terms and conditions being agreed. One survey of purchase order forms used in industry found that over a quarter of them had no printed conditions on them at all. Reasons given included this: 'we try to deal with our sources of supply in such a way that we can depend on them without a lot of foolish conditions'.

Many purchase order forms include a number of printed 'conditions', so-called, which are not really conditions of contract in the legal sense but general instructions or requests, such as that invoices should be despatched the same day as the goods, that any documents referring to the goods or to the order should mention the order number, and that the company will not be liable for goods supplied or work done unless an official order has been placed. The last statement can hardly be a condition of a contract which has obviously been made by means of an official order form, but is more a general notice to suppliers.

A minority of orders state that they are 'subject to our standard conditions of purchase', a formidable document supplied separately, while others have their reverse sides covered with a multitude of conditions in small print. Many suppliers also use sales documents listing in equally small print their standard conditions of sale. Mr Justice Winn spoke harshly of one of these sales documents in a 1959 case:

It may be remarked in passing, without any suggestion that the defendant intended their text to be a trap, that it conforms to customary mercantile practice at least in the regrettably normal respects, (1), that it is legible only by eyes with an acuity unlikely to be enjoyed by any individual possessing sufficient maturity of mind to understand it; (2), that it is verbose, tautologous and obscure; (3), that by internal evidence it has not been constructed but merely thrown together as an amalgam of phrases recklessly as well as fortuitously culled – with scant regard it may be for copyright – from other sets of trading conditions.

Despite these strictures, a great deal of business is done under standard form contracts, or contracts which include standard clauses, and some of these will now be considered.

'ROMALPA' CLAUSES

Retention of title clauses became popular with sellers after a 1976 case, *Aluminium Industrie* v. *Romalpa*. The seller supplied the buyer with aluminium foil, stipulating in the contract that the foil did not become the buyer's property until paid for. Before paying for the foil, the buyer went into liquidation. The receiver wanted to use money from sale of some of the foil to pay off creditors whose debts were secured by a floating charge. The seller wanted to recover the money on the grounds that the foil was his according to the contract. The Court of Appeal found in favour of the seller.

Since then a number of similar cases have come before the courts, and it has become clear that in addition to such well-established terms as 'ex works', where property passes to the buyer when goods leave the seller's premises, and 'delivered our works', where property passes to the buyer when goods arrive at the buyer's premises, it is legally acceptable for the seller to retain property in the goods until the buyer has not only received the goods but paid for them in full. As one judge said, if financial institutions are entitled to secure their loans to a firm by means of a floating charge, suppliers are surely entitled to seek some similar form of security by retention of title clauses.

And indeed a buyer in financial difficulties and threatened with insolvency may prefer such clauses to cash-with-order terms. But if the buyer is not in financial difficulties they are a nuisance, especially if they specify that both raw materials and goods made from them have to be segregated and specially marked for identification. The buyer then argues that there is no need for such clauses because his financial position is sound and that the seller is attempting to impose on all customers without discrimination onerous clauses which are appropriate only in special circumstances.

LIQUIDATED DAMAGES

A liquidated damages clause is a contract clause which specifies either a fixed sum or a percentage of contract price to be forfeited by the supplier if his product, system or work is not delivered or completed on time. Usually the forfeit increases with time – for example, £1000 a week, or $x\%$ of the contract price per week up to a maximum of $y\%$ of the contract price.

Such clauses are often called penalty clauses. They are enforceable in English law only if the 'penalty' is a genuine pre-estimate of the loss likely to result from lateness; hence the term 'liquidated' (that is, agreed in advance, pre-estimated) 'damages' (that is, monetary compensation for loss).

Liquidated damages clauses are mostly used in contracts for capital equipment, construction contracts, and in the purchase of requirements for project production, rather than batch production or continuous production or merchandising. They are common in international contracts, where the client often imposes a penalty clause on the main contractor, who in turn includes similar clauses in subcontracts and orders for material and supplies. Here they can be a protection to the supplier by limiting his liability for lateness to the amount stated in the clause, if this is less than the amount due from the main contractor when completion of the contract is delayed. Indeed if the penalty imposed on the main contractor is large and the value of the subcontract or order for materials is relatively small, it may be difficult to find a supplier willing to take on the work without the limitation of liability conferred by a liquidated damages clause.

The main advantage to the buyer of such clauses is that they help to get things delivered on time. A further advantage is that if delivery is not made on time, compensation can be obtained immediately by deducting the agreed sum from payment against the supplier's invoice, without the delays and expense of lawsuits.

FORCE MAJEURE

In agreeing to include in a contract penalties for delay, sellers usually wish to exclude delays due to circumstances which are completely outside their control and which could not have been covered by insurance. Such clauses are usually called *force majeure* clauses.

Here is an example:

Force majeure: if either party is prevented from carrying out its obligations under the contract by events beyond its reasonable control such as government intervention or strikes but not including weather conditions, then that party shall not be liable for the effects of any delay caused by such events. If the delay lasts for an unreasonable time the other party may cancel the contract without liability to either party and buyer shall pay to seller an equitable amount for work done before cancellation.

PRICE ADJUSTMENT

Many contracts incorporate price adjustment clauses, which are appropriate when the contract price is a considerable sum and the contract period covers a considerable time. A fixed price is more convenient administratively. But one which is adjustable according to clearly defined index-linking rules often gives a lower final cost than a fixed price which has to include safety margins and estimates of future cost increases which may be little more than guesswork.

Price adjustment clauses provide a formula for comparing actual costs incurred during the contract with the cost figures which were used in calculating the quotation or tender on which contract price is based, using published statistics, and for calculating what contract price adjustment should be made.

Many contract price adjustment clauses are based on a model devised by British Electrical and Allied Manufacturers Association (BEAMA) in 1940. This assumes that contract price is made up of three parts: labour cost, material cost, and a third part which is treated as invariable. Weighting these parts at 40% each for labour and materials and 20% for the invariable part gives a formula which can be written as:

Final price = quoted price $\times (0.4 \times MB/MA + 0.4 \times LB/LA + 0.2)$

In this, MA is the index of material prices last published before the date of tender and LA is the index of labour costs last published before the date of tender. MB and LB are the corresponding indexes published at an appropriate point in the contract period, or averaged over an appropriate part of the contract period.

The 40–40–20 weighting mentioned above was used from 1958 to 1972, when it was changed to 45–45–10. In 1975 a further change was made to 47.5–47.5–5. The current clause is given in Fig. 5.4.

Some buyers argue that this last version is too much in favour of the seller, and make counter-offers, usually in the form of an earlier version of the formula.

BEAMA price adjustment clauses have several advantages:

(1) They are easy to understand.

CONTRACT PRICE ADJUSTMENT CLAUSE
AND FORMULAE FOR USE WITH
HOME CONTRACTS

ELECTRICAL MACHINERY: (for which there is no other
specific Formula)

If the cost to the Contractor of performing his obligations under the Contract shall be increased or reduced by reason of any rise or fall in labour costs or in the cost of material or transport above or below such rates and costs ruling at the date of tender, or by reason of the making or amendment after the date of tender of any law or of any order, regulation, or by-law having the force of law in the United Kingdom that shall affect the Contractor in the performance of his obligations under the Contract, the amount of such increase or reduction shall be added to or deducted from the Contract Price as the case may be provided that no account shall be taken of any amount by which any cost incurred by the Contractor has been increased by the default or negligence of the Contractor. For the purposes of this clause 'the cost of material' shall be construed as including any duty or tax by whomsoever payable which is payable under or by virtue of any Act of Parliament on the import, purchase, sale, appropriation, processing or use of such material.

The operation of this Clause is without prejudice to the effect if any which the imposition of Value Added Tax or any tax of a like nature may have upon the supply of goods or services under the Contract.

Variations in the cost of materials and labour shall be calculated in accordance with the following formulae:

(a) Labour
The Contract Price shall be adjusted at the rate of 0.475 per cent of the Contract Price per 1.0 per cent difference between the BEAMA Labour Cost Index published for the month in which the tender date falls and the average of the Index figures published for the last two-thirds of the contract period, this difference being expressed as a percentage of the former Index figure.

(b) Materials
The Contract Price shall be adjusted at the rate of 0.475 per cent of the Contract Price per 1.0 per cent difference between the Price Index figure of Materials used in the Electrical Machinery Industry last published in the Trade and Industry Journal before the date of tender and the average of the Index Figures commencing with the Index last published before the two-fifths point of the Contract Period and ending with the Index last published before the four-fifths point of the Contract Period, this difference being expressed as a percentage of the former Index figure.

Fig. 5.4 Typical BEAMA clause for contract price adjustment.

(2) They are easy to calculate or check from publicly available statistics.
(3) They provide a workable approximation to actual increases in the cost of paying employees and buying materials, without contributing to unwarranted increases in profit.

In some circumstances they have disadvantages, which can usually be overcome by changes to the formula. For instance, part of the contract period might be waiting time while the contractor is busy with other work and has not actually started work on the contract. The clause can then be adjusted so that the contract period is deemed to start from a date agreed between buyer and seller to represent the start of manufacture. Or it may be argued that simply by delaying delivery, the contractor could increase the amount due to him, especially when costs are rising rapidly. To avoid this, the contract period can be deemed to end at the date the equipment is due for despatch or handing over, instead of at the date it is actually ready as in the standard clause.

CONSTRUCTIONAL AND ENGINEERING CONTRACTS

More complicated formulas are often used in building and civil engineering contracts, considered below in Chapter 17.

Standard form contracts are commonly used for constructional and building work. The best known are the ICE and the JCT forms of contract.

The ICE form is approved by the Institution of Civil Engineers (ICE), the Federation of Civil Engineering Contractors, and the Association of Consulting Engineers. Its full title is the Conditions of Contract, Forms of Tender, Agreement and Bond for use in connection with works of civil engineering construction. The current edition is the fifth, issued 1973 and subsequently revised. Copies are available from the ICE.

The JCT standard form of building contract is issued by the Joint Contracts Tribunal (JCT), representing the Royal Institute of British Architects (RIBA), Building Employers Confederation, Royal Institute of Chartered Surveyors, and other bodies. Six versions of contract in this form are widely used. Copies are available from RIBA Publications Ltd.

INCENTIVE CONTRACTS

Incentive contracts give the supplier an incentive for success, instead of penalizing failure as penalty clauses do. About 300 years ago Pepys used both methods in shipbuilding contracts, and the American War

Department in its contract with the Wright Brothers for one of the earliest flying machines in 1907 offered extra payment if it flew faster than 40 mph (18 m/s). So this is not a new idea; but it has been widely adopted in recent years as an alternative to cost plus contracts in cases where the cost can be estimated roughly so that a figure for target cost can be agreed but not with enough accuracy to arrive at a fixed contract price.

Cost incentive contracts are intended to motivate the supplier to achieve target cost by sharing with him any savings he manages to make, while obliging him to stand part of the expense if costs are above target. Multiple incentive contracts extend this by including in the contract monetary incentives for achieving other targets, such as delivery performance and quality performance. With multiple incentive contracts there is the problem of balancing one desirable objective, such as high performance, against another desirable objective, such as early delivery or low price; and the difficulty is, that if one is not careful in setting and balancing the monetary rewards embodied in the incentive clauses, then one will motivate the contractor to aim at a balance or pattern of objectives which is not the one preferred by the customer.

Terms used in this connection include:

(1) cost: prime cost and overhead, excluding profit or fee;
(2) prime cost: cost of labour and material charged directly to the project;
(3) overhead: costs which are apportioned to projects on some basis such as the ratio of direct labour costs of the project to total direct labour costs of the factory;
(4) fee: contractor's profit or monetary reward expressed as a lump sum;
(5) fee spread: the difference between greatest and least fees a contractor can earn;
(6) cost incentive range: the band of costs over which the cost incentives apply;
(7) delivery incentive range: the delivery period over which the time incentive applies;
(8) performance incentive range: the performance range, for example, range of speeds, over which incentive provisions apply.
(9) share formula: the expression normally in percentage terms, for example, 80/20, of the basis of the customer's and contractor's cost sharing arrangements. The first figure is the customer's share (80%) and the second figure is the contractor's share (20%).
(10) target cost (TC): the cost estimate used for devising a cost incentive

arrangement for the sharing by the contracting parties of excess costs and of savings.

(11) target fee (TF): the fee payable if actual cost equals the target cost.

(12) tradeoff analysis: the assessment of the effect on the net fee which a contractor could earn under a multiple incentive contract if he took a course of action which would result in an increase in the fee for one incentive element, e.g. by achieving an improvement in delivery, but a decrease in his fee for another incentive element, e.g. by reason of an increase in costs.

(13) tradeoff breakeven point: the point at which the increase in fee which would be earned by achieving an improvement in one incentive element would be exactly compensated by a reduction in fee due to a worsening of the position on another incentive element in consequence of that achievement.

The basic cost incentive contract

The parameters of a cost incentive contract therefore are:

(1) target cost – the best estimate at which the two parties can arrive of what costs will be incurred in executing the contract;

(2) target fee – the amount of profit which the contractor will earn if the costs come out at a target cost;

(3) a share formula, which determines how excess, or cost saving, in relation to the target cost, will be shared between the two parties.

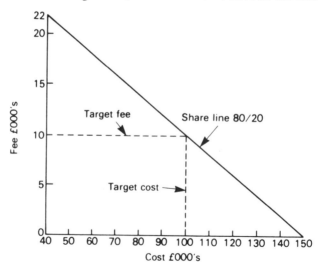

Fig. 5.5 Cost incentive contract; simple 80/20 fee structure.

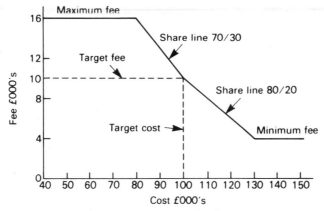

Fig. 5.6 Cost incentive contract; more complex fee structure.

If costs exceed the target cost, then the contractor gets his actual cost, plus his target fee, less a proportion of the excess cost, in accordance with the share formula. If costs are less than target cost, he gets his actual cost, plus the target fee, plus a proportion of the saving he has made. For instance, suppose the target cost is £100 000, and the target fee is £10 000, and the share formula is 80/20. If actual cost is £100 000, the contractor receives a total sum of £110 000. If actual cost is £120 000, he is paid a total of £126 000, his fee being reduced by £4000, his 20% share of the cost overrun. This simple arrangement is shown in Figure 5.5.

It is common practice to set maximum and minimum limits on the fee, although the unlimited share arrangements are also used, and sometimes different share formulas are used for cost overrun and for cost saving, as shown in Figure 5.6. This gives the contractor a greater fee for savings as well as greater protection for overrun, which he might require if the target cost were considered tight. If target cost is not too reliable, and actual cost could be considerably higher or lower, a 90/10 share formula would give less risk of loss as well as a lower profit incentive.

6

Planning the store

A store which has been properly designed or planned can be operated efficiently and makes economic use of space and equipment. Planning involves a number of compromises. Space can be saved at the expense of time. Time can be saved by using more space. Manpower usage can be balanced against labour-saving machinery; in countries where land is cheap, wages are low and people are looking for work, the automatic warehouses used in high-wage economies do not make economic sense.

Location of the store should be planned so that goods coming in from suppliers and goods going out to customers can be moved in and out freely. Inside the store, the internal layout and the equipment and operating procedures should facilitate off-loading, checking and putting away of goods coming in, and picking, issuing and despatch of goods going out.

The store should have adequate heating, lighting and ventilation. The floor should be dust-free and strong enough to support racks and fork-lift trucks. Security is important. It is a legal requirement that the health and safety at work of employees is fully provided for.

A typical central store serving several locations is an industrial building which allows four or five pallets to be stacked on top of each other, with some clear space above the stack for safety. (This corresponds to 5 to 6.5 metres, or 16 to 22 feet). Vehicle access needs to be convenient, with enough room for delivery vehicles to park, unload and turn. Loading bays should be about a metre above road level, and under cover.

STORE DESIGN

Much information needs to be collected and evaluated for the design of a new store; stock range, transaction volume, space requirements, and the extent to which mechanical handling is to be used. Four questions need to be answered:

(1) What things will be received, and in what quantities? Production inputs depend on what is to be produced. Each product would need to be broken up into lists of parts and materials needed to make it, multiplied by projected production rates, in turn depending on sales estimates. Maintenance requirements depend on the plant to be installed, plant utilization – single shift working or round-the-clock operation – and the importance of avoiding breakdowns.

(2) Which of these items will be stocked? Some requirements may be large enough and regular enough for arrangements to be made for suppliers to deliver direct into the production process, no stock, or just a buffer stock being held. At the other extreme, some requirements will be too occasional to be carried in stock and will be bought as needed. Between these extremes lies the broad range of stockable items.

(3) What are the average stocks, and the maximum stocks, to be carried of each item? Volume of usage, supply conditions, stock control policies, and cost factors affect this.

(4) How much room will these stocks take? This depends on stock levels multiplied by space requirements per item, and is also affected by holding and handling arrangements.

The next step therefore would be to plan the racks, pallets, tote-boxes, etc. in which the stock will be held, and the use of fork trucks, overhead cranes, conveyors, etc., for handling the stock.

Finally, the layout of goods receiving sections, issue areas, storekeeper's offices, inspection, and other auxiliary service areas need to be planned, and the gangway system laid out.

In practice, something like this has to be done when a new warehouse or a new factory is purpose-built for new products or processes. But when the new stores or factory is intended to replace or expand existing ones, stores design often starts with the shortcomings of the present arrangements, and aims at better ways to solve known problems.

Unit loads and containers

When goods are handled in large quantities, there are advantages in standardizing unit loads. The idea is to make a more convenient unit for handling and storage purposes by loading a certain number of goods into a container and keeping them in it as long as possible. The number of goods which make up a unit load depends on: the size of the item, the size of the container, storage, transport and handling methods, convenient delivery quantities for the supplier, convenient issue quantities for the user. Ideally goods are made up in unit loads at the point of origin and these are not broken into until the point of use, remaining in the standard lot through all intermediate transports, storages and moves.

Containers used with unit loads include: pallets, stillages, tote-boxes, freight containers. No-container unit loads are also made up by shrink-wrapping or strapping together such rigid items as bricks or cartons.

Freight containers are now widely used. Special container ships to take them, specially equipped docking areas to load and unload the ships, rail terminals and container trains, road terminals and fleets of special road vehicles for container transport have all appeared on an increasing scale. Freight containers facilitate transport rather than storage, but they have obviously influenced materials handling in the places which send or receive them. Many pallet sizes, including the standard European railway pallet, will not fit economically into the standard size freight container, which is 2.4 m (8 ft) high by 2.4 m (8 ft) wide by 3.0 m (10 ft), 6.0 m (20 ft), 6.0 m (30 ft) and 12.0 m (40 ft) long.

Pallets and stillages

Both pallets and stillages are types of load board, defined as 'a portable platform, with or without superstructure, for the assembly of a quantity of goods to form a unit load for handling and storage by mechanical appliances. Load boards include flat pallets, box pallets, post pallets and stillages.'

The meaning of the word stillage varies from one industry to another. A common type of stillage is a wooden platform mounted on wooden or metal skids which raise it 15 cm (6 in.) or so off the ground. This is used in conjunction with a stillage truck, often a simple angle iron frame on wheels with a tow handle. The operator pushes this frame under the stillage and pumps it from its low position to its high position, by a foot-operated hydraulic cylinder or a mechanical link with the towbar. The high position lifts the whole assembly off the ground on to the truck wheels, where it can be towed about. Semi-live stillages are also common, these are fitted with wheels at one end and the towing arrange-ment has only a single pair to take the front end load.

Any kind of frame for holding things can be called a stillage, and many types are made, with special attachments to hold bottles, carpet rolls, oil drums, etc.

Pallets are defined as 'a load board with two decks separated by bearers or a single deck supported by bearers, constructed with a view to transport and stacking, and with the overall height reduced to a minimum compatible for handling by fork lift trucks and pallet trucks'. Terms used in connection with pallets include the following.

(1) *Two-way entry:* the bearers allow the forks to enter from two opposite entry sides.
(2) *Four-way entry:* forks can be inserted from all four sides; on two sides known as 'restricted-entry sides' the truck's load wheels have to pass over the bottom slats of the pallet.
(3) *Bearers:* blocks or longer pieces which separate upper and lower decks or support the upper deck if there is no lower deck.
(4) *Deck:* top or bottom flat surface.
(5) *Stringer:* flat horizontal member connecting the bearers and supporting the deck.
(6) *Wings:* parts of the deck which project beyond the bearers.

Types of pallet include:

(1) *Flat pallet:* usually made of wood or plastic; can be single decked, if the goods will not be stacked, or are strong enough to support stacking – for example, wooden crates – or if the pallets are going to be held in pallet racks; can be double-decked, reversible, etc.
(2) *Box pallet:* these have at least three metal or timber sides, and are used to hold items which do not stack easily and would probably fall out without the sides; the sides can be solid, slatted or mesh; one or more can be removable to make it easier to put goods in and get them out; all the sides can be collapsible so that the pallet takes up less room when returned or stored empty.
(3) *Post pallets:* these have corner posts so that they can be stacked on top of each other, the posts taking the weight rather than the contents. Pallet convertors can be used to turn flat pallets into the equivalent of post pallets. The posts are usually made of metal and fitted with special feet which help in locating one pallet on top of another; sometimes lifting eyes or trunnions are also fitted.
(4) *Expendable pallets:* one answer to the problem of getting your pallets back from the customer when you send palletized unit loads to him, is to use non-returnable or expendable pallets. These have to be strong enough to stand the various moves and handlings they encounter en route, and are still in a state of active development. Another answer is the *pallet pool*: a group of organizations use a common pool of pallets on hire or loan arrangements of some kind. A national pallet pool for the United Kingdom has been discussed, but

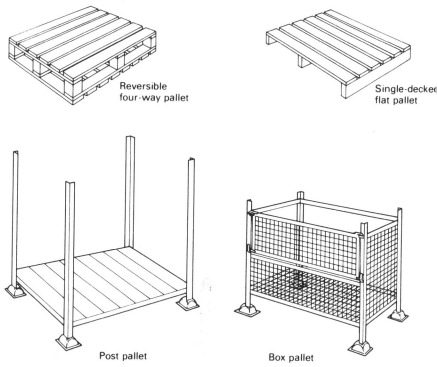

Fig. 6.1 Types of pallet.

firms are not willing to meet the cost and inconvenience of scrapping the 1200 pallet sizes they are currently using in favour of the two or three sizes a pallet pool would use. The two preferred sizes are 120 cm × 100 cm (48 in. × 40 in.) and 100 cm × 75 cm (40 in. × 30 in.).

Pallets can be stacked on top of each other, or where this would overload them or damage the goods, in pallet racks. Some pallets are shown in Fig. 6.1.

Storage racks

An extensive range of standard or semi-standard racks is available from manufacturers, as well as various kinds of slotted angle which can be cut and fitted together to make purpose-designed shelving. The main alternatives are:

(1) *No racks:* floor storage is used for very heavy goods.

(2) *Fixed and adjustable racks:* a popular choice is the double-sided rack 2.2 m (7 ft 3 in.) high, 2.7 m (9 ft) wide, and 0.9 m (3 ft) deep, allowing 45 cm (18 in.) deep shelves each side. Shelves are 0.9 m (3 ft) wide, the racks being made in 0.9 m (3 ft) bays bolted together. Distance between shelves can be adjusted to suit the size of the goods, and special drawers, dividers and cupboards are readily available. The overall height is fixed by the maximum reach of the average man standing on the ground. Heights greater than this can be reached by ladders, or by climbing up specially reinforced rack fronts, but a better way is to split high racks into levels with walkways or mezzanine floors at 2.0 m (7 ft) intervals, with at least two stairways and a gravity chute.

(3) *Sliding racks:* popular for items required infrequently. Small installations are moved by hand, larger blocks of shelves can be powered. Mobile racking saves space for storage, at the expense of time in getting goods out and putting them away.

(4) *Live racks:* a system useful when items are issued continuously in large quantities, providing automatic stock rotation. In one type, goods are accommodated on lengths of roller conveyor sloping towards the picking end.

(5) *Pallet racks:* fixed or adjustable racks designed to hold pallets.

Gangways between racks should be sited in line with windows to exploit natural light. Artificial light is best provided by lamps mounted above the ways, and also above receiving, checking, and issue points. Columns and stanchions should be in the rack area, not blocking gangways. Care should be taken that cables, pipes and sprinklers remain accessible.

The ways between racks and bins are usually divided into main roads and side streets. Main roads should be wide enough to take trucks and move the bulkiest goods: 1.5 m (5 ft) is the minimum practicable width; 1.8 m (6 ft) wide is a popular spacing for these main gangways. Side streets should be short to reduce walking, at right angles to main roads, and at least 0.7 m ($2\frac{1}{2}$ ft) wide; a width of 0.9 m (3 ft) is easier to work.

When several trucks are in use it is a good idea to make as many gangways as possible one-way streets. The width of one-way gangways should then be 0.6 m (2 ft) wider than the widest truck. Two-way gangways should be 0.9 m (3 ft) wider than two vehicles side by side. Provision should be made for trucks to turn round.

Clear spaces must be provided for receiving, unloading, unpacking, checking and inspecting incoming goods; for keeping returnable packages; and for assembling and making issues.

Stores location and centralized storage

Physical storage facilities are part of the organization's manufacturing strategy, in the case of production stocks, and part of its marketing strategy, in the case of stocks held for customers. They are links in the supply chain.

The basic principle is to store things where least work will be involved – where handling, rehandling and internal transport will be minimized and journey distances for the stores customers shortest. In a factory producing a single product or a group of similar products for instance, raw material might be stored near the first operation machines, work-in-progress between first and subsequent operations, finished product near the shipping and despatch area, and small tools and works supplies near the middle of the factory area. In a factory producing different products – for example, a textile factory producing jute yarn, woollen yarn, woven carpets, and operating a dyehouse – each department would store its own raw materials and central storage would be confined to common-user items such as maintenance and operating supplies. In an organization operating several establishments, each establishment except perhaps very small ones would store its own requirements.

That is one way to do it. There are others. Some very large organizations operating on a world scale, for instance armies and air forces, make extensive use of centralized storage. Local authorities and government departments have to consider the extent to which storage should be centralized. Even at the level of a factory it is common to find a single central store which receives all incoming goods, and makes issues either direct to users, or else in bulk lots to sub-stores like a wholesaler supplying retailers. Setting up a central stores of this kind adds another tier to the organization structure and another set of handlings and transports to the operations sheet, which must increase costs. Justification for a central stores must therefore be sought in those factors which may reduce costs by even greater amounts.

If common-user items are few and the combined demand for them small, centralization will not pay in the absence of special considerations – for instance maximum security for certain high-priced and readily saleable goods, or the need for special testgear and trained inspectors for certain deliveries.

But if there are enough common-user items, centralizing stocks of them can save money through lower stocks, lower prices, and perhaps other reductions in overhead. How can central storage reduce stocks? If four departments have independently stocked between three and 12 months' supply of an item they all use, obviously stocks come down if better stock control enables a central stores to supply them all with two months' stock. Departmental stores are usually small and their stock control may be amateurish. Less obviously, if four departments have independently kept three months' supply, and the item is switched to a central stores which still keeps three months' supply, there can still be a reduction in the quantity held. This is because the aggregated demand is stabler and hence more predictable than the four individual demands. The space saving may be greater than the direct stock reduction; bulk stocks take less room.

A switch to central storage should also mean fewer, larger orders – with possibilities of negotiating lower prices. Other considerations include:

(1) increased opportunities for standardization, leading to fewer stock items;
(2) greater security against pilferage and theft may be possible;
(3) overstocking and redundancy is usually easier to see and stop;
(4) administrative costs should be reduced, with fewer orders and fewer deliveries;
(5) there may be a net saving in space and personnel;
(6) materials which can best be bought forward in bulk on long delivery may be best handled centrally. This need not mean central storage, but sometimes it is a help.

Considerations which may weigh in the other scale include:

(1) extra transport cost;
(2) possible transport delays;
(3) possibly worse communications with users;
(4) unless there is excellent service and strict control, sub-stores will build up private buffer stocks and total stocks will increase, while the expected saving in space and personnel may fail to materialize;
(5) unless operating routines and paperwork are well designed, administrative costs may actually be increased.

Materials handling

Maximum use of space with minimum waste of time is the aim in planning storage and handling facilities. It is easy to save space by keeping goods in high-bay racks or in mobile racks which have to be moved to gain access. Whether it is more important to save space, or to save time, depends mainly on the throughput. For low transaction rates, over-the-counter service by hand is suitable. For high transaction rates, mechanization and automation can pay. In some applications goods are offloaded straight into conveyor systems which feed production, the stores being represented by loops and sidings in the system.

Four main types of materials handling are:

(1) *By hand:* widely used; goods are picked manually with the aid of steps, trolleys and ladders, and are carried to the issue point, with the aid of trolleys, sack trucks, etc.

(2) *Overhead cranes and hoists:* overhead travelling cranes have complete access to the area covered by their long and cross travel, without needing gangways except for storeman access.

(3) *Fork trucks:* these are available in considerable variety, both electric-powered and diesel-powered, as well as unpowered. They are primarily used for moving goods on pallets. Stacker trucks are mainly used for lifting or stacking pallets. Counter-balanced forklift trucks are perhaps the general purpose device for moving as well as stacking pallets, but there are several variations which operate in much narrower aisles than the counter-balanced type: for instance the reach truck, whose forks reach forward within the truck's wheelbase; the rotating-fork reach truck, which can work both sides of an aisle without the truck itself having to turn, and the stacker cranes, used in high-bay storage installations with narrow aisles.

(4) *Conveyors:* these include:
  (a) unpowered roller conveyors;
  (b) powered roller conveyors;
  (c) powered belt conveyors;
  (d) chain-driven overhead conveyors, which move goods in carriers suspended from trolleys linked by a chain running on an overhead track or rail;
  (e) underfloor dragline conveyors, in which trucks or trolleys are drawn round the floor by a chain in a channel in the floor. These are used in warehouses, where goods have to be picked from a number of different bays, the trucks being routed automatically to spurs in the bays required. Other materials-handling equipment is also used in stores, for instance dock levellers, mobile cranes, stillage trucks.

The objective is to arrange for material to be shifted over the shortest route in the safest manner, by the quickest means, in the largest convenient unit loads, and to cut out needless movement of men and materials.

Firms without a materials-handling engineer can obtain expert free advice from manufacturers of materials-handling equipment (who would not however be human if they did not have an unconscious bias in favour of mechanical handling), or can call in their own work study and industrial engineering department, since materials-handling engineers are simply method studiers with trade knowledge. Some simple rules which may be worth keeping in mind are these:

(1) Least handled is best handled. Every time parts and materials are handled, costs increase; and handling commonly accounts for 15%, occasionally as much as 85% of final cost. So eliminate unnecessary handling, and simplify necessary handling as much as you can.
(2) Try not to handle things twice. Some rehandling cannot be avoided if goods are to be stored at all, of course.
(3) Try to cut out bending and stretching, stooping, putting down and picking up. If incoming goods have to be held between unpacking and inspection, can they be held on bench-high roller conveyors? Getting things out of racks is usually easier than getting them off the floor. Floor storage usually requires goods to be stacked and lifted by hand.
(4) Avoid manhandling where possible; handle mechanically where justifiable on a cost basis. Mechanical handling devices include cranes, hoists, conveyors, forklift trucks and their attachments, jack trucks and stillage trucks, pallets and so on.
(5) Use gravity instead of muscle or motor where possible to move things. In a two-level stores, a gravity chute will bring things down quicker and more safely than a man.
(6) Try to handle in unit loads. Load standardization can save a lot of time in receiving, storing, checking and issuing goods. For goods of suitable size bought in adequate volume, the ideal is for the supplier to deliver palletized unit loads, which are not broken into until the actual production operation.

The changeover from manhandling to mechanical handling, apart from its cost advantages in an economy where men are not treated as beasts of burden, is part of the movement towards humanizing work, finding human uses for human beings.

Mechanical handling in the stores improves the storeman's lot, by taking some of the donkey-work out of his job. It should reduce labour costs. Whether or not it will reduce overall costs depends on a comparison of the wages saved, and perhaps other savings in time and space, with the depreciation and operating costs of the machinery.

AUTOMATIC WAREHOUSES

It is always interesting when considering the current state of the art in anything, to look at the leading edge, which in storage is the automatic warehouse. This is a warehouse in which a substantial part of the receipt, storage and dispatch functions are performed without manual handling of the goods. They are expensive installations, which pay only when a very high throughput of goods can be achieved – not less than 4530 kg (10 000 lb) per hour according to one estimate.

The history of the first of the automatic warehouses is instructive. This was designed by Donald Gumpertz for Brunswick Drug Co of Los Angeles and went into operation in 1957. The client supplied some 2000 retail outlets with a range of 1800 drugstore items, and increasing delays in filling orders from the central warehouse prompted the client to commission the design and installation of a highspeed automatic warehouse. The design solution was suitable for base stores handling upwards of a thousand issues a day. Each stock item was held in a steeply canted shelf or chute, loaded manually at the top by storemen, and unloaded automatically at the bottom by a solenoid-operated gate with remote control. Goods were discharged on to a system of conveyor belts leading to packing and dispatch bays.

Customers' orders were fed into data processing equipment which sorted the orders, printed advice notes and shortage notifications, updated stock records, and operated the gates at the appropriate locations. When the gates opened goods were discharged by gravity feed on to branchline conveyors, which fed mainline conveyors. Goods furthest from the output end were picked first, so that the whole order for a given customer would arrive together at the packing and dispatch bay, at rates of up to ten items a second.

The installation is reported to have worked well – only ten minutes lost through equipment malfunction in the first 18 months. But if its technical functioning was admirable, its economic viability became increasingly dubious. Los Angeles residents were moving further and further away from the city centre. So were the retail outlets which served them. Traffic congestion got steadily worse. Holdups in supplying goods to retailers were the result not of processing delays in the central warehouse, but of transit delays in moving goods from the central warehouse. The solution was to open warehouses in the outskirts of town. This reduced throughput in the costly high-volume automatic store until it became a white elephant and was shut down.

The optimum solution in this case turned out to be decentralization rather than automation. A successful technical achievement was a failure commercially. Storage facilities should be designed as part of a supply system. Designing them as a demonstration of what can be done with available equipment and techniques is not good business.

WORK STUDY IN THE STORES

The objects of work study have been defined as getting the most effective use of existing or proposed plant; the most effective use of human effort; and a reasonable workload for the people employed. These objects are as important in the stores as in any other part of the organization.

Work study has two aspects: work measurement, and method study. Work measurement consists in measuring and timing work with the object of setting standards of performance which a person trained for and used to the job can keep up day after day. These standards can be used for planning work, defining the size of the labour force, devising financial incentives and payment-by-result systems, and job costing. Work measurement begins by actually observing and recording what people do. Any storeman who knows his job could probably write down a list of the operations it entails; but actual observation is required to make the right allowance for delays, interruptions, waiting time, and frequency of various operations. A closely allied topic is job evaluation, or assessing the value of different jobs in relation to each other.

Method study also begins by observing how things are done, but with the object of devising better ways of doing them. Jobs which have for a long time been done in one way often turn out on examination to be capable of being done in a different way which is quicker and less tiring. After all it is obvious that the layout of many stores, factories, offices and indeed towns, just developed piecemeal, bits and pieces being added here and there wherever they could be fitted in. These haphazard arrangements have their own charm but things could be ordered better if thought were given to the functional aspects. Much work, especially work which is taught on a craft apprentice system, is equally piecemeal and haphazard in its organization. Method study entails a systematic consideration of process, procedure, equipment, layout, and anything else relevant, in order to make the work less tiring, more effective, efficient, and economical.

The work studier's main tools are analysis, ingenuity, and observation, together with a mind trained and skilled in work study. Nevertheless some tools or aids have been developed which all can use.

String diagrams to check travel distances, flow charts to devise optimum routes, scale plans and models aid in designing both stores layouts and materials handling.

PLANNING AIDS

The simplest planning aid is to make a map of the stores; the usual scale is 6.5 mm ($\frac{1}{4}$ in.) to 30 cm (1 ft). Walls, windows, doors, roads, railway sidings, lavatories, pillars and other obstructions should all be marked. Trucks, trolleys and equipment, racks, bins and fixtures are drawn to scale on thin card and cut out. The effect of various layouts can be tried out by moving the cardboard cutouts about on the base plan. When a good layout has been found the cutouts can be stuck down with transparent adhesive tape. A more permanent planning board can be made by using balsa wood, which is easy to cut, for the movable parts. Magnets set into the cutouts enable them to be moved about the metal-based board without falling off. This shows how much room for manoeuvre there is and whether alleys are wide enough to take trucks. By pushing truck cutouts along alleys you can tell when spacing between racks has to be increased and where trucks can go.

Some pins and a piece of string enable the same map to be used to check walking distances required for various jobs. The average storeman spends at least a third of his time walking from point to point either to get goods out or to put them away, so it is important to design stores layout and locate stock items in a way that will reduce this walking distance to a minimum.

One washing machine manufacturer used a string diagram to redesign their stores in this fashion. A scale map of the stores was made and pins were stuck in points corresponding with issue counters and storage locations. By running a string round the pins corresponding to the points a storeman has to visit, the distance he covers in doing his work can be measured. It turned out that to collect parts for the main assembly of the washing machine a storeman had to walk about 6 km (3.8 miles).

The string diagram also shows how alternative arrangements affect travel distances. By better stores layout and improved parts location, this company's work studiers were able to reduce this long walk by one third. In the course of the investigation they also saved a fifth of the space required for storage.

Flowcharts, diagrams showing where items go and what happens to them, are useful in plotting better layouts and improving work routines or forms routing. Scale models are useful in following three-

Table 6.1 A code for special hazards to which stock may be subject

Code letter	Keyword	
A	Attractive	Attractive to thieves – portable, high-value, saleable
B	Breakable	Easily broken – handle with care – for example, glass
C	Corrosive	Acids, other chemicals, which may corrode containers, etc.
D	Dry	Must be kept away from moisture
E	Explosive	Certain chemicals, gas cylinders, explosives
F	Fire hazard	Highly inflammable items – petrol, oil, paint
H	Heat-sensitive	Deteriorate above certain temperatures
L	Light-sensitive	Fade or deteriorate in strong light
M	Magnetic	Should not be kept in strong magnetic fields
W	Warpable	Bend or break if not supported properly
O	Other	Subject to special hazards not listed above

dimensional material flows through multistorey buildings, in devising applications for roller conveyors and gravity chutes, and in showing overhead obstructions and planning high stacks. Perspex, being transparent and easy to work, is a suitable material for walls and floors in the model, while racks, machines, raised loading bays and so on can be modelled in softwood. Making the model could be an interesting project for a management student or apprentice; or it could be made by the firm's joiners or pattern shop, or let out to a specialist firm of architectural modellers. The standard scale is again $\frac{1}{4}$ in. to the foot.

Certain stock items require special treatment. Rubber must be kept dark and within certain temperature limits, paper must be kept dry and clean, timber so that it will season and will not rot, inflammable and explosive goods out of harm's way. It is sometimes advisable to code stock items that call for special treatment, and Table 6.1 may be useful in this connection. Security must always be borne in mind when designing stores. According to J. Edgar Hoover, 25% of factory employees were dishonest and 25% were honest. He did not know about the other half. Even if 75% of employees can be trusted, we would not wish to put temptation in the way of honest folk.

Obviously thieves do not want to steal everything in the stores. Portability, desirability, cost and marketability are the key factors. Strict security regulations which would be appropriate for diamonds would not be suitable for 2 tonne lathe bed castings, for example.

It is standard practice to keep stock behind a perimeter fence or wall, with thiefproof windows and locked doors. Nobody is allowed into the stores unless they have business there which cannot be done over the counter. Goods receiving bays are walled off from actual storage.

7

Operating the store

The basic activities in a store or warehouse are as shown in Fig. 7.1: receiving goods, holding them in stock, and picking orders for issue or despatch. Other activities such as recording stock, checking stock, and replenishing stock, are really parts of stock control rather than store operation.

Factors which affect the design of procedures to carry out these activities include:

(1) the volume and frequency of transactions,
(2) the range of stock items,

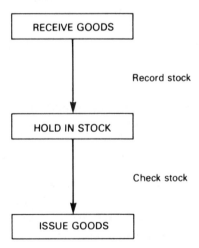

Fig. 7.1 Stores operation.

(3) the kind of demand on the store,
(4) the type of store,
(5) the stock control system,
(6) the materials handling system,
(7) value, weight, bulkiness of goods.

RECEIVING GOODS

Efficient procedures for receiving goods save time and trouble by ensuring that faulty goods are detected on arrival, not at some later stage such as issue or stocktaking, and that the quantity actually received is recorded.

After unloading, packages are counted and checked for visible damage before the delivery note is signed. Goods are checked for quantity and description against the delivery note, advice note, and purchase order. A goods-received note is made out, or the delivery is entered in a goods-received register.

If goods are damaged or defective they should if possible be sent back on the vehicle which brought them. Failing that, they are stored in a separate area, clearly labelled, until they can be returned, and both supplier and carrier are notified immediately.

After accepting, goods are moved to their proper location in the stores or to the department which requires them.

STOCK LOCATION

Three methods are used in deciding where to put things in the stores:

(1) *Fixed* location: every regular stock item has a fixed address or stock location, and can thus be found easily by experienced storemen. This is expensive in terms of space, since each location has to have enough room to accommodate maximum stock and most of the time stock will be well below maximum.
(2) *Random* location: any goods can be stored anywhere. Location records are essential; unless you record where things have been put you do not know where they are. Random storage makes better use of storage space and is the standard method when unit loads are handled mechanically.
(3) *Zoned* location: a compromise between fixed and random location is to allocate groups of goods to particular areas or zones; location within a zone may be fixed or random.

Fixed location

With fixed location, a specific place is assigned to each stock item, and there are several ways to do this. One study in a store holding quarter of a million items compared systems which:

(1) arranged items in part number order
(2) grouped products from each supplier together
(3) grouped similar things together
(4) located items according to their size and frequency of issue.

The latter system proved to be the most efficient: fast movers and bulk stores should be nearest the point of issue, and slow movers furthest away, it was found. This approach is sometimes called 'popularity storage' because the most popular items are located in the most accessible positions.

For quick and convenient operation, the following precepts are all important in deciding what items to put in which rack, though some of them conflict.

(1) Most frequently issued things nearest the issue point. In a tool stores for instance the most popular tools which are going in and out all the time could be kept in bins under the issue counter itself.
(2) Things issued together stored together. This cuts down walking time, speeds issues and reduces queueing.
(3) Keep things which are similar to each other near each other. Location in code order takes care of this automatically if a stores classification code is in use. But location in code order does not take care of other considerations some of which may matter more. Since deliveries of several similar items are often made at the same time, time is saved in putting goods away if like things are kept adjacently; time can also be saved in checking stock, and in hunting for alternatives.
(4) Store things in issue batches where possible. This is the principle of the unit load in another guise.
(5) Isolate dangerous stock – inflammable or explosive material like oil or cellulose paint; apply any special regulations which are relevant; can inert materials like sand be used as natural firebreaks?
(6) Change location when demand changes.

As well as deciding which rack to allocate to items, whereabouts in the stores to keep them, we have to decide which shelf in the rack to put them on – whereabouts in the rack to keep them.

In loading racks, put light bulky goods near the top; put smalls from waist to shoulder height; and put heavy goods in big compartments low down. Very heavy goods are best on the floor, not in the rack – for instance in a clear floor piling area near a hoist. Most frequently required goods should be in the most accessible position, which is usually between waist and shoulder height.

Random location

Random location means that stock can be stored in any vacant storage position. In the small store operated by one or two storemen, things are often put into the first vacant place and the operators rely on memory to find them. When memory fails they make a search. This system, or absence of system, has little to recommend it. Even in the small store 'a place for everything and everything in its place' is a good rule. The drawback is a somewhat wasteful use of space, since when stocks of an item are low the empty space cannot be used until that particular item is replenished.

Exaggerating a little, it could even be said that the average store using fixed location can be at the same time half empty – and short of space! The capacity of each storage location must be enough to accommodate maximum stock. But item stock is at its maximum only for a short time, just after a delivery has been received and before an issue has been made. As stock is issued, the level falls from maximum to minimum, and *average* stock is halfway between maximum and minimum – leaving a lot of storage capacity unused.

Admittedly, there is usually some floor piling, and for binned or racked goods some overflow on to adjacent bins and shelves is allowable; nevertheless space savings of between 20% and 30% have been made by using random location. A record has to be kept of where goods have been put. This can take the form of an indicator board.

One store which handled unit loads in pallets adopted random location, using two-part pallet tickets as the location record. As goods are received the fork-truck operator completes the pallet ticket, entering description of goods, quantity, date received, and location. He puts the top copy of the pallet ticket in a cardholder on the pallet itself as a contents label, and hands the second copy into the stores office. A third copy can also be prepared, for use in adjusting stock records kept somewhere else, or for costing and other statistical purposes including payment by results or productivity bonus calculation. Most stores work is not uniform enough for payment by results to be applied; but output bonus payments are obviously applicable to the work of storemen whose job is to drive fork-trucks and get out or put away pallets. The third copy of the pallet ticket which carries the operator's initials serves to record individual outputs for this purpose.

For describing locations a grid system can be used. For instance if we painted a grid on the stores floor by marking 26 lines a suitable distance apart from north to south, and at right angles to these ten lines from east to west, we would have 260 locations. If the north–south lines were lettered from A to Z, and the east–west lines numbered from 0 to 9, each location would have a two-element description. Location E3 would be where the north–south line E crossed the east–west line no. 3. Using two letters and two-figure numbers of course greatly increases the number of possible locations. Each location is the site of a pallet rack or stack, so if the pallets are stacked four high, and the operator knows the location, all he has to do is to check the pallet labels to see which of the four pallets on that location is the one he wants.

For filing and displaying the second copy of the pallet ticket in the stores office the type of board used for employees' clock cards has been adapted successfully. These are fitted with narrow slots for cards or tickets. One slot is assigned to each description of stock, i.e. each stock item. When goods are received, the office copy of the pallet ticket goes into the appropriate slot. To find what stock is held of any item, all that is necessary is to look at the tickets in the slot for that item. To make an issue, the oldest ticket is taken out and given to the operator, who drives his truck to the location shown on the ticket, forks out the corresponding pallet, makes the issue, and hands both ticket copies back to the office.

Stocktaking is reported to be simple with this system; it is only necessary to count the contents of the pallet which has been in stock longest for each item. Since issues are always made in order of receipt to ensure turnround of stock, this is the only one which may have been broken into for issues of less than a unit load. For the rest of the pallets containing that item, all we need do is to check that pallets are in the positions indicated by the location record, without counting their contents, and multiply the quantity of unit loads by the number of items which makes up a unit load.

Of course random location still provides a place for everything in a sense. Different lots of the same item may be in different places, but so long as each lot has a location shown on the indicator board, and is actually to be found in the indicated location, then there is a place for everything and everything in its place.

Zoned location

With zoned location the storage area is divided into a number of zones. There may be three zones: one for bulk stock, one for reserve stock, and one for picking stock. The idea is to get maximum use of space in the bulk stock area, which might comprise 21 m (70 ft) high racks, together with maximum accessibility in the picking area, where goods might be picked manually from 2 m (7 ft) high racks, or at two levels from 3.6 m (12 ft) high racks. Goods are initially put in the bulk storage zone, moving through the other two before issue.

Another method often used in large warehouses is to zone fast movers into a frontal zone, adjacent to the issue and receiving bays, so as to speed up operations by reducing the time spent putting goods away and getting them out again. Medium slow movers are in the intermediate zone, and slow movers in the rear area.

Yet another approach groups similar products in particular product zones – all the steel bars together, for instance – with either random location or else fixed location within particular zones.

ISSUING GOODS

The simplest way to issue goods is for those who want things to go or send to the stores and either help themselves or ask the storeman to get what they want.

Self-service storage racks for fitters' sundries are often kept in assembly bays, and maintenance men usually have a small open-access stores for their regular requirements. These are substores drawing supplies from the main stores; they are topped up regularly, often by some version of the imprest system described later (p. 128).

Storeman-controlled stores with counters at which goods are issued on request are often used for electrician's requirements, maintenance sundries, stationery, and tools. These single-purpose stores are sometimes open only part of the day – it would be wasteful to keep a small special stores open all day or employ a full-time storeman there, unless issuing and receiving goods is a full-time job.

Simply relying on the storeman to control issues and see that requests are reasonable may suit a small business where the storeman knows his customers and understands their requirements. But two complications occur in larger stores.

Firstly, storemen cannot control issues when there are many varied requirements. The solution is to make foremen and department heads responsible for authorizing issues to their section, by signing a stores requisition.

Secondly, cost clerks find that delays and inaccuracies are caused if they rely on lists prepared by storemen of what materials and supplies have been used on which jobs, or by which departments. The usual solution kills two birds with one stone by using the stores requisition. Signed by the appropriate authorizer, this shows what goods are wanted, the job number or cost allocation, and serves as an issue record for adjusting stock records and for job costing after it has been dealt with in the stores. In a small to medium stores, the routine would be:

(1) Section foreman writes out requisition, inserts job number or cost class, dates and signs.
(2) Section labourer takes requisition to stores issue counter.
(3) Storeman collects and issues specified goods; labourer takes them to section.
(4) Completed requisition passed to stock clerks, who adjust stock records to show new balance after issue and copy price from stock record to requisition.
(5) Priced requisition passed to cost clerks.

For regular batch production, preprinted requisitions or picklists are used. For mass production, requisitions are not used at all. Materials supply must deliver what is needed to the point of use at the scheduled time.

STOCKTAKING

Stocktaking means counting or weighing or measuring what is actually held in stock in order to verify records or provide a factual basis for the value of stock shown as an asset in the balance sheet of a trading company. Both the Inland Revenue authority in connection with tax, and the company's shareholders as represented by the auditors, are interested in the accuracy of these lists, because stock is an asset and appears as such in the balance sheet. If the figure shown for this asset is not correct, the profit shown will also not be correct. Undervaluing stock makes profit appear less than it should be and sets up a hidden reserve; overvaluing stock exaggerates profits.

The list of items in stock and the quantity on hand for each item can either be copied from records or obtained by checking the contents of the stores. If it is copied from records a physical check is still needed to prove the records are right. This physical check, actually counting or weighing or measuring everything in stock, must therefore be done at least once a year, and is called stocktaking.

If detailed records of stock are not kept the whole stocktaking job must be done at the same time, and while it is being done the stores must be closed for receipts and issues. All available staff must be drafted on to the work whether used to it or not. Counting and listing, though not hard, is tedious, and this together with the volume of work to be got through, usually over a weekend, does not make for accuracy. A recheck of sample items, say ten to a rack, carried out during the stock-taking, helps to encourage accurate work.

Stocktaking is easier to organize and interrupts normal work less when records are kept. The checking can be spread over a week or two; it can be done by storemen who know what they are checking; it is less rushed. The records can be checked in sections so that only parts of the stores have to be immobilized at a time. The most valuable or market-able goods should be recounted by accounting, purchasing, or internal audit personnel as a cross-check on storemen's honesty, on which the existence of records also provides a check.

Continuous as opposed to periodic stocktaking is possible when records are kept. Each week all-the-year-round selected items are checked. The selection of items can be random or items can be checked in sections in turn. Major items should be checked oftener than minor items, and a labour-saving way to achieve this is to check items when they are reordered.

Continuous stocktaking is particularly desirable when records are used for stock control, because errors then lead both to stock-outs and to overstocking, and stock records tend to be full of errors unless some continuous method of detection and correction is applied. Auditors however may not be satisfied to rely entirely on continuous stock-taking, and sometimes insist on a once-a-year complete stocktaking as well.

OBSOLESCENCE

Every store suffers from obsolescence. Retailers hold sales to clear their shelves of material which has not sold. Factory stores must also clear out obsolete and surplus and excess stock regularly, because it takes up space, makes some demands on stores labour and record-keeping, and contributes nothing to operations.

How does this dead stock cease to be live? Progress, fashion, im-provements in available materials may be the reason. Alterations to designs or to manufacturing policy or in sales are the most usual reasons; these all change or abolish requirements for certain items. As requirements alter, so must stocks; new stocks must be bought in, old unwanted stocks disposed of. There is always the temptation to hang on to goods because they are sure to come in useful one day. So they may; but meanwhile they are wasting a valuable asset – space – and they are not likely to be improving in stock.

Purchasing should insist on being informed by the department which institutes a change affecting requirements, at as early a date as possible, so that goods do not go on being bought after they have ceased to be required. Purchasing people themselves should keep reminding other departments of the importance of this.

But it is not enough to try to keep up with changes as they happen; some will slip through undetected and others will happen gradually. Systematic checks should be made on stock periodically, to identify the items for which stock levels have got out of step with demand. This is often done in conjunction with periodic stocktaking.

A three-way check after each 6 monthly stocktaking can be made. First, the two previous inventory sheets are compared with the one just completed, and a list extracted of items whose stock-level was similar on all three occasions. Second, the chief storekeeper makes an independent list of items which to his knowledge have not moved for months, or are moving but not fast enough to clear existing stocks inside a year. Third, the stock record section prepares a similar list from records by comparing stock balances with consumption. The lists are then compared and reconciled to give a final list of surplus.

Then steps are taken first of all to see that no more is bought of any of these items. (This sounds obvious and it is; but it can still happen that a stock clerk ignorant of the true position will requisition more of an item which is already overstocked simply because the balance is below a maximum stock figure or near an ordering level which is no longer appropriate.) Second, an effort is made to use up the excess material. Perhaps the design department can suggest a way to use some of it. The sales department may also be consulted; it may be possible to dispose of excess stock occasioned by discontinued or modified products by making a few more of the old products, perhaps for sale at special prices. Third, if all else fails, the rest of the dead stock is sold or scrapped and cleared out of the stores.

VARIETY REDUCTION IN STOCK PURCHASING

Most industrial stores stock a great variety of things; 10 000 items is quite common in small or medium-size engineering stores. In many cases this variety is greater than it need be; items are duplicated or triplicated under slightly different names, or the range of sizes is uneconomically large. A determined attempt at variety reduction can then be well worth while.

Variety is not of course in itself good or bad, and the mere fact that variety exists is no reason to try to reduce it. As consumers we all want a choice. One of the early steps in variety reduction, Henry Ford's famous dictum that his customers could have their Model T any colour they wanted so long as they wanted black, was a long step in the wrong direction. As now practised, variety reduction may actually increase the *useful* variety of end-products; it is the useless variants it aims to eliminate, and it ought also to reduce cost to the consumer. Steps in the right direction are simplification, specialization, and standardization.

Specialization is restricting the range of products coming from a particular group of productive resources, as when a plant specializes in screws and studding and refuses to branch out into turned products generally. *Simplification* is achieved by reducing the types and sizes made, although the word obviously has wider meanings some of which are relevant even in this connexion. *Standardization* is the process of agreeing and adopting precise detailed specifications or descriptions, whether of procedures, products or components. The dimensions, composition, quality, performance, method of manufacture or method of test may all be standardized.

Variety reduction has several advantages. With a smaller range of stock items, the demand for each item tends to increase and also to become more predictable. For instance, demand for items which are components in several end-products may well be easier to forecast than demand for any one of the end-products; consolidating the requirement tends to smooth out the fluctuations. Having fewer items in the stock range is likely to lead to lower total stocks even if total demand is not reduced. Making fewer and bigger purchases provides opportunities to obtain lower prices.

Prevention is better than cure, so care should be taken, when authorizing additions to the stock range, to avoid duplication and redundancy. Periodic re-examination of the whole range of things held in stock remains a necessity. Materials coding and classification provides an opportunity for this.

8

Materials
coding
and
classification

The straightforward and obvious way of referring to things as well as to people is to call them by their names. Despite this, we live in a coded world. Goods in stock are not the only items referred to by codewords. Our cars and telephones have code numbers. We ourselves are referenced by several codes – one for bank account, another for health service purposes, others for credit cards and so on. In work we encounter many codes, from the red paint that picks out firefighting equipment to pay codes, account codes, job numbers, part numbers, and vendor ratings.

Why? Short description is often the main reason. The more things we have to refer to, the longer the full name has to be if it is to describe a particular thing with no risk of confusing it with some other thing. A materials code such as '1333–114' is a lot shorter than a full description such as 'round brass rod to BS 249, 18 mm diameter'. Using short codewords instead of long names can save time in preparing documents such as requisitions, goods-received notes and stocktaking sheets.

When there are few things to refer to, names can be short and coding may not be needed. For instance the codeword above, '1333–114', is no shorter than 'brass rod', and would not save any time if only one type of brass rod were stocked.

A second reason for coding materials is certainty of description. People do not always call the same thing by the same name. When many users draw on a common stock of goods, several names are likely to be used for a single thing. Duplication of items, and apparent shortages of goods which are in fact in stock under a different name, can be prevented by assigning codewords to stock items on a one-for-one basis. Any stock item has one and only one code designation, however many names and descriptions are used for it in ordinary language. This may help in variety reduction and standardization.

A third reason is to arrange descriptions of items in an order that can be used for filing records and classifying goods. Useful information such as customer, supplier, end use, annual demand, Pareto classification, can be included in the code number.

Systematic materials coding gets more useful as the stock range gets bigger. In a small stores with a limited range of stock, plain language descriptions could be preferable. For larger stock ranges, the main advantages of materials coding are, as stated above:

(1) short description, combining complexity of reference with brevity of codeword, thus saving time in processing transactions and saving space in records;
(2) certainty of description, thus avoiding confusion and misunderstanding;
(3) order, providing a single definite filing order for materials records.

CODING FAULTS

Codes are easy to devise, but hard to devise well. Two common faults are:

(1) making codewords too long;
(2) not leaving room for expansion.

If codewords are too long they are hard to remember, and time is wasted looking them up, as well as writing them out. Codes must allow for future additions and changes. One electrical manufacturer replaced various existing product codes by a new single product code on a classification basis using nine-figure code numbers. Within two years the new code proved unable to fit in new products at the right places. It had to be redesigned, and a lot of large thick illustrated catalogues had to be replaced at considerable expense. Whether the chief engineer who devised it was replaced as well is not known.

Most article codes are made up either of letters or of numerals or of both. But colours can be used if all we want is an identification code.

COLOUR CODES

Factories often use colour coding to distinguish different specifications of bar and rod. High-alloy steel bar looks just like mild steel bar but costs much more and has different uses. If storemen saw slices off steel bars to make issues, they need some means of identification which lasts right to the end of the bar, like the name in Blackpool rock. A stripe of coloured paint down the full length of the bar will identify it when only a stub is left. A single stripe will identify six specifications, using six colours. Two stripes will identify 21, or 36 if the stripes are of different width.

Adhesive colour tabs are sometimes used for age-coding articles, so that the oldest stock can be issued first. Eight colours denote the eight quarters over 2 years.

Colour coding is also used for electrical wiring and for pipelines. Factories paint pipes black for drainage, white for compressed air, yellow for town gas, brown or pink for various oils, and dark grey for chemicals and industrial gases. Additional colour bands specify which gas; for instance, a yellow band means methane, a wide black band and narrow bands of yellow and red mean ammonia gas.

Electrical manufacturers pack a lot of information into the colour codes printed on resistors. Eleven colours in four bands state both the value of resistance, from 1 ohm to 9000 million ohms, and the tolerance, in one of nine ranges.

NUMERIC AND ALPHABETIC CODES

Most stock codes are either numeric, or alphabetic, or alphameric. Numeric codes use the familiar arithmetical digits to a base ten. (Internally, computers may operate in binary arithmetic, to a base of two. Binary codes are efficient for internal machine processing but unsuitable for use by people because the codewords are too long.) Alphabetic codes use the 26 letters of the alphabet, or a selection from them; letters which are easy to mistake for other letters may be avoided. Capital letters are commonly used. It is a mistake to use lower case letters or italics as if they were different symbols from capital letters, since they are pronounced the same and mistakes are likely to occur. It is also undesirable to use Greek, Russian or Hebrew letters, which would baffle those of us who do not have the advantage of knowing these languages or even how to pronounce their alphabets. Roman numerals are simply groups of letters and do not extend the range of available symbols. Punctuation marks are used as spacers but not as significant symbols.

Alphameric (also known as alphanumeric) codes use both letters and numerals. One chain store, for instance, used a five-character alphameric code. Codewords have three letters followed by one numeral followed by a letter, such as BAC4J.

A big advantage of alphabetic codes is that codewords are short, and consequently easy to recognize and remember. There are nearly half a million four-character combinations of letters. This does of course include some four-letter words best reserved for moments of stress. But when the combinations unsuitable for use in a materials code because they have meanings in plain language have been eliminated, we are still left with many more four-character codewords than if we used numerals. Binary codes using the characters 1 and 0, in contrast, have only 16 four-character codewords.

The relationship between the range of characters used, the length of codewords, and the number of possible codewords, can be expressed simply in mathematical terms. Let a denote the number of characters in a codeword, b denote the range of characters used, and c denote the number of codewords possible. Then:

$$c = b^a,$$

and consequently

$$a = \log c / \log b.$$

For instance, using the ten numeric digits the value of b is 10. If 10 000 codewords are required, the value of c is 10 000. The value of a is given by $\log c / \log b$, that is, 4/1, so that four character codewords are adequate. Or if a million codewords are required using the 26 letters of the alphabet, a is given by 6/1.415, that is, 4.25. Five-letter words would be needed if all codewords were to be the same length.

It is common practice in stock coding to make all codewords the same length, but some firms prefer variable length codewords: short codewords such as two-figure numbers for the high velocity lines, longer numbers for the slower movers. In principle, the time taken in processing codewords is minimized when the length of a codeword is inversely related to the logarithm of its frequency of use.

It might appear that alphanumeric codewords would be the shortest of all since the 26 letters plus the 10 numerals provide a base of 36 characters. But in practice such letters as I, O, Q are often excluded since they can easily be misread as numerals, and in constructing codewords groups of letters and groups of numerals are normally used, rather than having letters and numerals freely intermixed. It is apparently easier to remember a grouped coding such as AVX703 than a mixed coding such as A7V3X0.

CODE CONSTRUCTION

Three common methods of devising codes are:

(1) mnemonic,
(2) random or sequential,
(3) classification.

Mnemonic coding chooses codewords so that the letters used suggest the item referred to.: SB for steel bar, etc. They have been widely used for stock coding in the smaller engineering works, but they are increasingly difficult to devise as the range of items increases.

Random coding assigns codewords to items arbitrarily. Sequential coding uses the next number in sequence when a new item needs to be coded, and is the most common sort of random coding. In one carpet factory for instance, all of the thousands of colours and shades to which yarn is dyed are assigned code numbers. Any new colour is assigned the next number in sequence, and the dyer's recipe for producing it is recorded in the colour register under that number along with a sample.

Classification codes are much more difficult to devise, but they have certain advantages in variety reduction. The best-known example of classification coding can be seen in public and college libraries, where the stock is arranged in code number order. This automatically groups books of the same kind together, since the whole basis of the library code is classification. A well-known library code is the Dewey Decimal.

Melvil (he was christened Melville, but to save time shortened his name by two letters) Dewey was born in 1851, surviving undaunted to 1931. No doubt partly in the time saved by shortening his name, he devised a decimal classification code for the whole of human knowledge so simple and effective that it has been translated into ten languages including Chinese. An updated version of this, the Universal Decimal Classification (UDC), is published by the British Standards Institution as BS 1000.

Classification of stock goods can be either by use or nature. If they are classified by use, all the items used in making a particular end product would be grouped together. This presents problems when items are used on more than one end product, and classification by nature is generally considered better for stock.

Using a decimal base, the first step is to decide on ten broad classes. In an engineering factory these might be:

(1) raw materials,
(2) made-to-order production parts,

(3) off-the-shelf production parts,
(4) works supplies (MRO),
(5) office supplies and stationery,
(6) work-in-progress,
(7) jigs, fixtures and special tooling,
(8) packaging,
(9) byproduct, scrap,
(10) general.

Next, each class is subdivided. Raw materials might for instance comprise:

(11) steel,
(12) brass,
(13) aluminium; and so on.

Up to ten classes are available at each partitioning. Some can be left empty. When more than ten are required, two numerals can be used; for instance if there are more than ten grades of steel:

11.32 steel bars to BS 970 En 32B
11.36 steel bars to BS 970 En 36T.

Instead of using numerals to label the classes we could use letters; steel bar could be SB, steel sheet SS, brass bar BB, brass sheet BS.

Classifying and labelling in this way takes longer than may be supposed and requires considerable intelligence to do well. Many existing codes are inept. For those who feel that more time and talent than they have available would be required, there are consultants who specialize in coding.

Classification codes derived in this way have two main advantages.

First, with practice people remember the main class labels, so that codewords become meaningful and hence easier to handle. Second, classification codes are extremely hospitable; they are, or should be if properly planned, 'unburstable'. New items can be allotted new codings which fit into the sequence at the right place.

Extraordinary savings are regularly reported to have resulted from the adoption of a systematic materials code – although it is not the code itself but the systematic classification underlying it which is responsible. One concern was surprised to learn that it had been using 32 different names, none of them unprintable, for 32 plain discs of sheet steel. Another found that eight names (axle, bolt, pin, pivot, spigot, stub, swivel) covered eight components so alike that one could replace the lot. An electrical manufacturer reported savings of 32% on stockholdings, which is certainly substantial, by disposing of items they had not known were redundant until coding brought it to light. Of course concerns which have managed to avoid redundancy and confusion by intelligent and careful stock control cannot reap the spectacular savings reserved for those who have allowed things to get in a mess.

MIXED CODES; BLOCK CODING

These different approaches are not mutually exclusive. For instance a paint factory coded its materials in the following way. The block of numbers from 1000 to 2000 was reserved for liquids; the first 100 numbers in the block (1000 to 1100) were allocated to alcohols, the next 100 to esters, the section from 1200 to 1400 for hydrocarbons, and so on. Other main blocks of numbers were reserved for dryers, plasticizers, pigments, resins, and so on. This is partly a classification code and partly a random code. If a new specification of hydrocarbon is adopted it is assigned the next vacant number in the 1200 to 1400 group; the codeword 1374 tells us that the item is a hydrocarbon, but nothing more than that since the assignment of codings within each block is arbitrary.

SELF-CHECKING CODES

If in writing the description of an item out in full, two letters are accidentally transposed, or a word is spelt wrong, the meaning is still usually clear enough. But codewords are so boiled down that the slightest error can be serious.

Accuracy bonuses to machine operators have been tried to prevent such errors, and it was standard practice with punched card operations to have all entries verified. Even then errors occur. If the punch operator hits the wrong key once in a thousand strokes, and the verifier operator hits the wrong key also once in a thousand strokes they will both hit the same wrong key and let an error through undetected quite regularly. The machine itself can introduce errors, perhaps through faulty components or electrical disturbance or even floor vibration.

The next best thing to preventing errors is to arrange for them to announce themselves promptly. If you dial 60590 instead of 60950 on your telephone, you find that you have dialled the wrong number almost as soon as the call is answered. But if someone enters codeword 60590 instead of codeword 60950 in a stock record system, it may be months before the error comes to light. Meanwhile a train of resultant errors may be smouldering away: orders placed too early or too late; costs wrongly allocated; stock running out or piling up; culminating perhaps in some colossal and ridiculous bloomer which gets into the papers and adds to the mirth of the nation.

To prevent this, much thought has been given to so-called self-checking codes, incorporating check digits.

Check digits

It is standard practice to incorporate a check digit in codes that are processed by machine. This is a character derived by calculation from the other characters in a code designation. The machine repeats the calculation whenever a codeword is read in, thus detecting errors in the input.

For example, suppose we have a codeword (whether denoting an article, an invoice or a goods received note) of 100. We derive a check digit very simply by including one additional digit arrived at by adding together the other digits. The codeword 100 would become 1001 and on the same basis 101 would become 1012, and 102 would become 1023. Now if through operator error or other mistake the number 1001 is incorrectly input as 1101, the machine would automatically repeat the calculation, and on finding that the sum of the first three digits is not 1 but 2 would detect an input error.

Long before data processing machines were available, a somewhat similar practice was used by bookkeepers. Inevitably errors occurred either in adding up columns of figures or in transferring totals from one account to another. Such errors came to light at trial balance, but to locate them could be very time-consuming. To reduce the time it was common to post along with a total the number of pence required to make the total divisible by 13, what would now be regarded as a mod 13 check digit.

Data processing machines do not make errors in adding up figures or in transferring them from one location to another unless some malfunction or interference occurs. By far the most common source of errors is in the input of data. Consequently the usual procedure is for the program to repeat the check digit calculation as data is read in, and to discard the check digit in further processing if no error is disclosed.

A common type of input error occurs when an operator inadvertently transposes two digits when entering a number, inputting 60950 as 60590 for instance. All the digits are correct although they are in the wrong order, and a check digit derived by simple addition of the digits would consequently not detect the error. To overcome this, before adding the digits they are weighted, that is each is multiplied by the appropriate number for its place. If for instance the simplest series of weights were used, 1 for the first digit, 2 for the second, and so on, the check digit for 60950 would be $6 \times 1 + 0 \times 2 + 9 \times 3 + 5 \times 4 + 0 \times 5$, which equals 53. To reduce this to a single digit it is divided by some number and either the remainder, or the amount required to make the remainder zero, is taken as the check digit. The divisor is known as the modulus or mod. Using mod 9 and taking the remainder as check digit, the code number becomes 609508.

ARTICLE CODING IN SHOPS

Retailers have made great strides in using code numbers that are common both to suppliers and purchasers. Universal Product Code (UPC) in America, and the European Article Number (EAN) in Britain and other European countries, is preprinted on articles by suppliers in machine-readable form. In America 12-digit code numbers are used, and 13-digit code numbers in Europe. The first two digits indicate the country of origin, with 50 denoting the United Kingdom. The next five digits identify the manufacturer and the five after that identify the product. The last 13th digit is a check digit.

The article code number is converted into a bar code, a pattern of light and dark bars of various widths which can be scanned backwards or forwards, upside down or right way up, by laser scanners at the point of sale. The information can be sent to the in-store computer and used to tell the cashier what the price is while updating stock records and providing data for management reports.

9

Stock control: management and planning

Stock planning and control directly affect both the value of the assets used in a business, and the quality of the service given to customers. The importance of service should need no emphasis. The way assets are managed can account for the difference between success and failure; and stock is a sizeable asset for all trading organizations. Two thirds of a manufacturer's working capital may be invested in stock, and for retailers and wholesalers as much as nine-tenths of working capital may take the form of stock.

Stock has been defined as all the tangible material assets of a company except the fixed assets. It thus comprises any finished products or merchandise ready for sale, any parts or material to be incorporated into the products, and anything consumed in the process of manufacturing the product or carrying out the business.

A thought-provoking description of stock control is due to Dr Lewis. He defined stock control as: 'the science-based art of controlling the amount of stock held in various forms within a business to meet economically the demands placed upon that business' (Lewis 1970). This makes several important points. Despite its extensive scientific basis, stock control continues to call for human judgement, experience and expertise; it remains an art. And what it aims to do is to meet demands, and to meet them economically.

How can we tell if these aims are being achieved? Two measures are in common use.

PERFORMANCE MEASURES

The first measure is the *service level*. This is the proportion of demand which is met off the shelf, from stock, as a percentage of total demand. Unless shortages are kept to an acceptable minimum, production will be disrupted or halted, customers disappointed or lost. Less than 90% is poor service. Everyone would like 100% service level, but the cost is prohibitive.

The second measure is the *stock turn rate*, which measures how fast stock turns over. It is usually calculated on an annual basis by dividing average stock for the year into total demand for the year – figures readily available from the accounts.

Thus if total demand for the period January to December is £1m, and if average stock for the year is £250 000, stock turn rate is 1 000 000/250 000, that is 4. The stock is turned over four times in 12 months.

The reciprocal of the stock turn rate multiplied by the number of months in the relevant period of time gives a figure for months-on-hand:

months-on-hand = (average stock for n months $\times n$)/(demand for n months)

Thus, using the same figures as above:

months-on-hand = $(250\,000 \times 12)/(1\,000\,000) = 3$

A stock turn rate of four in twelve months thus indicates that three months supply is held in stock: three months-on-hand.

STOCKHOLDING COSTS

It costs money to hold stock. Space must be provided to house it, people and equipment to handle it. Stock is subject to deterioration, theft, 'shrinkage', loss, damage, and may be superseded or become surplus to requirements. The biggest cost element is usually the imputed cost of the money invested in stock. At the very least this is the 5 to 10% the money could earn if used to reduce the overdraft, or invested in short-term loans instead of in stock. At the most, when the organization has pressing opportunities to employ capital profitably and few opportunities to raise the capital, the rate will be much higher: 25% or more.

But exaggerating or overstating the rate in order to impress on people the need to keep stocks down may not be a good idea. Even at 20% interest money will double itself in less than five years. If you use the wrong cost figures in stock control calculations your decisions may well increase operating costs rather than reduce them.

Then there is the cost of storage space and of employing storemen. For many stock control decisions these may be regarded as fixed expenses, rather than costs which are affected by the decisions, so that to ignore them in taking these decisions does not affect the result. In a small organization the stores staff is usually a fixed expense, and even in a large organization the extent to which the number of storemen can be varied with changes in stockholding is limited. As for storage space, most stores are allotted a fixed area which does not change unless there is a substantial change in requirements, so that space requirements vary, not continuously with stock held, but in widely spaced steps.

However, allowance may need to be made for the fact that the value of goods taking up the same space may vary considerably. If £1 worth of cornflakes occupies as much space as £100 worth of brandy, using space to the best advantage may require a much faster stock turn rate for the low value item unless it carries a much higher margin.

Shelf life may also need to be taken into account. Some goods such as adhesive tape, photographic paper, paint, today's newspaper and fresh vegetables do not last long in stock, or 'on the shelf'. Others actually improve with age. Many industrial goods depreciate slowly, if at all.

The stockholding cost figures used for stock control purposes are as much a matter for management to decide as for cost accounting to calculate.

THE RIGHT STOCKS

Things should be stocked only if it pays to stock them. If it costs money to carry stock, at least it ought always to cost more to do without it. Every item in stock ought to be justifiable. It should be stocked for a reason. If something is required for production, sale or the operation of the business, that is a reason for procuring it. What further reason is there to procure it in advance of the time of requirement and keep it in stock?

Stocks are kept for many reasons, which can be grouped under two main headings: economy and protection.

Economy means the saving in time and money that can be made by buying for more than the immediate need. Protection means insuring against delay and uncertainty by providing a buffer against fluctuations in demand or supply – and even sometimes in price.

So inventory is held to reduce costs? Cost reduction programmes usually aim to cut stocks rather than create them. But perhaps this is because stocks are not always well managed. More weeds seem to grow in the store than elsewhere. Weeding-out routines must be included in any programme to improve stock control performance.

Every organization sometimes finds itself with too much stock of some items, often while it is short of other items. Inventories have a natural tendency to get out of balance. Users pull for more stock;

financial people pull for less stock. This tug of war can happen in a thick fog of uncertainty as to what is actually required.

FORECASTING REQUIREMENTS

Better forecasting can cut stock levels. A forecast is defined in the *Concise Oxford Dictionary* as a conjectural estimate of something in the future. It has also been defined as a statement about the future which is wrong. Certainly, we cannot hope to get it right every time.

So how do we forecast requirements? Two main groups of requirements are those due to *independent demand* and those due to *dependent demand*. The forecasting methods used for the first group treat each item independently and try to forecast future usage from past usage. Statistical methods are used: moving average, exponential smoothing, etc. For the second group of requirements, the demand for each item depends on the quantity of the item required to produce whatever quantity of the end product has been scheduled in the master production program. The process is called materials requirements planning (MRP).

Forecasting requirements for the first group, those which are not dependent for their demand on other items, is based on the assumption that future requirements will be more or less the same as past requirements. Allowance can be made for trend – whether demand is going up or down – and for variability: the extent to which actual demand for a period varies from average demand for the period. But there is not usually enough information to do this properly.

The standard forecasting method for stock items uses moving averages, modified by judgement. A 6 month moving average is the average monthly demand over the last 6 months. If the monthly demands for each of the last 12 months are added together and divided by 12, we get a 12 month moving average. It is called moving because a month later the figures used will move on a month, the oldest demand being dropped and the new latest demand being included.

A short period moving average adjusts more quickly to changes in demand, but is also affected by short-term fluctuations which do not indicate a long-term change in demand. A long-period moving average is less affected by short-term fluctuations, but takes longer to adjust to permanent changes.

Exponential smoothing is an alternative method which probably owed its original popularity mainly to the fact that it makes less demand on computer memory than moving averages. Instead of recording actual demand for each of a series of past periods, only the last forecast is recorded. A new forecast is produced at the end of each period by multiplying the difference between the old forecast and the actual demand by a number between 0 and 1 called the smoothing constant, and using this to correct the forecast. The formula is:

new forecast = smoothing constant x (actual demand minus old forecast) + old forecast.

Suppose for instance that the forecast for a period is 100. Actual demand for the period turns out to be 102. The smoothing constant is 0.5. The new forecast will be given by:

new forecast = $0.5 \times (102 - 100) + 100$

which is 101. A smoothing constant of 0.5 corresponds roughly to a three-month moving average and a smoothing constant of 0.1 corresponds roughly to a 19-period moving average. (A smoothing constant of 1 would use this month's demand as next month's forecast, while a smoothing constant of 0 would amount to ignoring actual demands and keeping the forecast the same from month to month.)

Similar methods can be used to work out figures for trend, the extent to which demand is increasing or decreasing. Seasonal variations can also be allowed for.

PARETO ANALYSIS

Pareto analysis (named after an Italian philosopher and economist, Wilfredo Pareto) is the study and representation of the way some characteristic such as value of order is distributed among a population, such as all orders placed in a period. It is usually found that there are a few large orders and many small orders.

As applied to stock control, this is often called ABC analysis. The range of stock items is split into three classes, called A, B and C, as shown in Fig. 9.1. Typically 70% of the total demand for stock is due to only 10% of the items: class A. Another 20% of the items account for a further 20% of demand: class B. And that leaves class C, comprising 70% of the items or lines in stock, but accounting for only 10% of the demand in monetary terms.

Because most of the money goes on 'A' items, it is economic to order frequently, control tightly, calculate requirements as exactly as possible. Shortages are prevented by frequent checks and energetic chasing rather than buffer stocks.

Because very little money is tied up in 'C' items, it is economic to order infrequently, control loosely, estimate requirements roughly, and prevent shortages by ample buffer stocks.

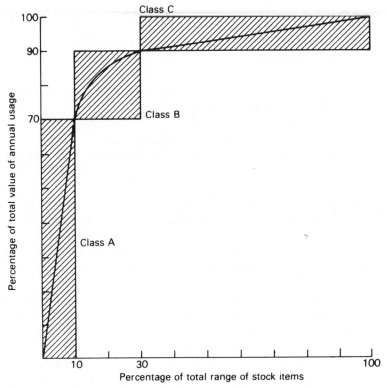

Fig. 9.1 Usage value distribution of stock items – ABC analysis, often known as Pareto analysis.

The aim is to save time in dealing with 'C' items and to reduce financial commitment in dealing with 'A' items. Because of the nature of the Pareto distribution, it is possible to reduce both the administrative cost of controlling stock and the size of the total stock investment by applying ABC analysis.

For instance 'A' items could be ordered once a month, 'B' items every three months, and 'C' items once a year. This results both in fewer orders and in lower stocks than ordering three months supply of everything.

ORDER QUANTITIES

Changes in order quantity directly affect average stock. For example, Abracadabra Product Co. have a labour-saving order system. They order a year's supply of everything. Carbothene, for which the requirement is £5000 a year, is ordered on 1 January. By the end of June stock is down to £2500 worth. By December the stores people are scraping the bottom of the carbothene barrel and the buyer is reaching for the order pad.

Of course stocks are high and the stock turn rate is only 2. How can Abracadabra cut their stocks by 96%?

Since this is a fictitious example, the answer is simple. They buy two weeks' supply at a time instead of 50 weeks' supply. (They work a 50 week year, with 2 weeks works holiday.) Carbothene stock varies from a maximum of £200 to nil, instead of from a maximum of £5000 to nil; average stock comes down from £2500 to £50.

But would this save money? The aim of *economic order quantity* (EOQ) theory is to find for each stock item the order quantity which gives the lowest cost, allowing both for stockholding costs that increase when we make the order bigger, because this leads to larger stocks, and for ordering costs that increase when we make the order smaller, because this leads to more orders.

Some practical people regard this sort of analysis as an abstruse and suspect method of taking half an hour to work out what quantity to buy when the time could more usefully be spent actually buying. Others recoil aghast from the sight of a square root sign. In fact the theory is simple and its application is straightforward. And buyers with little practical use for the EOQ still like to have it in the purchasing toolkit: it may not be applied much, but it sheds light on the principles.

To arrive at the EOQ, we have to weigh the costs of getting stock against the costs of keeping stock. To do this we need to establish how operating costs change when order quantities are changed. Stockholding costs were considered earlier in this chapter. Ordering costs also need to be considered.

ORDERING COSTS

It is not the average cost but the marginal cost which is needed for these calculations: how cost is actually increased by placing more orders, how cost is reduced by placing fewer orders. Fixed expenses should not be included. But the cost of receiving goods and processing invoices and paying bills should be included even if incurred by other departments. Within the purchasing function, the cost of postage and paperwork (requisitions, requests for quotations, placing and chasing orders, correspondence, envelopes) should be included. The main element is usually the cost of time: buyer's time, typist's, clerk's and expediter's time.

Now clearly if we save £1000 a year by reducing stock, and do it by spending £1000 a year on more frequent orders, the net saving is nothing and we are getting nowhere. This can be illustrated by returning to Abracadabra Product Company and their requirement for £5000 worth of carbothene. A cost investigation has shown that the ordering cost is £12 per order and the stockholding cost is 12%.

For the first plan of buying a whole year's requirement at a time, the average stock would be worth £2500 and at 12% this would cost £300 a year to carry. To this the cost of placing one order a year has to be added, giving a total of £312.

The second plan reduced average stock by 96%, to £100 worth, so this would cost only £12 a year to carry. But to achieve this 25 orders a year are placed, which at £12 a time would add £300 to the bill, giving the same total as before: £312.

Somewhere between these unsatisfactory extremes lies the best or most economic order quantity.

ECONOMIC ORDER QUANTITY (EOQ)

In this example, if you order twice a year instead of once a year this is a step in the right direction, because it reduces stockholding cost more than it increases ordering cost. If you calculate the costs for a series of order quantities you will find that the lowest cost is incurred when the order quantity is £1000 worth of carbothene.

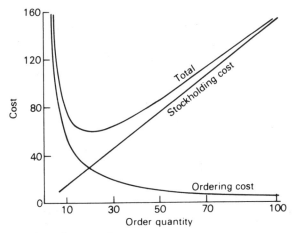

Fig. 9.2 Economic order quantity.

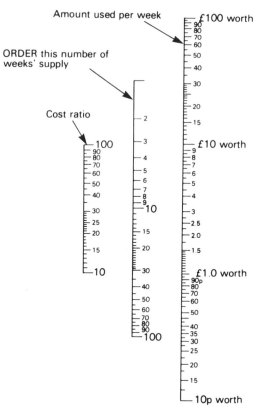

Fig. 9.3 Nomogram for order quantity.

Five orders a year will cover the annual requirement of £5000 worth, at an ordering cost of £60. Average stock is worth £500, so the stock-holding cost at 12% also comes to £60. Add these two, and the total of £120 is much below the previous figure of £312. If savings of this order can be made over the whole range of stock carried by an organization total savings could be substantial.

The way costs vary with order quantity is shown in Fig. 9.2. It can be seen that the lowest total cost occurs for the order quantity at which the stockholding cost curve crosses the ordering cost curve, that is, where these two costs are equal. This fact can be used to derive a formula for calculating the EOQ.

Writing u for the annual demand or quantity required
    p for the purchasing work and paperwork which makes up
        the ordering cost

c for price each or unit cost
s for stockholding cost
q for the order quantity,

then the annual total of ordering costs is up/q.
  The annual cost of stockholding is $sqc/2$.
  When these two cost figures are equal,

$$up/q = sqc/2$$

from which it follows that

$$EOQ = \sqrt{2up/sc}$$

Mathematicians derive the formula more rigorously, using differential calculus.

Equivalent formulas which state the EOQ in terms of how much money to spend or how many weeks' or months' supply to order, instead of what quantity to order, can easily be derived from this formula by transformation.

Mathematical presentations of the EOQ theory often take a simplistic view of the way orders are placed. As we saw in Chapter 4, many ordering policies are used. EOQ formulas can be adapted to several of them.

Years ago various calculating aids were used for EOQ calculations, such as special slide rules, or nomograms like the one in Fig. 9.3. Now that most stock control is done on computers, the problem has vanished. If stock is not controlled by computer, the calculating aid used today is the pocket calculator.

The EOQ formula is unsuitable for many stock control situations, for instance when demand is highly variable or seasonal. If price fluctuates, watching the market and seizing the moment matters more than balancing internal costs. If lead time is long or variable, making sure of supplies matters more.

QUANTITY DISCOUNTS

Lower prices are often available for larger orders. These may take the form of quantity discounts, or of a range of net prices which go down as the quantity goes up. To calculate the net saving we need figures for stockholding cost and for ordering cost, as previously discussed.

For example let us suppose ordering cost is £12 and stockholding cost is 12%. We have an annual requirement of 5000 articles costing £1 each, and the EOQ formula tells us to order 1000 at a time. We are offered a 10% discount if we take 5000 in one delivery.

The gross saving is £500 on purchase cost, plus a further £48 due to placing one order a year instead of five, which adds up to £548.

But average stock goes up from £500 worth to £2250 worth, an increase of £1750; which at 12% will add £210 to costs. That brings the net saving down to (548 − 210), that is, £338. It is still a worthwhile saving, so the offer would be accepted and an order placed for 5000 in one lot unless other considerations make this inadvisable.

A similar calculation shows that if the quantity discount offered is only 2½%, there is no net saving. The gross saving of £173 is wiped out by the extra cost of stock. The offer would not be acceptable.

Of course in addition to these cost considerations there are other things to consider, such as storage space limitations, risk of damage or obsolescence, possibility of a fall in price, etc.

DEPENDENT DEMAND: MRP

For many stock purchases each article or line can be regarded for stock control purposes as independent: the way the demand for it goes up or down does not depend on the demand for any other item. But in manu-facturing, the parts and material required to make a product cannot be regarded in this way. The demand for each part and for each piece of material depends on the demand for the product they are used to make (meaning the quantity of that product scheduled to be produced).

Item-by-item demand forecasting using moving averages or exponen-tial smoothing is not appropriate and leads to shortages as well as excessive stocks. Calculation of order quantities in the way previously described is also inappropriate. Requirements for parts and materials for the manufacture of a product to meet production schedules should be planned together as a single group, not as a lot of independent indi-vidual items. This is called *materials requirement planning* (MRP). Thous-ands of items may be involved, with varying lead times and other complications, and computers are a great help in processing the data and crunching the numbers quickly.

The first step is to establish a master production schedule, which is a programme showing what quantities of which products are to be com-pleted by what dates. Usually for each product the quantities due for completion are listed or scheduled week by week for the next three months, and then month by month for a further nine months.

The next step is to 'explode' this into detailed requirements for the parts and material needed, using bills of material (also called parts lists), which show what is needed to make each product. The bill of material

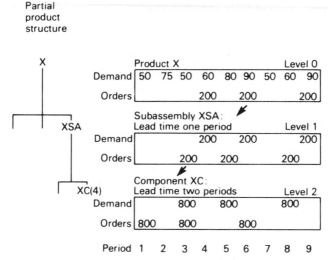

Fig. 9.4   Product structure and requirements planning.

for an end product is like the list of ingredients for a recipe; it shows what is needed to make it.

The bill of material (parts list) either incorporates or is used with a statement of product structure. For relatively simple products this can be shown in a diagram such as Fig. 9.4 showing what are called *levels* of structure. The explosion is done level by level, and at each level allowance is made for available stock and orders due in to get a net requirement.

Orders for the net requirement of each item are planned taking into account the 'lot sizing' rules which regulate order quantities, and also the item lead time so that goods can arrive in time for the end product to be completed by the date shown in the master production schedule.

ORDER QUANTITIES WITH MRP

The method most widely used for deciding order quantities in MRP systems is *lot for lot*: the net requirement for each period is ordered for delivery in that period, with no allowance for buffer stock.

Versions of the EOQ are also used. The *period order quantity* can be calculated as:

EOQ/(demand per period), rounded up to a whole number.

For instance if the EOQ is 110 units and the monthly demand is 50 units, the period order quantity would be 3 months supply.

The normal EOQ calculation assumes that demand is approximately constant in each period under consideration. This assumption is not valid for parts required for the batch production of a variety of products: product A may be made in January and March, product B in February and April, and so on. But it is possible to allow for this by calculating ordering and stockholding costs for each period in order to find the order quantity which minimizes cost.

There are several ways to do this. One is to calculate what is called the part-period value, obtained by dividing the stockholding cost multiplied by the price each or unit cost of the article, into the ordering cost. For example if the stockholding cost is 12% and the article costs £2.50 each, and the ordering cost is £12, then the part-period value is $12/(2.5 \times 0.12)$, that is 40. The part-period value indicates how many parts it is economical to hold in stock for how many periods. A figure of 40 indicates that 40 parts can be held for one period, or 20 parts for two periods, or one part for 40 periods.

If the demand is:

Period	1	2	3	4	5	6
Net requirement	0	40	20	0	80	35

then order quantities are calculated by applying the part-period value, giving:

Period	1	2	3	4	5	6
Net requirement	0	40	20	0	80	35
Order quantity	0	60	0	0	115	0

10

Stock control: practice and procedure

In theory, two systems for stock ordering are, first, to order variable quantities at fixed intervals of time; and second, to order fixed quantities at variable intervals of time. In practice a large number of different stock control methods are used, which may approximate to one or the other of these or combine features of both.

FIXED INTERVALS

Periodic review of stock at fixed intervals of time to decide what to order has many advantages. Ordering cycles can be varied by reviewing different classes of stock at different intervals. For instance, class A items can be reviewed frequently, class B items less frequently, and class C items every 6–12 months. Review work can be planned to give an even workload. Articles obtained from the same source can be reviewed at the same time and ordered together.

Since orders are placed at fixed intervals, variations in usage (or demand) have to be covered by varying the order quantity. Enough goods are ordered to replace what has been used and to cover expected requirements for the next cycle or period. It is not necessary to order every item which has been reviewed. A typical rule is to order enough to bring stock up to a preset maximum, unless this would give an order quantity below minimum order size.

FIXED QUANTITIES

In a simple fixed order quantity system, order levels are set for each item. When stock of any item falls to its order level, an order is placed

Fig. 10.1 Lead time.

for the fixed order quantity, which may be the EOQ. Abbreviations often used are: ROL for reorder level, and ROQ for reorder quantity.

This system is said to be easy to operate, clerically with manual records or electronically with computers, if lead times stay the same and demand is constant. But if lead times vary and demand varies too, both the reorder levels and the reorder quantities need to be amended several times a year. This is a lot of work, and unless it is done promptly the system does not give good results.

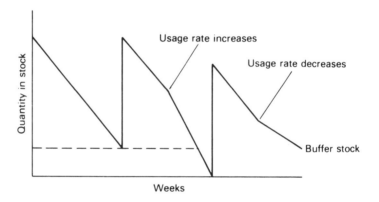

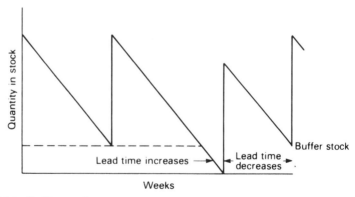

Fig. 10.2 Buffer stock.

The order level is the stock quantity at which we decide whether or not to order more goods for stock. For example, suppose we use exactly ten a week and our supplier takes exactly two weeks to deliver. No problem: the order level is 20.

Problems arise in practice from the fact that demand varies from week to week. Also suppliers sometimes deliver sooner than expected and sometimes later. How can order levels be set so that we do not run out of stock too often, and do not spend too much money on preventing shortages?

There are two parts to this answer. The first part is preventing shortages; the second part is doing this economically. With a demand of about ten a week and a lead time of about 2 weeks, we could set the order level at 200 instead of 20 and be pretty confident that we would never run out of stock. Average stock would, however, be very high in relation to demand, and thus costly to carry. It might be better to carry less stock and take the chance of occasionally running out of stock.

The ideal reorder level is: just enough to last until the order arrives. But how much is just enough? Stock on hand is a fact, but both lead time and the weekly requirements during lead time are forecasts. Like weather forecasts, they are not always right.

Lead time is the total time it takes to get items. Lead time, as shown in Fig. 10.1, includes the supplier's delivery period, plus transit time while the goods are on the way from supplier to customer, plus the internal lead time before the order is placed – the administrative delay in processing requisitions and orders within the organization.

BUFFER STOCK AND ORDER LEVEL

Buffer stock, or safety stock as it is often called, is a quantity of stock held to cover variations in demand or delays in delivery while an order is outstanding, as shown in Fig. 10.2.

If buffer stock is provided, order level is calculated as:

order level = (average demand per week)
$$\times \text{(lead time in weeks)} + \text{buffer stock}$$

So if we use 100 a week, and the lead time is 4 weeks, and the buffer stock is 200, what is the order level?
Substituting in the above formula,

order level = $(100) \times (4) + 200 = 600$

The order level is 600, which includes an expected demand during lead time of 400 plus a margin for variation of 200.

It is sometimes said, 'we don't provide buffer stock, we just order earlier'. This is a fallacy. If instead of using the actual lead time of four weeks in this example, we 'order earlier' by using a lead time of 6 weeks, the order level is still 600. And it still includes a buffer stock of two weeks supply – the two weeks added to the lead time.

The less buffer stock held, the lower the service level; the more buffer stock held, the lower the stock turn rate. Buffer stock can amount to as much as a third of average stock, which is often more than planned. Actual buffer stock, as distinct from planned buffer stock, can be found by averaging the stock on hand when deliveries are received.

STOCK VALUATION

Stock has to be valued for accounting purposes, for instance to get the total value of stock shown in the balance sheet, and to price parts and material used in production in order to calculate product cost. If stock is valued at market price or selling price for balance sheet purposes, this means that future profits that have not yet been made – because goods in stock have not yet been sold – are being included, which is not good practice. It is recommended that stock is valued at net realizable value or cost, whichever is lower.

Issues from stock are priced at cost, but there are several ways to do this, which can give surprisingly different results. One popular method is *standard cost*, used in budget control systems. Standard cost for each item is set annually when budgets are approved. Items are booked into stock and charged out to jobs or products at standard cost, and the differences between actual cost and budgeted standard cost appear as variances. These are considered in Chapter 23.

Three other methods for valuing stock are:

LIFO   – last in first out
FIFO   – first in first out
AVCO – average cost

If a business buys six lots of goods in successive periods of time and then sells three lots, the cost of sales would be regarded as that of the first three lots bought, under FIFO; of the last three lots bought under LIFO; and under AVCO the average cost of the six lots would be applied to the transaction.

This may be illustrated by an example. S. Tooth started business as a sugar importer in June, and by December had bought six lots on a rising market, as follows:

Tonnage bought	Price per tonne £	Cost £
10	124	1240
10	127	1270
10	130	1300
10	140	1400
10	136	1360
10	141	1410
60		£7980

Then 30 tonnes were sold at £150 tonne, realizing £4500. Clearly S. Tooth had made a profit, but how much? Consulting three accountants, Tooth got three different answers.

(1) The LIFO accountant says the cost of sales is £4170, so gross profit is £330.
(2) The FIFO accountant says the cost of sales is £3810, so gross profit is £690, more than twice as much.
(3) The AVCO accountant puts the cost of sales at £3990, giving a gross profit of £510, halfway between the other two.

But what if prices are falling? Suppose S. Tooth bought his sugar in six successive lots as follows:

Tonnage bought	Price per tonne £	Cost £
10	141	1410
10	136	1360
10	140	1400
10	130	1300
10	127	1270
10	124	1240
60		£7980

At this stage 30 tonnes are sold, and S. Tooth does a good deal and gets £133 a tonne, realizing £3990. Profit or loss?

(1) Loss, says the FIFO accountant: cost of sales was £4170, so you lost £180.

(2) Profit, says the LIFO accountant: cost of sales was £3810, so you made £180.
(3) Neither, the AVCO accountant says. Cost of sales was £3990. You broke even.

The LIFO method is not used much and is not approved by the Inland Revenue, who argue that stocks are not valued realistically if they are shown at prices paid a long time ago. The other methods are used widely, and although they give different short-term results this evens out in the long term.

DATA SOURCES

Applying stock control in practice requires a lot of data, for instance about what articles are in stock, what quantity of each article is on hand, and what the demand for each article is likely to be. Buyers need to know which things to buy; and knowing when to buy them requires information about lead times, although this may have been converted into order levels.

Basic stock control data can be obtained by stock count or by keeping records. Stock count was the universal method in shops until recently. Records can be kept clerically (manual records), or electronically (computer records). Computer records are normal, but manual records are still common.

STOCK-COUNT SYSTEMS

There are many stock-count systems which dispense with stock records. These include imprest methods, two-bin systems, and 'visual control'.

In the imprest system, stocks are topped up to a predetermined 'imprest' or maximum level after periodic reviews. The only stock control document is a preprinted sheet showing for each item its description, code number, and maximum stock level, as shown in Fig. 10.3. Two blank columns are headed 'In stock' and 'Required'. At regular intervals someone walks round and checks the stock, entering the figures in the 'In stock' column. Then order quantities are entered in the 'Required' column.

Normal order quantities are those which will bring stock up to the 'imprest' or maximum level. Adjustments are made if demand is expected to be higher or lower than usual. Dated and signed, the document serves as a purchase order, purchase requisition or requisition on central stores.

Description	Code	Max	In stock	REQUIRED	In stock	REQUIRED
WIDGETS	11207	100	80	20		
WODGETS	11208	50	20	30		
DIGITS	12000	25	20			
DODGETS	12001	50	20			

Fig. 10.3   Imprest stock control.

With extra blank columns, the same sheets can be used several times. Previous figures shown on the sheets can be used in deciding on order quantities. Or past demand figures, extracted from earlier sheets, can be included as a guide.

A typical application is when a range of articles obtained from a single source is held in quantities small enough to be checked visually. Sub-stores replenished from a central stores, branch shops drawing supplies from a central warehouse, garages getting their spare parts from the manufacturer of the vehicles they sell and service, all may use versions of this method.

TWO-BIN SYSTEMS

In two-bin systems, stock of an article is physically or conceptually divided into two bins. Issues are made from one bin until it is empty. An order is placed for more stock when issues begin from the second bin.

In principle a single bin could be used with a line painted round it at a level corresponding to the difference between the first and the second bin, as shown in Fig. 10.4. Racks or bags or drawers or bundles are also used instead of bins, but the stock of each article has to be divided into two lots: free stock and order level stock.

'Visual control' is a version of this in which colour coding in the form of coloured self-adhesive tapes or paint is used to identify free stock (green) and order level stock (yellow). A refinement is to have a third division (coded red), for 'danger level' or buffer stock.

When physical stock falls to a level which requires the contents of a yellow bin to be issued, or a yellow bag or yellow tape segregating order level stock to be broken into, storemen send the permanent requisition card from the bin to the buyer, who returns it after ordering.

If danger level stock has to be broken into, storemen send the red warning card to the buyer as a reminder that the order needs to be progressed.

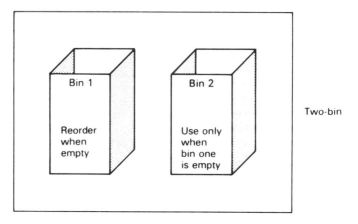

Two-bin

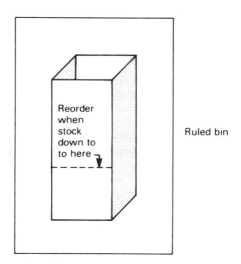

Ruled bin

Fig. 10.4 Versions of two-bin system.

The stock control document is a permanent order card or travelling requisition kept in the store with the goods, which shows description, code number, order level, order quantity, and has space to enter date requisitioned, store manager's initials, date ordered, order number, and buyer's initials.

This system is called visual control because a supervisor can walk round a store and see (visually) if the system is working. If anything is below order level, it is possible to tell at once if the order card is away in buying, or back with details of an order placed, or if nothing has been done.

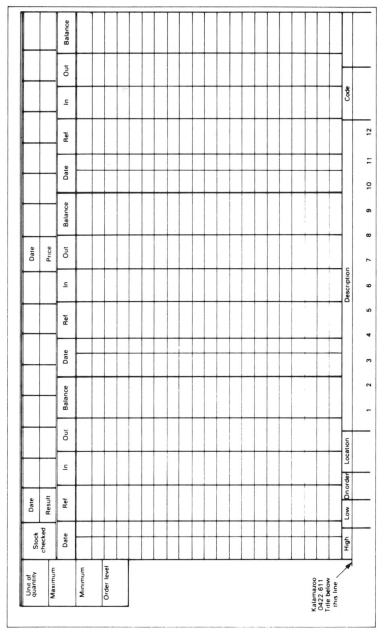

Fig. 10.5 Stock record: shows physical quantities, stock check results and dates and permanent descriptions.

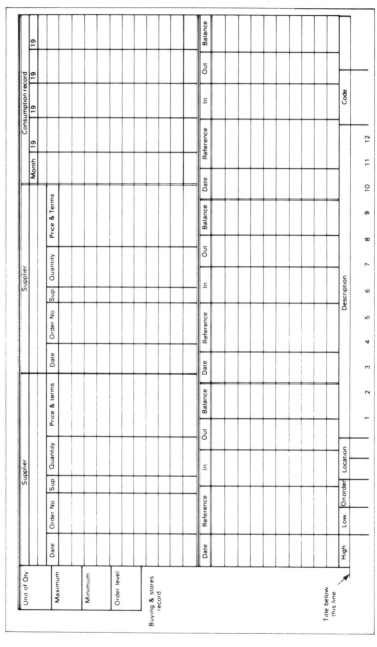

Fig. 10.6 Stock record: shows physical quantities, consumption record, order record and permanent descriptions.

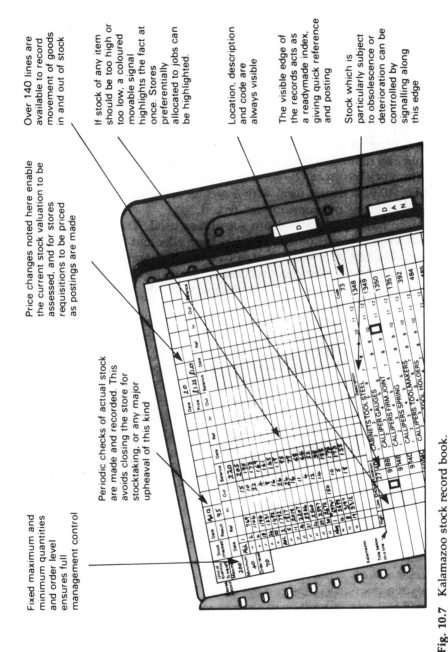

Over 140 lines are available to record movement of goods in and out of stock

If stock of any item should be too high or too low, a coloured movable signal highlights the fact at once. Stores preferentially allocated to jobs can be highlighted.

Location, description and code are always visible

The visible edge of the records acts as a readymade index, giving quick reference and posting

Stock which is particularly subject to obsolescence or deterioration can be controlled by signalling along this edge

Fixed maximum and minimum quantities and order level ensures full management control

Price changes noted here enable the current stock valuation to be assessed, and for stores requisitions to be priced as postings are made

Periodic checks of actual stock are made and recorded. This avoids closing the store for stocktaking, or any major upheaval of this kind

Fig. 10.7 Kalamazoo stock record book.

MANUAL STOCK RECORDS

Stock records posted manually by clerks are still quite common, and indeed still have advantages sometimes, although most times computers have the edge.

A typical stock record form with item description and code at its bottom is shown in Fig. 10.5, courtesy of Kalamazoo. The main part of the form consists of columns in which quantities in, quantities out, and stock balance are entered, with a 'REF' column for requisition number, job number, etc. Spaces are provided in which other data such as stock location, stock check dates and results, order dates and prices, maximum and minimum stock levels, and order level can be shown.

The stock record can be combined with the buying record, as shown in Fig. 10.6, a similar form with a section added at the top to record buying history and consumption record.

More complicated forms are sometimes used. They can show for instance which part of the stock has been allocated to or reserved for particular jobs and which part is free to meet demand. Or they can include costing and financial accounting data which can be used to cost issues from stores for job costing or other purposes, or to value stock for balance sheet purposes.

These stock records can be filed in special looseleaf books with the bottom edges overlapped to give a visible index. Kalamazoo's version is shown in Fig. 10.7.

Stock record cards are kept in card index boxes or drawers, or in cabinet-mounted or wall-hung trays with the lower edges overlapped to give a visible index. Card wheels or card drums are also used, and the 'Vistem' system of filing the cards vertically in grooves with the edges staggered sideways to give a visible index is a compact and convenient way to accommodate them.

COMPUTERS FOR STOCK CONTROL

Now computers have become so cheap and even small machines come equipped with large random access memories, they are becoming the standard tool for stock recording and stock control.

Very simple stock 'control' programs (so-called; they just record stocks) sell for a few pounds. More advanced ones cost from a few hundred pounds to considerably more. They can provide all kinds of useful features. In addition to recording items such as order level, order quantity, unit cost, allocated stock and free stock, what is on order, consumption record, and stock location, they can provide facilities for:

(1) Pareto analysis;
(2) stock-on-hand report;
(3) stock valuation report;
(4) shortage report;
(5) slow mover and non-mover report;
(6) analysis of delivery times (actual, as distinct from quoted, lead times);
(7) forecasting demand, using several methods;
(8) recommending order level and order quantity on the basis of forecast demand and preset parameters;
(9) calculating performance measures for the system, such as service level, stock turn rate, forecast accuracy;
(10) prompting cycle counts for continuous stock checking.

Questions
on
part one

(1) In what circumstances would a factory be likely to buy out parts which it is equipped to make internally?

(2) Is a purchasing manager ever entitled to recommend that his organization should invest in new manufacturing facilities in order to produce internally items which have previously been purchased?

(3) When one division of an organization makes goods for supply to another division of the company, what do you consider the best way to determine prices to be charged for the goods?

(4) What purposes does a purchase requisition serve? Is there any point in having special rules for requisitions for plant and equipment which will be treated as capital expenditure?

(5) How do buyers find sources of supply for items that they have not previously bought?

(6) There is evidence that many buyers will not change from their best supplier to a new source able to supply an identical product 'for a price reduction of less than 5%, i.e. on average 27% increase in profitability'. Explain the reference to profitability and account for the behaviour described.

(7) Do you consider it good practice for every purchase order to state the price for each item ordered?

(8) The purchase function is concerned with the supply of goods and the cost of goods; but it is the finance function which deals with the supply of finance and the cost of finance, as well as with payment for goods. Consequently terms of payment are exclusively a matter for the finance function; the buyer is not concerned with them.' Discuss.

(9) List the advantages and disadvantages of microfilm compared to files of full-size carbon copies for a record of completed orders. Mention some other methods of keeping old records so that they are accessible but do not take up a lot of space.

(10) Explain some possible uses in purchasing and supply of:
 (i) facsimile transmitters
 (ii) teletext information systems such as Ceefax, Oracle, Viewdata
 (iii) speech input to computers.

(11) Does the increasing use of information technology in purchasing and supply decrease the scope for the exercise of skill and judgment by the buyer?

(12) Chattanooga Railco Inc. expects increased demand for detonators, and the merits of internal manufacture are being investigated. Detonators are used to warn locomotive drivers of hazards ahead, such as fog, damage and accidents on the line. Currently they are supplied by Nobel Explosives for $2 apiece. A semiautomatic (SA) machine could be purchased to produce detonators at a direct cost of $0.80. Also available is a fully automatic machine (FA) which would produce them at a direct cost of $0.50. The annual operating cost of the SA machine would be $1500, as against $3000 for the FA machine. To assist management to reach a decision, you are required to:
 (i) calculate the annual requirement quantity at which total manufacturing cost would equal the cost of buying out, for each type of machine;
 (ii) calculate the expected annual usage of detonators, given the historical information that 3000 were used in a typical year with a bad winter, and 1000 in a year with a mild winter, and that in Chattanooga Railco's area 40% of winters are bad; and state with reasons which type of machine you would recommend;
 (iii) state the minimum annual amount of business required from Nobel to make it worthwhile to instal an FA machine, given that Nobel want to stop producing detonators and will assign their detonator orders to us free of cost provided that we buy from them exclusively the explosives used in detonator manufacture;
 (iv) list the advantages and disadvantages of making this requirement internally rather than buying it out.

(13) 'Purchasing is marketing too!' To what extent do you agree with this statement by a professor of marketing?

(14) Briefly explain with the aid of a sketch *three* of the following:
(a) reversible fourway pallet;
(b) single deck flat pallet;
(c) post pallet;
(d) box pallet.
Indicate briefly the circumstances in which each type of pallet might be used.

(15) Greanlea Ltd operate a wholesale warehouse which is due for demolition shortly because its town centre location is affected by Centreplan reconstruction. You have just been attached to a planning team which is to work out the details of the new warehouse to replace the old one. A site has already been acquired, with motorway access, situated 100 m from a local railway station on the outskirts of town. What would you expect the planning process to involve?

(16) Your employer has decided to set up an area distribution centre and needs to acquire warehouse accommodation for this purpose. The area in question has been industrialized for a hundred years, and you are asked for a preliminary report on the relative advantages and disadvantages of building a new warehouse as against renting or buying an existing older building. What would you write?

(17) Bulk Stores A is part of the Welsh Electric Motor complex and comprises a single storey rectangular warehouse measuring 45 × 182 m (50 × 200 yards). Stock location is random within three zones: fast movers, medium and slow movers. Stock range comprises full pallet loads of purchased components, manufactured parts and finished products, all handled by fork truck. Describe one type of stock location file and one type of stock location code number system which you would consider as suitable for Bulk Stores A.

(18) Three basic approaches to stock location are: fixed location, random location and zoned location. Explain and compare them.

(19) What is a unit load? Why is it useful in the storage and transport of goods?

(20) Explain the terms *mobile storage* (with sliding racks) and *live storage* (with goods moving in fixed racks) and discuss their applications.

(21) List some of the special hazards to which goods may be subject while kept in stock and suggest ways of minimizing the risk.

(22) What methods would you recommend for the detection and elimination of obsolete, obsolescent and redundant stock?

(23) The Ruritanian Oil Company is a nationalized industry which distributes oil and supplies central heating systems throughout the country of Ruritania. Consequently a large range of spare parts, equipment, pipe, and oil need to be available for supply in all towns and cities throughout the country. It would be possible to carry all this stock at: one central stores for distribution as required; or at five regional stores, since administratively the company operates in five regional divisions; or at a greater number of stores. What in your view are the key considerations in deciding the number and location of stores?

(24) List the main considerations in deciding on the location of stores, warehouse or physical distribution centre.

(25) Outline the kinds of information required to plan a new storage facility.

(26) Welsh Electrical Manufacturing Co. Ltd propose to appoint a stock control specialist because of dissatisfaction with current inventory performance. Responsibility for stock control is at present divided between purchasing, production planning and control, stores, and sales. You are required to draw up a preliminary job description.

(27) Explain ABC or Pareto analysis with the aid of a diagram, and outline its application to the design of stock control systems and records.

(28) Give a short general account of computer applications in stock control and storage; *or*
describe in detail one specific computerized stock control system.

(29) Explain the use of (a) moving averages, and (b) exponential smoothing, for routine forecasting of stock requirements, mentioning any advantages and disadvantages.

(30) 'So far as dependent demand streams are concerned, almost all the assumptions of traditional statistical inventory theory are invalid.' Explain this statement and indicate what could be used instead of traditional statistical inventory theory for dependent demand items.

(31) A certain stock item is bought on six-month contracts with deliveries every four weeks. In successive four-week periods, stock levels immediately before and after a delivery are as follows:

Period	0	1	2	3	4	5	6
Stock before	50	30	0	30	90	80	50
Stock after	250	230	200	280	290	230	250

Calculate:
(a) average buffer stock
(b) average stock
(c) service level
(d) usage rate.

(32) A company purchases 1500 castings a year for use in production at constant rate. The castings cost £10 each to purchase. The cost of placing an order is £15 and the cost of holding stock is 20% of average stock value per year. The lead time is 4 weeks. A buffer stock of 60 castings is to be held. The company works a 50 week year. Determine:

(a) the economic order quantity
(b) the number of orders to be placed in a year
(c) the order level
(d) the total annual cost for the item.

(33) (a) Item X82 is used at a constant rate of 400 a year, and is available at £1 each. Ordering cost is £0.60 per order and stockholding cost 30% per annum. What is the EOQ?
(b) The item is also sold in packs of 50 at £48 per pack, and in crates (one crate = 8 packs = 400 parts) at £380 the crate. Show whether it should be bought loose, in packs or by the crate.

(34) 'Whenever we take over a business we find invariably that we have to throw out two-fifths of the items on the shelves – the accumulation of many years' obsolescent stock.' Outline a systematic procedure to prevent this situation arising with stocks of materials and components in a factory.

(35) Stocks in a business often include: purchased parts and raw materials, semimanufactured parts and work in progress, finished product held for sale, maintenance stocks and works and office supplies. In view of this, discuss the relationship between the stock control function and the purchase department, production planning and control, sales department and other departments.

(36) You have been asked to evaluate a suggestion submitted by an employee that minor items be omitted from bills of materials and stocked as open inventory on the shop floor. What items would you regard as particularly suitable, and what items as particularly unsuitable, for this treatment? How could you arrange for such open-access stocks to be replenished as necessary without keeping stock records?

(37) Explain the uses and limitations of *either*:

(a) colour coding for stock identification, *or*

(b) check digits in material codes.

(38) You have joined Taj Mahal Ltd as a management trainee and your first assignment is to develop two coding systems, one to identify each cost centre in the company's nine factories, and the other to code each company product, indicating which it is and what factory produced it. Seven of the factories are in Britain, one in France and one in Holland. A factory has at least seven and at most 20 departments. Any department has from one to ten cost centres. There are six product groups, the smallest comprising 20 products and the largest comprising 100 products. Suggest a solution.

(39) List:

(a) two reasons for physically counting or checking stock

(b) two types of storekeeping error which could cause stock records to be incorrect

(c) two types of error which occur in posting manual stock records

(d) two stock check errors which would produce apparent discrepancies.

(40) As a management trainee with GB Ltd you have just been assigned the task of 'sorting out the stores', the previous manager having just retired early as the result of illness. The main problems in the stores are explained to you as: excess stocks (general manager); insufficient stocks and too many shortages (production manager); inaccurate records and low stock turn rate (accountant); too much work and not enough pay (stores personnel). What action plan would you adopt?

Purchasing practice and techniques

11

Specifications

Obtaining the right quality, that which is fit for the purpose and conforms to specification, is fundamentally important in purchasing.
Increasingly, the dynamic purchasing function aims to achieve improvements in quality without increases in cost. The aim is still the *right*
quality, but the goalposts which define the target for quality are moved
year by year.

Quality means in this connection both specification quality and conformance quality. Specification quality is the set of features and characteristics of a product or service which are specified by a purchaser and
thus required from a supplier. Conformance quality is the extent to
which the supplier complies with the specification and thus conforms to
requirements.

These two aspects of quality are both important, since a good specification is no good if suppliers fail to comply with it, nor will customers
be satisfied if goods received comply in full with a specification that is
not appropriate to requirements.

Purchasing often plays a big part in defining specifications in non-
manufacturing organizations which do not make products and have no
product design function. In manufacturing organizations the purchasing function has some involvement with the product design function in
defining specifications, especially as regards commercial aspects, but it
plays a bigger part in obtaining conformance quality, acting jointly with
quality control personnel.

This chapter is about specification quality, and also takes a look at
value analysis and quality circles which often involve a review of
specifications. Conformance quality is considered in Chapter 14.

DECIDING WHAT IS REQUIRED

Defining a specification is a two-stage process. The first stage is to
decide what is required: the second stage is to describe it.

Orders and contracts need to state clearly what is required. Materials
and services have to be described so that suppliers know what to

deliver. Standard descriptions such as type, class, style, grade, or other commercial descriptions that adequately identify the goods are often used. Special descriptions are also often required. These may take the form of documents such as written specifications, drawings, process requirements or inspection requirements, and are normally drawn up by the purchaser. It is good practice to identify these documents by title or number and to date them.

Both technical and commercial considerations are involved in deciding what to buy. Purchasing works jointly with other departments which also have important parts to play in specifying what is required from outside organizations. The right quality is not necessarily the best obtainable, nor is it necessarily the cheapest on the market, although it may happen to be either. It is the quality which is considered to be the fittest for the particular application, having regard both to cost and to technical suitability.

Deciding what is required may comprise a comparison of available merchandise and the selection of suitable brands or descriptions. Or it may involve design and development, with the production of engineering drawings and other forms of internally prepared specification. A specification of this kind is a detailed statement of the features or characteristics required in a material, part or product. Features or characteristics may include chemical composition, ductility, viscosity, conductivity, weight, colour, surface finish, physical size or dimensions – to name but a few. The tolerance may also be stated: that is, the range of values within which a characteristic may vary without making the product unacceptable.

In manufacturing firms, product design and the associated process of specifying parts and materials required to make the product, is normally the responsibility of a specialist department such as Engineering or Design. Such a department needs to make use of inputs from marketing (what can be sold) and from purchasing (what can be bought), as well as considering the manufacturing implications (how it can be made). It is difficult to generalize about the role of purchasing in this connection beyond saying that its concern is primarily with the commercial rather than the technical aspects of the product. Commercial aspects include the relative cost and availability of alternative materials or components, and also the feasibility of obtaining the quantities required for bulk production at an acceptable time and price.

Two examples may clarify the latter point.

Company A manufactures agricultural chemical products, some for sale to farmers and some for the home gardener. New products are continually being developed, and those which are approved by the new products committee for further test undergo two-year field trials intended to uncover any unwanted side-effects as well as to provide evidence that the product will in fact produce the result claimed. During the field trial period, a small purchasing research section within the purchasing department investigates the availability on world markets of the ingredients required for each product under trial, since at the end of the field test it would not be possible to change the formulation without starting again. Obviously management needs to know that all the ingredients can be supplied in sufficient quantities before authorizing bulk production.

Obvious as this seems, it is sometimes overlooked, whether because of insufficient attention to purchasing aspects or because of inadequate input from the purchasing function, as the next example shows. Company B specified an advanced input–output device for a new computer, only to find when purchasing began to negotiate a contract that the supplier did not have enough production capacity to meet requirements. The launch of the new product had to be deferred until the supplier had built up capacity.

EARLY SUPPLIER INVOLVEMENT

It is becoming increasingly clear that traditional views of the purchasing department's involvement in product design need to be revised, as product life-cycles shorten and competition sharpens worldwide. Key suppliers can play a significant part in product design and development, especially when new or rapidly developing technologies are to be used. Early supplier involvement in design and development makes it most desirable for purchasing to be involved from the start. This may make it necessary to redefine the role of purchasing and perhaps to recruit new purchasing staff with qualifications and expectations different from those considered suitable in the past.

Suppliers may be urged to join the design team. The purchaser may say: We know what we want to do, but, as you know the technology of glass, electronics, or whatever better than we do, will you use your expertise to work out the best way to meet our need? Suppliers will require something in return, usually most of the business resulting for a reasonable period, although not necessarily all of it, or for ever.

This tends to produce a situation in which the purchasing department has fewer suppliers to work with, many of them promised most of the relevant business. Yet purchase expenditure as a proportion of manufacturing cost will probably have increased. Such a situation makes much bigger demands on the skills of the buyer than just shopping round with a commodity type specification and picking the lowest quote. To ensure that the price is right while costs are low and supplier profits high, buyers need supplier management skills.

NON-PRODUCTION REQUIREMENTS

A large number of relatively low-value purchases both in manufacturing and in non-manufacturing firms are for MRO (manufacturing, repair and operating) supplies such as janitorial goods, office and works supplies. For these, unlike the parts and materials required to make a product, there is usually no department corresponding to a product design department which is specifically required to produce an authoritative specification.

Since the purchasing department has to write the order, it often falls to that department to draw up the specification. As many as 70% of purchase requests, it has been estimated, do not specify what quality is required. Purchasing is relied on to get the right quality. User departments have the last word in case of dispute. In the absence of dispute the buyer is left to find and obtain the right quality.

TYPES OF SPECIFICATION

Specification by sample is a simple method of specifying, which is often used for such characteristics as colour, feel, finish. Complicated minor components may be specified by sample to save the time and trouble of making sets of drawings if the quantity required is small. Some purchase departments keep libraries of samples for the convenience of colleagues and for use in talking to possible suppliers. Samples, however, can deteriorate; they may not be or stay uniform; and when several people need to use them they have obvious drawbacks as a form of specification.

Specification by brand name is another simple and convenient method, which however has two disadvantages. First, manufacturers sometimes change their internal specification without altering the brand name or notifying all those who might be concerned. A machine tool manufacturer lost four weeks production when his electric motor supplier upgraded the specification for the motor and incidentally altered the mounting dimensions. Second, a brand specification may lock the buyer into one source of supply, which has commercial disadvantages. 'Brand X or equal' increases the choice of supplier and gives the buyer more room for manoeuvre while putting on the buyer the onus to demonstrate that any alternative adopted is in fact equal to Brand X.

Purchase specifications may specify manufacturing method, composition, test procedure, dimensions and tolerances, etc. They should state precisely what is required, avoiding vague phrases. They should be clear and unambiguous, specific and positive. They should either specify the desired result and leave the method of achieving it to the supplier, or else specify the method and assume responsibility for the result.

An example of a specification follows:

Specification: black whole pepper

This shall be the dried fruit of *Piper nigrum L.*; it shall be subject to our approval of sample before delivery.

General requirements *shall*:

(1) have the characteristic colour and appearance of good quality whole black pepper;
(2) have the full characteristic odour and flavour of black pepper, free from mustiness and off odours and off flavours;
(3) be free from all harmful foreign matter such as stones and shall contain not more than 2% by weight of foreign seeds and no more than 0.1% by weight of harmless foreign material;
(4) be free from contamination by rodents or insects;
(5) contain not more than 1.5% of ash insoluble in hydrochloric acid;
(6) contain not more than 5 ppm arsenic and 110 ppm lead;
(7) comply with the requirements of the Food and Drugs Act 1955 and all subsequent amendments and conform to BS 4595:1970.

British or other standard specifications should be used if possible. Adopting standard specifications rather than developing special specifications unique to a single organization makes for easier purchasing and also utilizes national resources more efficiently. It also speeds the work of the designer, once he has done his research into available standards.

STANDARDIZATION

Standardization is a process carried out at many levels: within one organization, between all organizations that belong to one industry, nationwide and, indeed, worldwide.

The national standards body for the United Kingdom is the British Standards Institution (BSI). Founded in 1901, originally to serve the engineering industry, it has broadened its scope to all industries and also to some non-industrial areas. Standards, of which over 8000 are in print, are prepared by specialist committees, on which some 30 000 people serve. Draft standards are circulated to interested parties for comment and criticism before the final versions are agreed. Manufacturers and distributors are well represented, and the voice of the consumer is heard to some extent.

Most of the major trading countries have similar bodies (AFNOR in France, DIN in West Germany, JISC in Japan), which get together in an attempt to produce international standards. This is not easy. For example, it took years of work to agree on an international standard for colour coding electric wiring in the 1970s. No agreement has been reached on standardizing power plugs, which would be more useful but would involve much higher changeover costs.

The BSI is a chartered body supported partly by industrial subscriptions, partly by government grant, and partly by sale of documents and other services. It is a member of the International Organization for Standardization (ISO) and of the European Committee for Standardization (CEN).

Many organizations buy specials when standards would work as well, cost less, be delivered sooner, save both designer and buyer time, and enable stocks to be cut. Because of these economic advantages, buyers in many organizations have taken the lead in pressing for standardization, which facilitates bulk buying. They urge their specifying and design departments to adopt standard sizes or preferred size ranges and to adopt standard commercial specifications instead of specials. They look for opportunities to reduce needless variety in purchases.

VALUE ENGINEERING AND VALUE ANALYSIS

Price may be the buyer's particular concern, but price alone means little. It is what you get for the price that matters. Aiming for the best buy, the most value for money, requires consideration of technical features as well as of commercial features. It may call for a second look at the specification.

In the manufacture of engineering products, it is the job of production to make, and of purchasing to buy, what the design department specify. However production people can often come up with design modifications that will reduce production cost, and purchasing people can suggest changes that will reduce the materials bill. Suppliers can be a major resource in this connection.

Value analysis is a systematic reconsideration of specification and other aspects of purchased parts in order to get better value for money. It can be extended to things which are not purchased, when it may be called value engineering.

Lawrence D. Miles, then employed in the General Electric purchase department in America, invented the name 'value analysis' during the postwar reconstruction period. Other organizations were working on similar lines at the time. Cost reductions running into hundreds of thousands of pounds are claimed to have been achieved without reducing quality, and at a cost in salaries and expenses which is a small fraction of the savings realized.

TEN TESTS FOR VALUE

Miles defined value analysis as 'an organized creative approach which has for its purpose the efficient identification of unnecessary cost; i.e. cost which contributes neither quality nor use nor life nor appearance nor customer features.'

The basic organization for this 'creative' approach is to set up a team of people from design, production, purchasing, and perhaps marketing and management accounting, who meet periodically to examine a series of articles in the light of ten questions – ten tests for value, as they are called. Typical questions are:

(1) Can we cut it out altogether?
(2) Can we simplify it; does it need all its features?
(3) Is there anything better for the purpose?
(4) Can we replace it, or parts of it, with a standard part?
(5) Is it made on proper tooling considering the quantity required?
(6) Would some cheaper material do as well, or a dearer material be better?
(7) Would some cheaper production process give a satisfactory part?
(8) Do material, labour, overhead and profit add up to its price?
(9) Can we find a cheaper supplier who will be satisfactory?
(10) Is anyone buying it for less?

In this list the first two questions ask what function the item serves, how else the function could be achieved and whether it is worth what it costs. Question 6 is illustrated by Fig. 11.1. The eighth question is price analysis – building up a purchase estimate of price to compare with the quoted price, in order firstly to isolate the items that are high-priced,

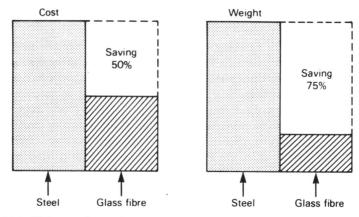

Fig. 11.1 Value analysis: alternative materials for a fan shroud.

and secondly to give the buyer a factual basis for his negotiations. The last question applies mainly when other factories in a group are buying similar components.

It is no accident that many of these questions resemble closely those asked by industrial engineers in a systematic method study. One work study questionnaire starts off:

'Purpose – WHAT is achieved? WHY? Is it necessary? If yes – why? Means – HOW is it achieved? Why that way?' – and goes on to ask WHEN, WHO, WHERE?

Suppliers are often canvassed for their suggestions. One factory (which incidentally spent five-and-a-half times as much on purchases as on direct labour) did this by displaying on a peg board in the entrance hall the 50 components on which the most money was spent. A notice addressed to visitors read: 'We invite your suggestions. These are some of the components we purchase. Can you suggest ways to improve their quality or reduce their cost? A description of how each part is used may be found in the handbook at the foot of the display. Our buyer will be happy to discuss your ideas.' Other departments within the organization were also asked for suggestions. These efforts do of course bring in usable suggestions, but they have the even more important effect of helping to get everyone value-conscious.

Value analysis should not be seen as a misguided attempt by commercial people to usurp prerogatives of technical people. It is a team job. Nearly always it is carried out interdepartmentally. In some large organizations value analysts have been attached to the purchasing department, which has initiated and organized the value analysis programme;

but the final say in specifications must remain with engineering design, which has also been responsible for initiating value engineering programmes in some firms.

One British firm organized value analysis by setting up fourteen teams, one for each of eleven major products, and one each for plastics, diecastings, and boxing and packaging. Each team had representatives from four functions: product engineering, design engineering, factory administration, and purchasing. All teams met fortnightly and reported through the four executive directors responsible for these functions to the deputy managing director. Considerable savings in cost and some improvements in quality were reported to have been achieved by the constructive, cost-conscious review of design and method these teams carried out. The changes in the attitudes and skills of those involved may be at least as valuable. It will be obvious that design people can gain much useful information about commercial considerations such as relative price of alternative materials, price variability and relative availability of materials; purchasing people can learn a great deal of technical and product knowledge; and both can gain new understanding of each other's objectives and skills. Often purchasing people also benefit from a radically new sense of participation. As one of them said, 'I have been a buyer for many years now and have seen new ideas come and go. Never in my whole career have I met one idea which has had as dynamic an effect on buying as Value Analysis.'

QUALITY CIRCLES

Value analysis continues to thrive, although despite the undoubted successes which it has notched up there is evidence that the success rate tends to fall off after the first year or two. Once the initial enthusiasm begins to wane, attendance at team meetings declines and before long the end is in sight for what will usually have been a very useful programme.

Quality circles seem to be a natural successor to value analysis programmes, although they probably developed independently. Following a visit to Japan, Mark Barratt wrote about them as follows:

The standard operational unit for improving quality on the Japanese shop floor is the quality circle. In leading companies, membership of quality circles is voluntary, unpaid (though there may be work time set aside), and almost universal at shop floor and clerical level.

In some companies, Quality Control Circle (QCC) leaders are self-selected, in others they are appointed by the line manager. Similarly, some groups set their own tasks, and some have tasks suggested to them. Generally, but not always, they are focused on production/performance problems – at Sony, for instance, groups work on what we would call welfare problems as well.

QCCs work at their own pace to solve problems and report upwards with suggestions. They investigate forwards or backwards in the production process to report problems to their 'suppliers', who may be on the production line or in some cases a similar group in a supplying company, and to their 'customers' to check that they are delivering the right goods or services. Apart from the basic techniques (see below) for investigating defects, they have access to skills in, generally, production engineering or quality control departments.

The QCC is equipped, generally through its leader, with some training in statistical techniques. The key tools in their activity are, again, statistical. They are:

- histograms
- cause and effect diagrams
- check sheets
- Pareto diagrams
- graphs
- control charts
- scatter diagrams

Correcting faults, is, it is hoped, the least part of the QCC's work. More important is a combination of, first, changing working methods to do a job with less effort/resource and, second, identifying variables in the production process so they can be eliminated – ie, 'squeezing' the normal distribution of output (performance, dimension, etc) so that, first, every item is within design tolerance and, second, so design tolerance can be narrowed to aid the next operation in the production process.

Success in QCC is rewarded by management with a pat on the back. It is also rewarded by the recognition of the QCC members' peers. Large companies have periodic gatherings of their better QCCs, at which medals are distributed. There are also group, regional, and national quality meetings at which successful QCCs explain their achievements and are applauded. If material rewards are involved, they are either indirect (a cruise or trip to 'study quality'), or purely nominal.

The use of QCCs works, particularly in the series production of physical goods, where marginal improvements at each stage of production contribute to major improvements in the finished product.

More than this is necessary, however. An elaborate consultative process is needed to coordinate design, purchasing, and production engineering, together with feedback from a company's suppliers and customers.

If the information flow within the company and between the company, its suppliers, and its customers is good, there are contingent benefits, which appeared to be achieved by some of the companies we visited.

Successful Japanese quality control methods have been based on knowledge acquired in the USA and, according to Dr Hajime Karatsu, 'there have been many failures too'. Success or failure, argues Dr Karatsu, is determined not by cultural factors, but by the attitudes and methods of top management. Good management is good management wherever you go, he says, and a good plant can be distinguished from a bad one easily. 'The basic things,' he explains. 'Clean plants, well maintained machines.'

'People have difficulty in understanding the term quality control. It is simple. The purpose of quality control is to supply good quality products to the customer. There are many ways of doing it: for instance by inspection and throwing away bad products, or by repairing defective items. Many people believe this definition. Lots of people understand quality control as groups of inspectors.

'In fact it is the manufacture only of quality products. In Japan, factories doing strict inspection are considered inferior and not something to be proud of.

'If products are designed with the wrong machine or a badly maintained machine to produce them, this will produce bad products. Vendors must supply to zero defects, the after-sales service must work. To supply a satisfactory product to the user the entire company must work together.

There are, says Hajime Karatsu, two ways of solving problems on the shop floor – by technological means, and by statistical means. It is statistics which he feels is extremely underrated by western companies. More than that, it must be statistics in a form which ordinary folk can understand and use. 'What is crucial is the "reduction" of complex statistical methods to visual forms: the graph, the histogram, the pareto diagram, the scattergram, the fishbone diagram, and so on.'

In the hands of assembly and clerical workers, he says, these tools are immensely powerful, and solve problems which stump the engineers. The 'seven tools of quality control' taught to most Japanese workers, he claims, 'transform quality from a stick to a more and more exciting process. It becomes a sport.'

Whatever the reason, there does seem to be in practice a willingness among workers to cooperate in projects which are good for the company. We were told by Tohio Takai, executive vice president of the Electronics Industry Association of Japan (EIAJ), that the quality circle is the key to higher prosperity . . . each staff member finds joy in participation, the improvement of his work with others. From the management side, it is important to create an atmosphere of participation.' They don't do it for money, he said – they want to be recognised by management as someone important.

12

Suppliers

The main factors in choosing suppliers are quality, delivery, service and price, although there are others.

Quality means both the quality which is offered or specified and the quality which is delivered or received. Specification quality and conformance quality are the technical terms used in other chapters for these two aspects of quality. When something specified by the purchaser is bought for the first time, quality capability is also important: can the supplier make it to the standards required?

Delivery means both how long the supplier says is required to complete the order and also how reliable is what he says. Quick delivery is always preferable. It simplifies forward planning, increases flexibility, means the buyer has fewer orders outstanding and less to worry about. Often the best suppliers are the busiest, but most buyers prefer a 6 week delivery period which can be counted on to the day, to a shorter quoted delivery period which is not so reliable. For regular purchases, just-in-time-delivery systems require absolute reliability from suppliers.

Service means whatever makes for good relations between buyer and seller and the smooth flow of goods from one to the other. This varies in detail with the type of purchase. Good service may include the provision of technical assistance and expert advice before and after the sale. Or information about new technical developments, and help in improving the quality or cutting the cost of the end-product. For equipment and machinery, ready availability of spare parts, and of service engineers to sort out operating problems, is important. Good service includes prompt attention to queries, accurate paperwork, reliable promises; rush orders *are* rushed, special orders *do* get special treatment; and perhaps the buyer gets advance word of changes, for instance in price or lead time, in time to do something about them.

Price has to be considered in relation to what it buys. The best suppliers are usually not the cheapest. For what they offer, they can afford to charge more, and perhaps they need to charge more. But some suppliers make a better-than-average product at a lower-than-average price. It is the buyer's duty to find them and his delight to encourage them.

Increasingly buyers try to build up balanced portfolios of reliable, profitable, low-cost suppliers. To do this they have to do a lot more than comparing bids and picking the cheapest. They have to take part in the management of outside production. They may have to develop new suppliers.

SUPPLIER DEVELOPMENT

Just as management development programmes aim to develop the kind and quantity of managers an organization needs, so supplier development programmes aim to develop the kind and quantity of suppliers the business needs. Supplier development is often stated as one of the objectives of the purchasing function.

The basic idea of supplier development is to treat supply markets not as given, but as something to be shaped. Suppliers themselves are regarded as capable of improvement. Behrmann (1970) found that manufacturers in Australia 'have demanded of their suppliers a higher quality of raw materials and have assisted them in producing such qualities; they have insisted on prompt delivery and have helped reduce delays; they have helped in the construction of the supplier's plant and equipment layout, even assisted in the purchase of production equipment.'

Buyers for British food factories have developed new bulk sources for tomato paste, traditionally sourced in Italy, in other parts of Europe.

Marks and Spencer plc have been developing suppliers for 60 years or more, since in 1928 they first cut out the middleman and dealt direct with the manufacturer. As Tse (1985) records, Marks and Spencer has no financial stake in their suppliers, but 'does invest very substantially in them in terms of technical support, management advice, and . . . a thorough educational process to bring the manufacturer's outlook and operating policy close to that of Marks and Spencer'. These are seen as long-term investments. Long-term relationships with the supplier are needed if the investment is to pay off.

Supplier development in this sense is a planned process of getting suppliers to produce the things the purchaser wants, to the purchaser's quality standards, in the quantities and to the delivery schedules required, by providing *technical* assistance and advice, *commercial* help with procurement and perhaps transport, and possibly also *financial* assistance in the form of loans or equity investment to pay for new equipment or tooling.

It is a way to shape the supply markets of the future. As Leenders (1965) argued, 'a company can, through its marketing efforts, develop new customers. Exactly the same opportunity exists on the procurement side. A company can, through its procurement efforts, develop new suppliers.'

SUPPLIER APPRAISAL AND VENDOR RATING

The systematic evaluation of suppliers is known as *supplier appraisal* if done before an order, and *vendor rating* if done in numerical terms after an order. Vendor rating is the measurement of actual performance; supplier appraisal is the assessment of potential performance. Supplier evaluation includes both, but is often used as just another name for supplier appraisal.

Supplier appraisal is important the first time you pick a supplier for something new. It is particularly important when you have to assess a new supplier's capability to meet special requirements. Investigation is required as well as the use of informed judgement by experienced people. The quality aspects of this are considered in Chapter 14. Other aspects include financial soundness, technical ability and management ability. Some firms prepare *key supplier profiles* – a typical form is shown in Fig. 12.1. Figure 12.2 shows a firm used for supplier appraisal.

Vendor rating summarizes actual performance by suppliers into numerical scores. Two problems with these systems are, what attributes to include and how to weight the attributes included. Price is

| Key supplier profile | Name | |
	Category	
		Ref.
(1) Parent organization and affiliates		
(2) Products and markets		
(3) Other customers		
(4) Financial information		
(5) Organization chart		
(6) Personality profiles, executives and contacts		
(7) Visits: who went, persons seen, dates		
● Visit reports		
(8) Forward plans		
(9) Alternative suppliers		
(10) Alternative materials		
(11) Purchase history: dates, prices and terms		
● Delivery performance		
● Quality performance		
(12) Other data		

Fig. 12.1 Key supplier profile.

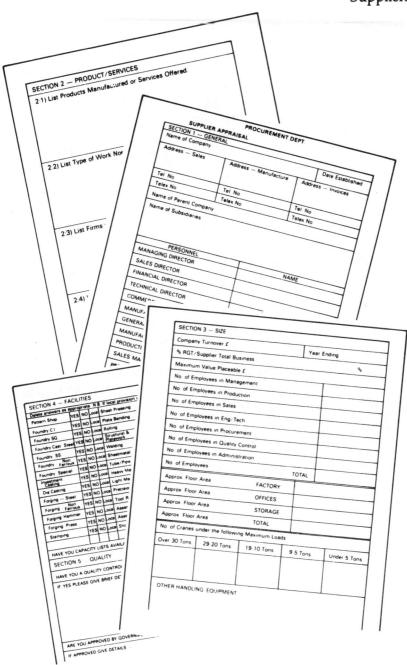

Fig. 12.2 Supplier appraisal forms.

sometimes included because of its obvious importance. But it is also sometimes not included because direct comparison of price is possible, while delivery performance or quality conformance are not so easy to compare unless records are kept and summarized into scores. In weighting the scores, we have to decide if delivery performance for instance is of the same importance as quality conformance, or twice as important, or only half as important.

It is not mathematics we are doing here, but management. The aim is not to find a way to make some theoretically perfect numerical evaluation of the merits of rival suppliers.

The main aim is to get suppliers to do better, by showing them how their performance compares with targets, or with how they performed in previous years, or with how their rivals performed. A subsidiary aim might be to help in selecting suppliers. But this is feasible only when several firms are supplying the same thing at the same time, otherwise the figures are not comparing like with like.

WHAT ATTRIBUTES TO INCLUDE

Quality and delivery are attributes which are nearly always included. Quality rating is usually the percentage of inspected items which have been accepted. Delivery rating is the percentage of deliveries that arrived on time. One firm uses the following vendor rating system at all its establishments. Three attributes are rated: quality, packaging and technical service. Each attribute is given a mark or score ranging from 1 to 5. The score for quality is weighted most heavily, multiplied by six, and the scores for packaging and technical service are each multiplied by two. The resultant figures are added up to give a total mark or score between 10 and 50, which is used to put the supplier into one of four groups, A to D.

Whenever a supplier's rating changes from one group to another the buyers tell the supplier and discuss it with the supplier. The objective is obviously to get the supplier to perform better on the three attributes which are included in the calculation.

The attributes which are included are the ones in which improvement is desired.

WEIGHTING

Weighting means in this connection the multiplier applied to the raw scores for each of the attributes included in the vendor rating. In the last example, a multiplier of six for quality meant that it was considered three times as important as either packaging or technical service, which each had multipliers of two.

One firm which was trying hard to get its suppliers to carry stock for immediate delivery allocated a high weighting to this attribute. The result was that suppliers with an excellent performance on quality, ontime delivery, and service still got a poor vendor rating score if they were not willing to carry stock for immediate delivery.

Weighting reflects the current priorities of purchasing.

Example

One firm uses the form shown as Table 12.1 for rating about 200 suppliers (out of over a thousand) which account for 80–90% of the total spend.

Table 12.1   Vendor rating example

	Maximum points
A. Quality performance	30
B. Right time delivery performance	30
C. Part shipments (made only when required by customer)	5
D. Ability to carry out paper work correctly (reference numbers stated on letters and invoices, shipments made according to instructions, test certificates sent without delay, etc.)	5
E. Ability to answer telegrams, telex, telephone calls, letters and orders promptly	5
F. Delivery follow-up (informing customers in advance of expected late shipments)	5
G. Sales policy and sales ethics	5
H. Performance of the salesmen	5
I. Ability to assist the customer in reducing costs (value analysis)	10
Total	100

Delivery performance and quality performance are assessed factually from goods received notes and inspection records. Between them they account for 60% of the overall score. The remaining 40% of the score covers various aspects of service which are assessed subjectively by buyer judgement.

Delivery performance is measured by the percentage of deliveries which arrive on time. On time could mean within five minutes, five hours, or five days of the target. Quality performance is measured by the percentage of deliveries which were not rejected by inspection.

ADVERSE COMMENTS

Many purchasing managers dislike in principle these numerical scoring systems for suppliers, and others think that in practice they cannot be applied to their own purchasing situations.

One said (Williams, 1977):

much of what has been published is impractical or meaningless in an industrial environment other than repetitive engineering. . . . Ultimately it is a matter of judgement whether one buys from a source or not. We try to develop buyers who have experience in special fields, eg paper and board packaging, plastics, chemicals, etc. They have seen many factories producing such products and can assess with reasonable accuracy whether a supplier has adequate premises, equipment, staff, quality control, etc., for the type of business we intend to place. We would make at least one visit, probably several visits with technical personnel, before orders are placed. Sometimes things go wrong, but this is rare, and we often find that we are at least partly to blame in that we have failed to make clear some feature of our requirement for fluctuating quantity or a vital element of quality.

Some respondents just said that vendor rating schemes did not apply in their businesses.

There are only three manufacturers of cellulose film in the UK and all three make to international specifications.

In buying steel from the UK for export, or from other countries for import or sales abroad, we are guided by previous experience. In the case of new suppliers, we visit the works and then place a trial order.

As suppliers of commercial vehicles and luxury coaches, we have a long association with our main suppliers and know a lot about their size, financial status and ability to produce goods of the right quality at the right time. In selecting suppliers of sundries we have no formal method of appraising them apart from their general reputation in the motor trade.

Most of the buyers here at Bakery Centre are specialists. Personal knowledge and experience are the key to success.

We do not use simple forms for evaluation, but in-depth feasibility studies. Purchasing research evaluates world sources.

One of the techniques used for supplier evaluation in this general sense is financial assessment.

FINANCIAL ASSESSMENT

Businesses are interested in the financial assessment both of customers and of suppliers. The credit rating of customers may seem more important. But it is also important to know if a potential supplier is likely to run into financial difficulties in meeting obligations under purchase contracts.

A valuable source of information in this connection is the trade knowledge which buyers derive from talking to their suppliers and competitors of their suppliers, and perhaps other people who deal with their suppliers. Word gets round. It is hardly possible to employ auditors to go through a potential supplier's detailed accounts before signing a contract. But some information can be obtained from the published annual accounts. These tell us about the past, when we want to know about the future; but that may be better than nothing.

Annual accounts are often obtainable from the company representative or the company secretary. Limited companies have to file copies of their audited annual accounts with the Registrar of Companies in Maindy Way, Cardiff, where they are open to public inspection.

Annual accounts can be made to yield a little more information than appears on the face of them by ratio analysis. Buyers may consult colleagues who are qualified accountants for help with this.

Profitability is perhaps the first thing to examine, and the two ratios used to assess this are profit in relation to capital employed and profit in relation to sales turnover. Return on capital employed is obtained by dividing capital employed into profit. The figure used for profit is preferably the figure before deduction of interest and tax. The figure for capital employed is preferably fixed assets plus net current assets. Other methods of calculation are legitimate, but comparison between figures for different periods or different companies is only valid if the same method is used in deriving the figures being compared. Return on sales is obtained by dividing sales turnover value into profit. These ratios are usually expressed as percentages, so that:

return on capital = 100 (profit/capital)
return on sales   = 100 (profit/turnover)

Profitable suppliers are a better risk than unprofitable firms, which may quote low prices to get orders and then plead for price increases to avoid collapse.

A business has to make enough money to keep going if it is to avoid liquidation. The ratio of current assets to current liabilities is an indicator of its liquidity position. Preferably current assets will be at least 2.5 times current liabilities. If the ratio is 1 or less the business is probably in trouble. The acid test or quick ratio is the ratio of cash plus accounts receivable to current liabilities, a more severe test of the short-term ability of the business to pay its way. Preferably this ratio will be at least 1.5. It is also possible to estimate how much credit customers are taking by dividing sales turnover into the figure shown for trade debtors and multiplying by 365, which gives the answer in days.

Other ratios include the asset turn rate, obtained by dividing total assets into turnover, and the stock turn rate which can be estimated by dividing stock into cost of sales.

LOCAL SUPPLIERS

The best suppliers may be half a world away. But they may also be just across the street. Local suppliers are preferred if they can supply acceptable goods at competitive prices. Factors that strongly favour suppliers in the local area are quicker and more reliable delivery, better communications by personal visit or local phone call.

If local suppliers are not as good in terms of quality, price, service or delivery as other sources located further away, public service institutions such as local authorities or universities still find themselves urged to patronize them. It is necessary to be firm about this, although of course a fair hearing must be given to any potential suppliers in their local area.

When a large factory opens in a new industrial area local firms are often encouraged by a process of supplier development to become suitable suppliers. This is a short-term investment to produce long-term benefits, not a permanent subsidy. As with the 'infant-industry' argument for protecting new industries against foreign competition; infants are protected so that they grow up safely, not so that they do not need to grow up.

DISTRIBUTOR OR MANUFACTURER?

Industrial distributors are middlemen who stock and sell goods to factories and other users. Some specialize in particular products such as steel or stationery, others carry a wide range in stock (and so are often called stockists or stockholders).

It appears that while the role of the wholesaler in supplying the retail trade has declined, the role of the distributor in supplying industrial customers has increased. Small occasional purchases are welcomed by distributors, who can handle them cheaper and quicker than manufacturers who prefer large orders. A wide variety of MRO requirements are often bought from one or two distributors rather than from dozens of manufacturers, with appreciable savings in time and usually no increase in cost.

SMALL FIRMS AS SUPPLIERS

Not very long ago it was thought that the small firm was finished. The future lay with the big firms, it was believed, because their large scale production and in-depth support in research and development made their products and prices more attractive and ensured that they could compete in world markets. Whether or not this is true for mass producers of consumer products, no-one now believes it applies to the firms which are their suppliers.

Most big producers have a network of small suppliers, and actually prefer supplier factories with about 500 employees. Low prices, fast delivery, and good service make small suppliers attractive. While a big supplier can afford to rest on its laurels, a small supplier has to work hard 'to keep the contracts we have got and to win the ones we haven't'. It is also said to be easier for the buyer to contact the manager and make things happen.

It is good to benefit society while at the same time doing the best for one's own organization. Small firms are now seen as the main creators of new jobs, as well as assisting in the 'dispersion rather than the concentration of economic power and decision-making; plants near optimal size; short lines of communication between head office and factory floor . . . the individual's freedom of choice and satisfaction, as consumer and producer of goods and services' (Moos, 1971).

RECIPROCAL TRADING

Another problem in selecting suppliers is whether to give preference to potential suppliers who are also potential or actual customers.

Naturally many organizations have suppliers who are also customers. It would be surprising if none of Ford's suppliers drove Ford cars. But would it be sensible for the company to discriminate in favour of Ford car-users in awarding supply contracts?

Reciprocal trading or reciprocity is the practice of linking sales to an organization with purchases from that organization, and making one conditional upon the other. This practice – I'll scratch your back if, and only if, you scratch mine – can be a problem in businesses which both buy from and sell to other businesses. There is no harm in using trade contacts to get introductions which could lead to sales. But it is different when the seller dangles the carrot of further sales to his organization as an inducement to buy from him, or waves the big stick by threatening to withhold purchases by his organization or its associates unless his sales offer is accepted. It also happens that buyers make similar threats – to switch to a different supplier unless the current supplier comes up with some orders.

A sensible rule is not to pay any more for purchases made on a reciprocal basis and not to accept anything less in quality or service. Perhaps better yet is to take no account at all of whether potential suppliers are potential or actual customers in deciding whether or not to buy from them.

But reciprocity is not a matter of ethics, or what is right or wrong. It is more a matter of expediency, or what pays. Many firms are not strong enough to ignore the balance of power in the market structure. Purchasing executives should, however, insist that costs and benefits are properly weighed up. Factual performance records should be kept and the reason why the supplier was chosen should also be on record. Negotiations must and can be done without losing goodwill or antagonizing customers, and without losing sight of purchasing objectives.

ONE SUPPLIER OR SEVERAL?

For major purchases, should you stick to a single supplier or use several? Sometimes you do not have a choice. Only one supplier is available, or is acceptable. Sometimes you have a choice at the start, but once you have made the choice you are committed to one supplier for a considerable time. For instance special tooling, dies or moulds may have to be made, which even if it is the buyer's property may not be suitable for use by another supplier. Or there may be a strong learning curve effect which makes it very hard for any new supplier to quote prices as low as the established supplier.

The increasing use of just-in-time systems that require close cooperation between buyer and seller has made single-sourcing more attractive. There may also be cost advantages in giving all the business to a single source; although there could also be cost advantages in having several suppliers competing for the business. Progressing and quality control are simpler when there is only one supplier. But there is a lot to be said for not having all the eggs in one basket, as the saying goes: if strike, fire or breakdown stop supplies from the main source, it may be much easier to build up supplies from a secondary source than to start from scratch with a new supplier.

Traditionally purchasers like to have several satisfactory suppliers competing for their business, which could be shared or rotated between them. But in recent years there has been a swing towards single-sourcing, mainly because of changes in supplier policy.

Supplier policy

Relationships with suppliers can be just as difficult and complicated as relationships with customers or employees, and large sums of money may be at stake.

Suppliers are a major resource both for manufacturing and distributive firms. Successful and profitable operations in sales markets depend at least to some extent on the arrangements which have been made in supply markets. There is an increasing tendency to examine the whole supply chain, back from the final customer right through to supplier's suppliers.

Two basically opposed policies are both popular at present in this connection: competitive and cooperative.

Competitive policies are traditional in many leading British, European and American industries, such as vehicle manufacture. The basic strategy is to develop or support a number of competing sources for each major purchase requirement. Orders may be split between two or more sources. Tapered integration may be used to strengthen the purchaser's hand in negotiations: part of the requirement is manufactured internally so that the buyer knows from experience what production costs actually are and is able to build up internal production and phase out purchases if suppliers are unwilling to supply at competitive prices.

Dependence on suppliers is avoided: some alternative supplier, or alternative material, or else the option of internal manufacture, is always kept available. Contracts usually provide for every conceivable contingency, in detailed legal terminology. Such a supplier strategy is seen by Porter (1979) as an integral part of the general competitive strategy of a firm in highly competitive markets.

Cooperative policies are particularly associated with Japanese firms, which certainly sell against stiff competition, but which seem to establish long-term stable relationships in their supply markets. Single sourcing rather than multiple sourcing is the norm. This leads to mutual dependence. Contracts are informal and contingencies are dealt with as and when they occur. This depends on mutual trust.

Negotiations in competitive situations are win–lose contests, where in a typical outcome when the buyer 'is gone his way then he rejoiceth', and presumably the seller weepeth. But is this appropriate when both parties are locked together in continuing relationships? Perhaps the seller too should rejoice, or at least both parties should feel reasonably satisfied with the outcome.

Negotiations in cooperative situations are on a win–win basis, with both parties aiming to do well. In no way does this imply that suppliers can expect an easy ride when they put in for a price increase. 'We will consider a claim based on an increase in the cost of materials, if the supplier can show that it was unavoidable,' said one buyer. 'But we won't consider a claim based on an increase in the cost of labour. That should be offset by increased productivity, not passed on to customers.'

The proper management of supplier relationships requires more time and more ability in cooperative situations than in competitive situations, not less. Forecasts of demand and future plans may need to be shared. Continuous dialogue between buyer and seller is required. Strong-arm tactics are not suitable; buyer and supplier have to work together. Price competitiveness for instance has to be discussed and price adjustment arrangements made. This is not needed when orders are placed with low bidders from several possible sources.

MARKET STRUCTURE

When economists speak of market structure and performance, they refer mainly to the number of firms both on the buying and selling sides which constitute a market, the market shares of the leading firms, and whether or not the result is satisfactory to customers.

Monopolies

The number of firms can be one, few, or many. A market dominated by a single firm is called a monopoly (some writers use the word monopsony if the firm is a monopoly buyer). Substantial monopoly power may also be exerted by a cartel, which is an association of firms acting together as if they were a single firm, to fix prices and perhaps control output or distribution.

The traditional objection to monopoly power was that it would lead to high prices and excessive profits. As Adam Smith wrote over two centuries ago, 'the price of monopoly is on every occasion the highest which can be got. The price of free competition . . . is the lowest which can be taken, not upon every occasion indeed, but for any considerable time together.'

Recent experience has been that monopoly sellers and cartels do charge high prices, but not so much to make excessive profits as to support large underemployed workforces and huge management superstructures, to reduce uncertainty and prevent the weakest going to the wall.

American antitrust legislation (trust in the sense of cartel or merger) began with the Sherman Act of 1890, which declares flatly that 'every person who shall monopolise or attempt to monopolise or combine or conspire with any other person to monopolise any part of the trade or commerce . . . shall be guilty of a misdemeanour'. Some 50 or 60 years later, Britain and the rest of Europe followed suit.

In Britain, the law did not intervene in these matters until 1956, when the Restrictive Trade Practices Act was passed. It caused major upheavals in British industry, which had been heavily cartelized. In the European Economic Community (EEC), unfair prices and conditions of contract, whether imposed by buyer or seller, are condemned by the Treaty of Rome. Articles 85 and 86 define the basic Common Market competition policy. Regulations made under the Treaty and policed by the European Commission are intended to promote competition and prevent price rings and monopolies. High fines have been imposed on offenders. For instance in 1986 15 polypropylene producers were found guilty of rigging the market and fined £37.2 million.

Perfect competition

At the opposite pole from monopoly is what economists call perfect competition. As the word perfect suggests, this does not actually exist; but some markets for primary commodities come close to it, with many sellers, standard commodities, good information and so on.

Oligopolies

In between the two are markets with few sellers that economists call oligopolies. The relative size of suppliers is at least as important as their absolute number. A 100-supplier market would still be an oligopoly if the three largest suppliers accounted for 90% of the output, leaving the other 97 to share the remaining 10% of output, because of its high concentration.

Ease of entry is another important consideration. It is impracticable to maintain a high price for long if newcomers attracted by the prospect of high profits find it easy to enter the market. Barriers to entry take many forms: in the mass production of motor cars, the immense capital investment required by the technology; in detergents, the heavy advertising budgets of the two main producers; in the supply of roadstone, the high cost of haulage from a distance; in the early days of a new product such as xerographic copying, patent protection; all these have served as entry barriers. Domestic producers are sometimes protected from foreign competition by such barriers as tariffs, quotas, prohibitions, and Kafkaesque devices such as unexplained delays in providing the necessary paperwork.

The buyer who cannot find an alternative supplier may find an alternative material; high and unpredictable prices for wool have led to increasing use of synthetic fibres in carpet manufacture, for instance. Availability of substitutes is thus important. So is the price elasticity of demand, which expresses the sensitivity of sales to price changes.

Oligopoly sellers are in active competition with their rivals and need to consider how they would match possible moves by the competition, and how rivals will react to their own actions. It is a risky situation which tends to lead to cartels or information agreements unless these are illegal (and sometimes even when they are illegal). For instance, a price *reduction* by one supplier of a product which is not differentiated, that is to say, a commodity exactly like that supplied by other firms, needs to be matched quickly by the other firms if they are not to lose business; but a price *increase* need not be matched by rivals, when it is the price changer who loses business. This accounts for the two-way entry for elasticity in Table 12.2. Obviously this tends to lead to level pricing; prices tend to level out in the long term, although in the short term suppliers may quote a high price if they have full order books, or a low price if they are short of work.

Suppliers escape from this situation and increase their security by making their product in some way different from what their rivals offer. Products can be differentiated by technical specification, as with comparable machine tools or motor cars which serve the same purpose but with different features. Since customers purchase a package in which product characteristics are only part of the deal, supplier characteristics

Table 12.2 Types of market structure; a simplified view of supply markets

Structural type	Number of sellers	Entry barriers	Availability of substitutes	Demand elasticity	Scope for price negotiation
Monopoly	One	Very high	Very low	Low	Very little
Differentiated oligopoly	Few	High	Low	Fairly high	Some
Undifferentiated oligopoly	Few	Low	High	High for increase, low for price decrease	Considerable
Perfect competition	Many	Very low	Very high	Very high	Very little

can also differentiate the 'product'. Suppliers can build up a reputation for quality or reliability or superior service after sales which enables them to retain customers, even when undercut on price. Product differentiation can even exist almost entirely in the eye of the beholder, as when advertising creates imaginary differences which lead buyers to form distinct preferences between suppliers.

The four types of market structure shown in Table 12.2 may suggest a basis for the buyer to analyse his own supply markets. The most notable omission from this diagram is the structure on the buying side. There are two sides to any market, and a further important structural parameter is the number of buyers and their relative market share. Table 12.2 states that there is very little scope for negotiation with a monopoly seller; but this is not the case for the monopoly buyer.

Examples of monopoly buyers are: for power stations in Britain, the Central Electricity Generating Board (although suppliers also sell abroad); for much telephone equipment, British Telecom. There are also situations where an industry has many customers, but one takes such a large proportion of output as to have considerable monopoly power as buyer – for instance, conveyor belts and British Coal.

A common market situation for the industrial buyer is bilateral oligopoly, in which there are only a few significant firms on both sides of the market. For instance, many parts and components for motor car manufacture are purchased in significant quantities within the United Kingdom only by the four major car producers, although some purchases are also made by the smaller producers, by garages for the replacement market, and by producers abroad. The number of suppliers capable of meeting the quality standards and the large quantity requirements of major car makers is inevitably restricted, so that the market is oligopolistic on both sides.

Such markets, according to Joe S. Bain (1959), are characterized by two sets of active price-making policies, those of the sellers and those of the buyers. We tend to find a 'total conduct pattern . . . of bargaining and negotiation between buyers and sellers'.

The Monopolies Commission went so far as to find the non-competitive supply conditions for most motor car electrics were potentially advantageous to the public interest if not abused. Abuse there might be in the replacement market, where a consumer buys a single replacement component from a garage; but in the original equipment market the *countervailing power* of the industrial buyer prevented abuse. Vehicle makers all appear to be satisfied that the prices at which they are able to buy and the service they receive in present conditions are at least as good as they could get by breaking down the monopolies of leading suppliers. In part this is due no doubt to their evaluation of the advantages of large scale production and of continuity of service which are features of the present concentrated structure, but it is also a measure of the pressure which they can bring to bear on the suppliers without actually setting up or strengthening competitive suppliers.

To sum up, important structural characteristics of a market include: the number and concentration of sellers; the number and concentration of buyers; product differentiation; availability of substitutes; entry barriers; and price elasticity of demand. A number of other characteristics are important in particular cases; for instance, the location and availability of raw materials, the rate of growth or decline in demand, the type of technology and whether or not it is capital intensive, the normal purchasing method (sealed bid, negotiation, list price with discounts, etc.).

MARKET POLICY

We turn now to consider the market policies adopted by purchasers with significant market power in dealing with sellers who also have significant market power, or who for one reason or another are in a sole source position. The dangers are that without the stimulus of competition, the supplier will make unduly high profits, will become inefficient and overstaffed so that costs are high, will fail to innovate, and that generally his market performance will be unsatisfactory, with (for instance) a poor delivery record and inadequate service.

US government buyers have made extensive use of cost incentive contracts and mandatory value analysis clauses to motivate defence contractors to make active efforts to innovate, to reduce costs and to pass cost reductions on to their customer. The example has been followed to some extent by other public sector purchasers, in the United Kingdom and elsewhere.

In mass production industries, especially vehicle manufacture, cost analysis (or price analysis) is widely practised. Cost estimators attached to the purchase department prepare detailed cost statements for purchased parts. These are used both to strengthen the buyer's hand in negotiations, and to set price targets for him to achieve. Suppliers are also pressed to support their price quotations by cost breakdowns. Somewhere in the background to discussions is an implied threat that if the supplier cannot make the part on an agreed cost basis plus an agreed profit, the purchaser will make it internally.

Some large purchasers also practise tapered integration, as it is called when a firm produces some of its requirement of a particular part or material internally, and buys the rest externally. The buyer has considerable bargaining power since he knows from internal experience what costs are and can make convincing threats to increase internal production at the expense of purchases. In times of shortage he is guaranteed at least some supplies from the internal manufacturing facility. There is also the possibility of running internal production at near-capacity constant load, transferring demand fluctuations to the outside market.

The key feature of these and other policies is that the buyer maintains, in a market from which active competition is absent or is not strongly present, the equally effective discipline of potential competition. Potential competition can be provided as above by the make-or-buy option. It can also be provided by one form of dual sourcing, where a relatively small proportion of the requirement for a part or material is bought from a small supplier. It may be necessary to pay a somewhat higher price because of the low volume requirement, although this is often not the case. Even when there is a cost differential this may be a small price to pay for the potential threat to transfer more and more of the business to the small supplier until it becomes a big supplier, if the existing bulk supplier does not meet requirements. Or there may be one main source for most of the requirement, with the rest of the requirement spread around alternative sources just to keep in touch and to let the main source know that he does not have a monopoly.

Supplier development provides another possibility. At one time, lathe manufacturers in the United Kingdom were concerned by their dependence on a monopoly source for large lathe chucks. Although the quality was excellent and there was no objection to the price, very long delivery periods were the cause of much concern. The chuck manufacturer was unwilling to invest in extra capacity. Several lathe manufacturers then jointly encouraged a manufacturer of small drill chucks to extend his production to progressively larger chucks. A similar case occurred when vehicle buyers dissatisfied with the service given by the sole source of crankshafts, persuaded a large manufacturer to diversify into crankshaft production. The incentive offered was a promise of large orders over a 2 year period.

13

Professional
ethics
in
purchasing

People who buy on behalf of organizations cannot afford to give anyone cause to believe that their buying behaviour is not completely ethical. Spending millions of pounds for their employers, they are exposed to temptations that few of their colleagues face. They have to be honest; but more, they have to be seen to be honest.

This brings problems of definition. It is easy to say that taking a bribe for awarding a contract is sufficient reason for instant dismissal. But is a small Christmas present a bribe? Is there such a thing as a free lunch?

It was partly to help in deciding policy for these grey areas that the Institute of Purchasing and Supply published its Ethical Code, shown in Fig. 13.1.

There is evidence that many buyers follow the example set by their supervisor or manager (as in the old saying: *cuius regio eius religio,* or the cruder version *monkey see, monkey do*). Bad examples are followed too, for as the poet says:

Wronged shall he live, insulted and oppressed,
Who dares be less a villain than the rest.

As well as setting a good example, purchasing managers:

(1) Install departmental routines which discourage improper behaviour; documentary justification should be on file when the supplier selected is not the low bidder.
(2) Have some kind of outside check made on the work of the department, by internal or external auditors for instance, picking at random any six orders for more than £600 placed in the last six months and requiring the responsible buyer to justify the price paid and the

THE ETHICAL CODE OF

THE INSTITUTE OF PURCHASING AND SUPPLY

Introduction
1. In applying to join the Institute, members undertake to abide by "the Constitution, Memorandum and Articles of Association, Rules and By-Laws of the Institute". The Code set out below was approved by the Institute's Council on 26 February, 1977 and is binding on members.
2. The cases of members reported to have breached the Code shall be investigated by a Disciplinary Committee appointed by the Council; where a case is proven, a member may, depending on the circumstances and the gravity of the charge, be admonished, reprimanded, suspended from membership or removed from the list of members. Details of cases in which members are found in breach of the Code will be notified in the publications of the Institute.

Precepts
3. Members shall never use their authority or office for personal gain and shall seek to uphold and enhance the standing of the Purchasing and Supply profession and the Institute by:
    (a) maintaining an unimpeachable standard of integrity in all their business relationships both inside and outside the organisations in which they are employed;
    (b) fostering the highest possible standards of professional competence amongst those for whom they are responsible;
    (c) optimising the use of resources for which they are responsible to provide the maximum benefit to their employing organisation;
    (d) complying both with the letter and the spirit of:
        (i) the law of the country in which they practise;
        (ii) such guidance on professional practice as may be issued by the Institute from time to time;
        (iii) contractual obligations;
    (e) rejecting any business practice which might reasonably be deemed improper.

Guidance
4. In applying these precepts, members should follow the guidance set out below:
    (a) *Declaration of interest.* Any personal interest which may impinge or might reasonably be deemed by others to impinge on a member's impartiality in any matter relevant to his or her duties should be declared.
    (b) *Confidentiality and accuracy of information.* The confidentiality of information received in the course of duty should be respected and should never be used for personal gain; information given in the course of duty should be true and fair and never designed to mislead.
    (c) *Competition.* While bearing in mind the advantages to the member's employing organisation of maintaining a continuing relationship with a supplier, any arrangement which might, in the long term, prevent the effective operation of fair competition, should be avoided.
    (d) *Business gifts.* Business gifts, other than items of very small intrinsic value such as business diaries or calendars should not be accepted.
    (e) *Hospitality.* Modest hospitality is an accepted courtesy of a business relationship. However, the recipient should not allow him or herself to reach a position whereby he or she might be or might be deemed by others to have been influenced in making a business decision as a consequence of accepting such hospitality; the frequency and scale of hospitality accepted should not be significantly greater than the recipient's employer would be likely to provide in return;
    (f) when it is not easy to decide between what is and is not acceptable in terms of gifts or hospitality, the offer should be declined or advice sought from the member's superior.
5. Advice on any aspect of the precepts and guidance set out above may be obtained on written request to the Institute.

6/77

Fig. 13.1 The ethical code of the Institute of Purchasing and Supply.

supplier selected, is a more efficient method of control than elaborate and detailed rules and procedures plus searches for deviations. Of course you cannot spring this on your staff without notice. They have to be told in advance so they can keep the records they will need. Also, the checks should be made by someone with common-sense.

LEGAL AND MORAL

It is now considered to be the legal and moral obligation of those who buy for organizations not to accept any gift or favour which goes with a particular contract, or puts them under an obligation to a particular supplier, or amounts to a secret profit for the individual concerned.

This was not always so. Pepys was considered by his contemporaries to be a most conscientious public servant; 'discharging his duty . . . with a religious application and perfect integrity, he feared no one, courted no one, neglected his own fortune'. Yet his diary shows that he did not in fact neglect his own fortune quite as scrupulously as those responsible for naval procurement nowadays are expected to do.

Parts of the world still remain in the Pepys period, or even further back. International traders and multinationals have to allow for the custom of the country in which they operate. In some countries personal commissions and large gifts are customary when contracts are awarded.

And there are always people who take a different view of their obligations. In one survey (by *Purchasing Magazine* of New York), one buyer stated that his company's no-gift policy was not realistic and not fair, and he had no intention of complying. Another said 'Any gift regardless of size may be accepted without violating purchasing ethics so long as it is accepted after the purchase is made'. A third regarded gifts from suppliers as fringe benefits of the job.

Part of the difficulty is that gifts and favours, which it would be proper for the proprietor of a business to accept, cannot properly be accepted by an employee who is not a principal but an agent. In a large organization a further consideration is that the greatest care must be taken not to give scandal to colleagues in other departments who do not have outside contacts. Nor is it always easy to distinguish between gifts or favours intended as a kind of bribe to gain business, and those intended as commercial civility. Of course suppliers want their customers to feel that it is a pleasure to do business with them; and Dean Ammer (1974) warns American buyers that they must adapt

to foreign business customs. In Japan, in particular, business is mixed up with a great deal of wining and dining. . . . In fact, while American buyers usually grow genuinely fond of their Japanese suppliers, they often return from visits to

Japan in a state of complete exhaustion from the continuous hospitality of their hosts. . . . It is not at all uncommon for businessmen to exchange gifts in Japan and Europe. The American buyer who visits Japan, in particular, should have a gift for each of his hosts which he can present at the time of his departure. The practice is also not uncommon in Europe.

This may seem hard on the American buyer, precluded by his company ethics from receiving gifts but required by the custom of the country to give gifts; still, as we know, it is more blessed to give than to receive.

The business lunch

Even the harmless business lunch comes in for hard words from those who are not in a position to enjoy what they describe as expense-account junketings. Discussions that run into the lunch hour can conveniently be concluded over the luncheon table. Salesmen, being professionally sociable creatures, usually prefer to eat their meals with acquaintances, and in a strange town the only people they know may be their customers. The selling company pays the bill, which makes some buyers wary: they would rather take turns to pay than feel under an obligation. As they do not see why they should pay out of their own pocket when the other person is paying on an expense account, they arrange for their own company to accept such hospitality as legitimate expense.

Some buyers get so many lunch invitations that they decline them all, either because they object to spending the lunch hour as captive audience for a salesman, or because they do not want to give scandal to colleagues in other departments, or to set an example to their junior staff, who might be found reeling into the office at half past three somewhat the worse for wear unless their chief adopted a hard line. Some companies with impressive executive dining rooms insist that any entertainment of other companies' representatives must take place on the premises. Quite commonly it is left to the purchasing manager to lay down sensible policies in this apparently trivial matter. Given a sense of proportion and the will to avoid the appearance of abuse as well as the reality, no competent manager should find this hard.

Christmas presents

At Christmas buyers, specifiers, and senior managers are apt to receive whole cargoes of unsolicited gifts, from calendars in questionable taste and pocket diaries packed with useful data about the phases of the moon, to whisky, cigarettes, and even more lavish aids to festivity.

The donors, who are suppliers, explain this open-handedness (which amounts to little in relation to turnover) sometimes as a trade custom; sometimes as a token of esteem, although there must be many people they esteem who do not receive tokens; and sometimes as an acknowledgement of prompt and courteous reception of their representatives. They do not explain it as an attempt to induce buyers to give them more business.

The professional attitude is that only gifts of nominal value or which are advertising in character are acceptable. Even advertising novelties such as pencils, diaries and calendars are sometimes declined. This may seem needlessly high-minded, but, to take an example: the buyer for a small firm adopted the same policy in his second year with the firm. In the first year he was given 30 pocket diaries. He put them on a tray and sent his secretary round to all the foremen and the offices of his colleagues. There was not enough to go round, and the foremen and colleagues who did not get a diary were so annoyed that he had to buy a lot more out of petty cash. This annoyed the company secretary, and in addition the buyer had to suffer a lot of cracks about the presumed gifts he had not shared out. After that he sent everything to charity with a polite note to the donor and a copy of the note in the files. 'I've got to live with these people,' he said. 'It just isn't worth it.'

The legal position is that no buyer is entitled to accept items for his personal benefit without the consent (implied or explicit) of his employer, although any buyer is entitled to refuse even trivial gifts. In large purchase departments some buyers refuse gifts with considerable indignation while others would be equally indignant not to receive them; which makes the distribution of the seasonal largesse a delicate task, unwelcome to the sensitive salesman. It also makes the position of the purchasing manager quite clear. He must lay down a no-gift policy, not because he suspects his staff of corruption, but because others will. It is sad that a harmless and pleasant sign of the Christmas spirit, which helps to humanize business transactions, should have to be outlawed like this. As one reader wrote to *Purchasing Magazine* after its 'annual attempt to slaughter Santa Claus':

Why don't you quit hounding purchase agents about the insignificant little gifts they get at Christmas? You should take a crack at executives who set up their own small companies and force their purchase departments to buy from them.

Conflict of interest

Buying from relatives, and owning shares in a supplier, are other situations of a similar kind in which a conflict of interest occurs. The transactions are not in themselves dishonest, but they put the agent in a position where his private interest may conflict with the interest of the principal on whose behalf he is acting.

The chief buyer of a machine tool manufacturer was found to be buying large quantities of supplies from several suppliers unknown to the trade. These firms existed; they were companies registered and owned by the chief buyer himself. In effect he was buying goods on his private account, and then selling to himself as the machine tool company's agent. This was of course a swindle.

The buyer for an iron foundry while walking over the moors one weekend happened on a patch of sharp sand. He hired a lorry, engaged some labour, and went into business as a foundry sand supplier. As he was also engaged as a buyer of, among other things, foundry sand, he might appear to have had it made. In fact he had cleared the whole deal with his managing director, he sold at standard price or lower, and (most satisfactory of all, to his colleagues) he made little or no money out of it. This was not a swindle, but a conflict of interest situation.

Anyone responsible for placing advertisements would be pleased to find an advertising agency which always gave him priority, always rushed his rush jobs, for which at least one customer – himself – was always right. A certain marketing director brought about this desirable state of affairs by running his own agency. When it was discovered that he had channelled a large part of his advertising budget through his own advertising agency, he was forced to resign – much to his annoyance; he brought an action for damages.* Again, such a situation involves a conflict of interest, in which the agent's private interest is bound at times to clash with the interest of the principal on whose behalf he is acting.

In the larger organizations especially, it is important to avoid behaviour that arouses the reasonable suspicion of one's colleagues. As an old Chinese proverb says, 'when passing through a neighbour's melon-patch, don't bend down to tie up your shoelaces'. There is no difficulty if a purchasing officer who owns 100 shares in ICI buys 1000 litres a year of paint from ICI Paints. The situation becomes suspect when the orders placed are significant in relationship to turnover and the shares held are significant (3% or more) in relation to capital.

---

* This was part of a notorious row in a firm which was at the time the third biggest car maker in the world and ninth biggest business in the United States. The newly appointed company president flew by company plane to a New York board meeting. There, only ten days after a press conference to explain his plans for the company in the coming year, he resigned all his offices in the company and the six-figure salary that went with them, flying home by commercial air service. It was later announced that he had agreed to refund private profits exceeding £150 000 that he had made from interests in suppliers.

14

Quality
assurance
in
purchasing

The purpose both of quality assurance and of quality control is to ensure that the customer gets the quality required and specified. Quality assurance aims to make sure that everything is right. Quality control aims to sort out things that are not right. The difference is in emphasis more than techniques. Quality assurance is more comprehensive than quality control, and indeed includes quality control along with other management techniques.

'Right first time', and 'quality is everybody's job', have replaced the traditional approach of weighing on the one hand the cost of inspection and other aspects of quality control against on the other hand the cost resulting from defective items quality control fails to detect.

Quality control used to be seen as a balancing act. The lowest cost could be achieved by balancing inspection cost against other costs such as the cost of rectifying defective parts missed by inspection but found later in the production process, or of aftersales claims, or of losing sales because defective parts which get through to the customer give a company a bad reputation for quality.

Now the emphasis is on quality assurance rather than quality control. We expect our suppliers to deliver goods that we do not need to inspect because we know they are right. Dynamic purchasing departments aim for continuous reductions in reject rate at the same time as continuous improvements are being made in productivity, so that total unit cost comes down at the same time as product quality goes up. We think in terms of a few defective parts per million instead of a fraction defective of 10%. We expect this to cost less rather than more.

INSPECTION METHODS

Three methods are in common use for inspection:

(1) examination of every article, that is 100% inspection;
(2) spot checks;
(3) statistical quality control by inspection of samples according to some systematic plan based on probability theory.

A fourth option is to accept goods without inspecting them, used for two main types of purchase. First, many requirements are well within the range of what is commercially available. Technical inspection is not considered appropriate for most supplier-specified articles, such as typing paper, carbon paper, chalk, machine screws, standard paints, and lubricating and cutting oils. Second, even when requirements are not commercially available but are purchaser-specified, the trend is to make the supplier fully responsible for ensuring that the goods conform to specification. The purchaser does not need to carry out acceptance inspection if completely satisfied that the supplier's quality control system guarantees acceptable parts.

For isolated purchases or occasional small lots, 100% inspection is usual. It is also preferred if a defect would be dangerous for people using, maintaining or depending on the article, or likely to prevent performance of the function of a major product.

Even then inspecting every article is not feasible if the inspection method results in the destruction of the thing tested. If anything is to be available to the customer or user after inspection, destructive testing can be applied only to a sample of the output. Special sampling plans are available for such situations.

Unfortunately, 100% inspection is not 100% reliable. Also it takes time and costs money. Research has shown that even 300% inspection lets defects through undetected, because of human errors or faults in test equipment. When articles are in continuous production and are presented to the inspector in a series of lots or batches, sampling inspection is thought to provide better control of quality, despite the inevitable risk that some defective parts will get through undetected.

Spot checks are used to keep people reasonably satisfied that no major change is occurring in a process which has already been tested and proved to be satisfactory.

STATISTICAL QUALITY CONTROL

Statistical quality control provides systematic methods for devising plans for acceptance inspection by sampling and also for ensuring that production processes are not deviating from target. The sampling plans are based on probability theory, developed by statisticians and mathematicians.

Sampling methods can be used both for inspection by attributes, which classifies the article (or one of its attributes) on a straightforward yes/no basis – either accept or reject; and for inspection by variables, where a single quality characteristic such as ductility or tensile strength is measured on a continuous scale.

Statistical quality control is applied to any repetitive process which produces large batches of similar items. Although the main application area is to physical articles such as bars of steel or electronic components, the technique has also proved useful in other connections, such as complaints, reservations on aircraft, or errors in purchase invoices. It provides simple standardized methods for making decisions about:

(1) process control,
(2) acceptance inspection.

PROCESS CONTROL

Process control is concerned with future performance. Control charts (originally developed by Walter Shewhart in the United States in 1924) are used to check that a process is not getting out of control and becoming likely to produce unsatisfactory results. Sample checks of successive process results are plotted on charts which indicate immediately whether or not the results are as expected. The process is 'in control' statistically if the variations that actually occur are such as would normally occur in random samples from a stable process.

The principle of control charts is illustrated by Fig. 14.1. This relates to a continuous process in which at regular intervals a small sample, usually four or five pieces, is inspected. The average of the test results is plotted on a control chart. In the example shown, all the results lie well within the expected range, even though random variations exist.

The process mean, which should be about the same as the average test result, is shown along the centre line. Superimposed on this graph at the right-hand side is the curve of the normal distribution, to illustrate the principle. Sample means tend to be normally distributed and consequently nearly all of them will fall within plus or minus (±) three standard deviations of the process mean.

American practice is to draw upper and lower control lines on the graph at ± three standard deviations. Any results which fall outside these limits call for immediate corrective action since they indicate with

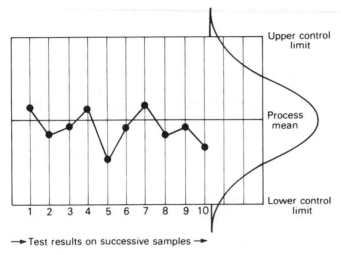

Fig. 14.1 Control chart with normal curve superimposed.

a very high degree of probability that the process is getting out of control.

British practice differs slightly: action limits are drawn at a level corresponding to a 1 in 1000 probability of occurring by chance (3.09 times population standard deviation divided by the square root of sample size), and additional warning lines are drawn at a level corresponding to a 1 in 40 probability of occurring by chance (1.96 times population standard deviation divided by the square root of the sample size). If the chance of sample means lying above or below the warning lines is only 1 in 40, many test results in the warning area are not significant. If one occurs the usual procedure is to take another sample immediately. The chance of sample means occurring above or below the action limits is about 1 in 1000 so that a test result in this area signals the need for immediate corrective action such as shutting down the process to check tool setting or sharpness.

Control charts are plotted for the range, as well as the mean, of sample results, to detect any changes that occur in the variability of the process even though process mean stays about the same. When inspection is by attributes rather than variables, control charts are plotted for number of defects.

ACCEPTANCE INSPECTION

Acceptance inspection evaluates past performance, but it is not confined to sorting good from bad and deciding whether goods delivered are to be accepted or rejected. The aim of quality assurance is to prevent defective parts from being produced rather than to reject them after they have been produced.

When successive batches from one production process are being checked, accept or reject decisions are usually made by inspecting a sample selected in accordance with some plan: for instance, take a random sample of 125 from the batch, inspect each one, and either reject the whole lot if there are four or more which fail to conform or else accept the whole batch if fewer than four fail to conform. Sampling plans can be taken from published tables such as those in British standards 6001 and 6002. BS 6000 explains clearly how BS 6001 works.

Sampling plans are used to assess the quality of a large batch by inspecting relatively small samples. Single-sampling plans rely on checking a single sample from each batch. The whole batch is rejected if the sample contains more than a specified number of defects; otherwise the whole batch is accepted. Single-sampling plans are simpler, and consequently more widely used. Other sampling plans use double, multiple or sequential sampling. In these the test results can lead not only to yes or no but also to don't know verdicts: the decision is either to accept or to reject the whole batch, or else to check some more. For instance in one such plan if inspecting a sample of 120 finds three or fewer defectives, the whole batch will be accepted. If six or more defectives are found, the whole batch will be rejected. But if four or five defectives are found, a further sample will be taken and inspected.

Sampling inspection plans cannot guarantee that no part which fails to conform to specification will ever slip through inspection and get accepted when it should be rejected. Consequently it is usual to start by

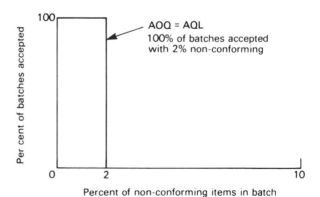

Fig. 14.2 Ideal operating characteristic for sampling scheme.

deciding what proportion of non-conforming parts is just acceptable as process average. This is called the acceptable quality level (AQL). The difference between zero defects and the AQL is the price that has to be paid for the economic advantage of inspecting a sample instead of the whole batch.

The supplier is expected to aim for zero defects. A high proportion of batches will be rejected unless the actual proportion of items which fail to conform is well above the AQL. The average outgoing quality (AOQ) is consequently higher than the AQL.

In Fig. 14.2, an idealized operating characteristic is shown in which every batch having more defectives than the AQL is rejected, and every batch having less non-conforming than the AQL is accepted. In this situation, which is impossible to achieve in practice with sampling inspection, the AOQ is the same as the AQL.

In Fig. 14.3, an actual operating characteristic is shown. Corresponding to any percentage of non-conforming items in a batch, there is a probability of acceptance, which can be read off from the graph by going up from the proportion of non-conforming items on the horizontal axis to the curve, and then across to the probability of acceptance on the vertical axis. In the example marked on the figure, if batches contain 2% non-conforming items, one in every four batches will be rejected

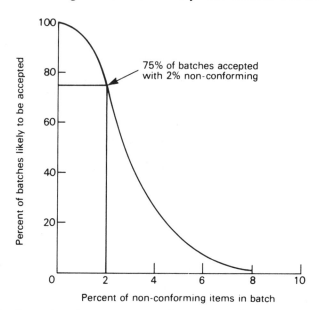

Fig. 14.3 Operating characteristic, single sampling (batch size 2500, sample size 125, reject batch if four or more non-conforming in sample).

and only three-quarters of batches will be accepted. This is drastic and would in practice lead to investigations, tighter inspection, etc.

Standard sampling plans allow for three inspection levels: normal, tight, and reduced. If two out of five successive batches are rejected, the inspection plan is tightened by increasing the sample size. This continues until five successive batches have been accepted. Reduced sampling applies when few defects are found, making it safe to reduce the size of the sample.

The operating characteristic of a sampling plan shows how it works. It can be calculated or taken from the tables. Adjustments are made to the plan to give risk levels considered acceptable in relation to design tolerance and process variability. Both supplier and purchaser are at risk.

This can be seen from Fig. 14.3. Almost every batch with fewer defectives than the AQL of 1% will be accepted, but a very small proportion will be rejected. This is the producer's risk: that a good batch will be rejected, with the resultant expense of 100% inspection, transport, etc. Similarly at the lower end of the curve, some bad batches will be accepted: this is the consumer's risk (or purchaser's risk).

CAPABILITY ASSESSMENT

The risk of inadvertently accepting faulty goods can be much reduced by selecting reliable suppliers whose quality capability and performance has been thoroughly checked and found satisfactory.

Many organizations have their own methods for doing this, but use is also made of a 1979 British standard, BS 5750. This is used both in specifying quality assurance requirements in contracts, and in assessing the quality capability of suppliers before making contracts with them. It can also be helpful in devising sound quality assurance schemes.

Three 'levels' are used in checking a supplier's quality capability. At the simplest level only final inspection facilities and methods are examined. At the intermediate level, when more complicated things such as subassemblies are to be supplied, which may need to be inspected at several stages during manufacture, the whole quality control system including arrangements for correcting faults occurring during manufacture is examined. Both these levels apply when the supplier is not responsible for design. At the highest level, when the supplier may be handling design, development, installation and field trial, as well as manufacture, the supplier's entire organization may need to be vetted.

Examining organizations and their capabilities to make these assessments is expensive and time-consuming for both parties – supplier and purchaser. When several purchasers want to examine one supplier,

Fig. 14.4 BSI symbols.

they can save time and money by using a third party to make the assessment. This service is available to purchasers from the BSI and other
organizations.

Figure 14.4 shows the well-known BSI Kitemark, safety mark, and
registered stockist symbol. The Kitemark indicates that the BSI has
tested samples of the product against the relevant British Standard and
found them acceptable, and that the producer operates a quality system
based on BS 5750.

The safety mark appears on products that conform to standard safety
requirements. The registered stockist symbol is claimed to indicate that
goods 'have been manufactured, stored, handled and packed to the
highest standards'.

QUALITY AUDITS

Periodic reviews of quality assurance systems are known as quality
audits. In addition to verifying final accounts, financial auditors review
the operation and design of the whole accounting system which produces final accounts. In the same way, quality audits both verify that
goods which have passed inspection are in fact free from defects, and
review the operation and design of the whole quality assurance system,
including the calibration of test equipment and the implementation of
the quality control manual.

15

Buying
abroad

Increasingly, buyers source and operate in world markets. Purchasers buy *from* abroad: these are imports into the purchaser's country and exports from the supplier's country. They also buy *for* abroad, for delivery to some country and thus for import into that country and for export from the country of origin. Multinational organizations, for instance, often buy for delivery to overseas locations. In major international projects such as turnkey contracts for the Middle East or China, contracts are made in many countries for completion in the country of destination.

ORGANIZATION ASPECTS

Multinationals which employ people and operate factories in several countries usually try to optimize at least part of their sourcing and supply arrangements on a worldwide basis. There are several ways to organize this.

One way which used to be popular was to establish a corporate or headquarters department with authority to insist that purchasing managers in the various countries make sourcing decisions in the best interests of the organization worldwide, as perceived by the headquarters department.

Another way is to have an international purchasing coordinator, whose job is to collect information, draw conclusions, and persuade people in the various national operations to sign contracts which make the best, rather than the traditional or locally biased, source decisions. The coordinator may operate from a small office with just a secretary and a desktop computer with a lot of information on hard disk, and needs to be a most persuasive person.

Many groups of companies set up international procurement committees, which meet periodically to review sourcing and supply. Meetings are usually held in turn in each of the countries where factories are.

WHY BUY ABROAD?

Purchasers increasingly look abroad when sourcing, whether or not in the end they buy abroad, because this gives a wider choice and could give better value for money. There are several reasons why the search area for sourcing has become worldwide. These include:

(1) the arrival of new contenders on world markets;
(2) the progressive reduction in barriers to international trade.

Newly industrialized countries on the shores of the Pacific are knocking hard on our doors. Singapore, Taiwan, Korea, Malaysia, Hong Kong are some of the South-east Asia countries whose manufacturers are now competing successfully in world markets.

Free trade is obviously good for buyers, although it may have disadvantages for some sellers. Attempts to liberalize the world trading system by dismantling barriers to trade have been made by the General Agreement on Tariffs and Trade (GATT), which covers 122 countries and at successive meetings had approved seven rounds of tariff cuts by 1986. Common market areas are also developing, of which the largest is the European Economic Community (EEC).

The EEC is dedicated to the notion of free trade between member countries, on the model of the United States. It was hoped that this would make war between European countries as unthinkable as war between American states. It was also expected confidently that the larger market would benefit consumers, users, customers generally by giving them more choice of goods and facilitating more efficient production. However, in all American states people speak English and have the same constitution and come under one federal system of law. The European states on the other hand speak many languages and have different legal systems. These things constitute to some extent natural barriers to trade. Artificial barriers are also set up both by governments wishing to benefit their economies at the expense of foreigners, and by domestic producers wishing to protect their patch.

FREE TRADE AND PROTECTION

The traditional ways to protect domestic producers, by imposing import taxes to make foreign goods more expensive, or quotas to restrict the quantities of them which can be imported, have declined because of GATT and the EEC. 'Voluntary' restrictions in place of mandatory quotas, the use of technical standards and specifications to hinder imports, exchange controls which restrict the availability of currency, administrative regulations and other ingenious devices have taken their place. Most countries speak in favour of free trade but few countries do not protect domestic producers.

The demand for protection comes mainly from pressure groups of domestic producers who are up against international competition. Producers obviously benefit when foreign competition is shut out. Less obvious is the considerable cost to the rest of the economy.

The basic argument for free trade is well known. Some countries are better at producing certain goods and services than others; they have a 'comparative advantage' in the production of such products. Specialization between countries, each of which exports items in which it has a comparative advantage, raises the standard of living in all countries. If each nation specializes in what it does best, everyone benefits – except the unfortunate producers who have a comparative disadvantage. They cannot compete. But they can be protected from international competition, if their government can be persuaded to make people pay the price of protection: prices are higher, and other industries become less competitive and thus produce less and employ fewer workers.

DON'T BUY ABROAD!

American steel producers sponsored a brilliant advertisement years ago when some of their customers were starting to source overseas.

Once deep in the forest there lived an industrious beaver. He not only felled trees and built dams, but on the land he cleared he grew produce for a hungry family of rabbits. How they loved his fat, juicy carrots!

But one day Father Rabbit found that by crossing the river on a fallen tree he could buy carrots more cheaply from a raccoon who lived on the other side. Soon he was racing back and forth across the river. The beaver shrugged his shoulders and went into the dry goods business.

Then came a terrible flood. The fallen tree was swept away and the rabbits could only gaze longingly across the river. They went back to the beaver, who said: 'Sorry, folks, but I'm out of the carrots business. Could you use a dozen hand towels?'

One cold day Mr Beaver met Father Rabbit foraging for food. The rabbit was near starvation. He looked at the beaver with tears in his eyes and wailed: 'Where were you when I needed you?' And the beaver replied: 'Where were *you* when I needed you?'

Whether your needs be carrots or steel, your safest, most reliable suppliers are right here at home. To serve you, and serve you well, is our primary concern – not just today and tomorrow – but year after year.'

This makes the point that buying abroad just because a lower price is available from a foreign supplier brings a short-term cost advantage but may in the long-term result in the disappearance of domestic sources, with their claimed advantages of safety and security, and incurs the risk that foreign sources might also disappear from the scene for a variety of reasons, leaving the purchaser bereft.

SHIPYARDS MAY BUY ABROAD

By MAURICE WEAVER   Industrial Staff

BRITISH Shipbuilders will look abroad for equipment supplies if British standards do not improve, says Mr Graham Day, chairman of the State-owned yards.

He stressed in an interview that patriotic considerations and long-term trading arrangements would not prevent him looking abroad for alternatives.

He was not prepared to tolerate a situation in which it was "not unusual" for British suppliers to quote prices ten per cent higher than foreign competitors and in which delivery schedules were not met.

He said: "I would rather deal with someone I despise who delivered on time and at the right price than with a good friend who could not meet these requirements."

For that reason his managers would be doing more "shopping around."

Regular reports

Mr Day has introduced a "vendor rating system" to monitor supply contracts. Yard managers deliver regular reports on suppliers.

Of £563 million spent by British Shipbuilders on equipment, materials and services in 1984-85, about £48 million went overseas and this percentage is expected to show a rise this year.

Mr Day disclosed that in order to beat foreign competiton for two ships for the Sunderland yard of Austin and Pickersgill earlier this year it had been necessary to buy 25 per cent of the equipment from overseas.

"In the light of this experience we must look for better prices, guaranteed delivery and absolutely consistent quality from all our suppliers, whether British or foreign."

One unnamed British supplier which had for years provided the corporation's shipyards with between 10 and 15 units annually, each costing several hundred thousand pounds, had already been sacked.

Mr Day said it had been a major blow to the company concerned which had regarded British Shipbuilders as its major world customer, but its quality, delivery and technical support had simply been inadequate.

Mr Day declared: "For the next year or more we will not buy from them. We told them "if we deal with you again we are going to want to monitor your manufacturing and, if we do contract with you again, there will be very considerable monetary damages if you fail to perform properly."

He held up British Steel as an example of what can be achieved if management gets to grips with its problems. "Going back about two years we had serious problems with them, but the efforts they have made since mean we now have very few problems."

"The quality has improved, we have a much better commercial relationship with them and the important thing is they wanted to understand what our problems were and then moved in to address them."

Fig. 15.1 'Shipyards may buy abroad' – a 1985 example.

Can we import foreign goods without importing unemployment? If a foreign source offers goods at substantially lower prices than domestic sources, other things being equal, is there any way a buyer can justify not buying abroad?

Most buyers would prefer to deal with domestic suppliers. But if they are not competitive a buyer makes his own firm uncompetitive by dealing with them. The point was made forcibly in an interview with the chairman of British Shipbuilders in 1985, as shown in Fig. 15.1.

POSITIVE PURCHASING

Buyers sometimes urge domestic suppliers to improve their performance or their products so that their market offering will be the 'best buy' next time. This may result in reduced imports or increased exports. 'Positive purchasing' was the name given to this policy by public sector purchasers in the 1980s.

Such a policy should not be regarded as a crude 'Buy British', 'Buy French', 'Buy American', campaign. The purchaser will not buy from domestic suppliers unless what they offer is technically and commercially the best buy. But if the business is placed abroad, that is not the end of the matter. Dangling the carrot of future business, the purchaser will urge domestic suppliers to make whatever changes are needed to product range, design, quality assurance, delivery, reliability or price, in order that their market offering will be the best buy next time round. Foreign producers may also be encouraged to license domestic producers to make products to their specification and standard, or to establish a manufacturing subsidiary in the purchaser's country.

Positive purchasing has much in common with the techniques of supplier development mentioned in Chapter 12.

But it should be borne in mind that 'English soil won't grow everything'. It is futile for every country, large or small, to attempt to produce within its frontiers everything it needs, from food and raw materials to consumer products.

PROBLEMS IN BUYING ABROAD

Most of the problems that occur in purchase transactions with firms in other countries come under one or more of the following six headings:

(1) identifying and evaluating foreign suppliers;
(2) language;
(3) legal system;

(4) currency;
(5) method of payment;
(6) transport arrangements and type of contract.

In identifying foreign suppliers, buyers use the same information sources they use for domestic suppliers: directories and buyer's guides, advertisements, trade shows and exhibitions, direct mail contacts and catalogues, calls by salesmen, their own trade knowledge and advice from colleagues. Also for foreign suppliers they consult embassies and commercial attachés, the United Nations and other international services in the case particularly of developing countries. They make missionary purchasing visits to investigate potential suppliers and to get them interested.

In evaluating foreign suppliers, the methods used are again the same as for domestic suppliers, although they may be more difficult to apply because of distance and language problems.

Language and law

English-speaking countries are fortunate in that English has become to a large extent the international language of business. Fluency in foreign languages is not essential to the conduct of international transactions. Letters and other documents can readily be translated; the names of qualified translators and recommended fees are available from such bodies as the Institute of Linguists.

Of course a working knowledge of the local language is a help when travelling abroad, as well as in the social and informal contacts which oil the wheels of business.

It is always desirable to establish if a contract is made under English law or under some other legal system, and specialist advice may be necessary. The seller may wish to have payment guaranteed by a British bank. If a dispute occurs, it will be necessary to decide if an English court has jurisdiction to hear the case, and if so whether English law or the law of another country applies.

Arbitration

International contracts often stipulate that any disputes should be submitted to arbitration. Arbitration is usually quicker and cheaper than litigation. It is subject to the Arbitration Acts 1950 and 1979. English arbitration is widely respected for fairness and efficiency, and many contracts refer any disputes to it even when the contract is not itself made under English law. The International Chamber of Commerce, based in Paris, also offers a widely respected arbitration service. A typical contract clause reads: 'all disputes arising in connection with this contract shall be finally settled under the rules of conciliation and arbitration of the International Chamber of Commerce by one or more arbitrators appointed in accordance with the rules'.

Currency problems

The rate at which money current in one country exchanges for money current in another country has been subject to considerable fluctuations in recent years. If a customer in country A accepts a quotation from a supplier in country B, and places an order at a price stated in the currency of country B, and if between contract date and settlement the rate of exchange between the two countries alters, the result is equivalent to a price change imposed on the customer, although the supplier receives no more and no less than the amount originally quoted.

If on the other hand the order is placed at a price stated in the currency of country A, a price change is imposed on the supplier.

Suppose for instance the wine buyer for a hotel chain goes to France and places orders with a cooperative for delivery three months from now for £10 000 worth of wine. The rate of exchange is 10 francs to the pound. Three months pass, and the rate of exchange is now 12 francs to the pound. If the contract is made in pounds, the buyer will pay £10 000 as agreed, but the seller will receive 120 000 francs, which amounts to 20% more than expected. If on the other hand the contract is made in francs, the seller will receive the 100 000 francs as agreed, but the buyer will pay only £8334.

Various ways have been devised to share the risk of loss or windfall profit between the two parties, for instance by averaging the rates of exchange at contract date and at completion date. However if the price is stated in the supplier's currency, the most popular technique is for the customer to make a forward purchase of the amount of currency required. By doing this the amount which will eventually have to be paid is made definite, without the need to lay out the whole amount in advance. Rates are quoted in the media, as shown in Fig. 15.2.

METHOD OF PAYMENT

The normal method of payment for contracts within the United Kingdom is by monthly account. Suppliers allow one month for payment after the date of the invoice, and payment is made by cheque. Payment

FOREIGN EXCHANGES

STERLING SPOT AND FORWARD RATES

	Market rates day's range November 28	Market rates close November 28	1 month	3 months
N York	1.4315-1.4380	1.4350-1.4360	0.58-0.56prem	1.80-1.75prem
Montreal	1.9859-1.9901	1.9859-1.9887	0.41-0.33prem	1.36-1.21prem
Ams'dam	3.1985-3.2150	3.1986-3.2030	1½-1⅜prem	4⅜-4⅛prem
Brussels	58.90-59.15	58.92-59.03	20-15prem	56-47prem
C'phgen	10.7130-10.7315	10.7137-10.7284	1⅜-⅝prem	2-1¼prem
Dublin	1.0422-1.0460	1.0428-1.0438	24-30dis	71-88dis
Frankfurt	2.8275-2.8415	2.8298-2.8339	1⅝-1⅜prem	4⅝-4⅜prem
Lisbon	210.75-213.35	210.80-212.03	79-117dis	221-341dis
Madrid	191.75-193.00	191.79-192.06	14-32dis	25-115dis
Milan	1960.20-1972.50	1960.21-1965.88	1prem-2dis	3prem-1dis
Oslo	10.7625-10.8060	10.7840-10.8059	3¾-4¼dis	9¾-10¾dis

Sterling index compared with 1975 was same at 68.1 (day's range 68.0-68.1).

OTHER STERLING RATES

Argentina austral*	1.6895-1.6966
Australia dollar	2.2049-2.2083
Bahrain dinar............	0.5380-0.5420
Brazil cruzado*	20.2505-20.3653
Cyprus pound 0.7280-0.7380
Finland marka..........	6.9910-7.0310
Greece drachma.......	196.75-198.75
Hong Kong dollar...	11.1686-11.1779
India rupee	18.60-18.80
Iraq dinar.............................	n/a
Kuwait dinar KD	0.4190-0.4230
Malaysia dollar..........	3.7317-3.7372
Mexico peso	1220.0-1270.0
New Zealand dollar....	2.7972-2.8102
Saudi Arabia riyal......	5.3630-5.4030
Singapore dollar.......	3.1481-3.1518
South Africa rand	3.1747-3.1912
U A E dirham	5.2520-5.2920
*Lloyds Bank	

DOLLAR SPOT RATES

Ireland	1.3735-1.3765
Singapore................	2.1938-2.1948
Malaysia	2.6005-2.6025
Australia..................	0.6503-0.6508
Canada	1.3843-1.3848
Sweden...................	6.8800-6.8850
Norway	7.5100-7.5150
Denmark	7.4560-7.4610
West Germany..........	1.9750-1.9760
Switzerland..............	1.6430-1.6445
Netherlands..............	2.2330-2.2340
France	6.4725-6.4775
Japan	161.95-162.05
Italy.......................	1368.5-1369.5
Belgium (Comm).........	41.05-41.10
Hong Kong	7.7830-7.7840
Portugal	147.30-147.60
Spain......................	133.50-133.55
Austria.....................	13.92-13.94

Rates supplied by Barclays Bank HOFEX and Extel.

Fig. 15.2 Exchange rates, spot and forward.

may be made sooner, especially if discounts are offered for early payment, or later, if the purchaser is able to use the supplier as a source of cheap credit; and other methods of payment are used, especially for large projects, as discussed in Chapter 17. Such methods are also in common use for contracts between organizations in the EEC, in Britain and Australia, etc. It is when there are doubts about the purchaser's willingness or ability to pay or about the willingness or ability of the purchaser's country to make available foreign currency in which payment can be made that it becomes necessary to agree on other methods of payment.

Bills of exchange

Bills of exchange, although not much used in domestic trade, continue to be popular in international trade. A bill of exchange is defined as: 'an unconditional order in writing, addressed by one person to another, signed by the person giving it, requiring the person to whom it is addressed to pay on demand or at a fixed or determinable future time a sum certain in money to or to the order of a specified person or to bearer'. They may be payable ten days after sight, or three months after date, or however specified. The person to whom the bill is addressed accepts it by writing 'Accepted' on it with his signature, and then becomes liable to any third party, who can in turn endorse the bill and use it in payment of any amount due from him.

Documentary credits

Documentary credits are often used. These are arrangements by which the purchaser instructs his bank (the issuing bank) to open a credit account in the seller's name in another bank, usually in the seller's country (the correspondent bank). The seller can draw money from this account only by presenting documents of title to the goods consigned to the purchaser. This is a high security payment method, especially the irrevocable letter of credit, which cannot be cancelled or modified unless the seller fails to present the appropriate documents to the bank within the contract period.

TRANSPORT ARRANGEMENTS AND FORM OF CONTRACT

Transport arrangements in buying abroad can present no more of a problem than when buying from a domestic supplier. But for island economies such as England or Japan, buying abroad means buying from overseas, and this is largely true for the United States too.

For these countries the carriage of goods from supplier to customer assumes much greater importance than in a normal domestic transaction, and if goods have to be transported for long distances, possibly using several modes of transport, then insurance against loss or damage in transit becomes an important feature of the contract.

Of critical importance in this connection is when property passes, as lawyers put it: that is, when the goods cease to belong to the seller and become the property of the buyer. For domestic transactions one of two extreme cases usually applies: either the goods cease to be the seller's property when they leave his establishment, or else they cease to be his property when they arrive at the buyer's establishment. The first case may be stated in quotations from suppliers as *ex works*. Even if the supplier arranges transport for the goods, as does quite often happen, he is doing so on behalf of the buyer, as an agent. Any claim for delay or damage in transit is made by the buyer against the transport firm, which makes its own arrangements for insurance. In principle, it is the buyer's responsibility to collect the goods or arrange transport for them from the seller's establishment.

The second case may be expressed by the purchaser as 'delivered to our establishment', or 'delivered buyer's works' or 'delivered to this address'. Here it is the seller's responsibility to make or arrange for delivery, and any loss or delay in transit is the seller's liability, whether or not it can be recovered by a claim against a transport firm. The buyer claims against the seller rather than the carrier.

Between these two extremes a large number of cases exist in international trade, the differences between them being differences in the point at which responsibility for transport and insurance changes hands. For instance *FOB* (free on board) makes the seller responsible for transport and insurance until goods are loaded onto the ship. *FAS* (free alongside ship) is a very similar form of contract. The seller may have to hire lighters to take the goods to the point at which the ship's lifting tackle can hoist the goods aboard. *CIF* (carriage, insurance, freight) contracts make the seller liable for all insurance and transport costs up to the port of delivery. *C and F* contracts are similar to CIF contracts except that the buyer is responsible for insuring goods in transit between port of loading and port of delivery.

About 90% of goods imported into Great Britain come in by sea, to which these forms of contract are mainly applicable. But an increasing proportion of international trade is transported by air, road or rail. Airway bills or consignment notes, and consignment notes for road or rail transport, differ from bills of lading for shipments by sea mainly in that they are advices of goods shipped rather than documents of title conferring property in or ownership of goods shipped. Much use is made by British importers and exporters of 'Ro-Ro' (roll-on-roll-off) arrangements, which use road transport but include provision for the channel crossing.

Differences exist in the way some of these trade terms are used, and to avoid dispute it is good practice either to spell out in the contract what they mean, or else (preferably) to refer to Incoterms, a widely recognized set of standard international definitions of trade terms in common use. First published in 1936, revised in 1953, and subsequently added to by incorporating new terms such as 'FOB Airport', Incoterms are published by the International Chamber of Commerce in Paris. They state precisely the responsibilities both of buyer and seller – 'the seller must:'; 'the buyer must:' in connection with each of the terms defined.

FREIGHT FORWARDERS

Companies which frequently have large international transactions may employ expert staff to handle the details, but most companies will go to outside help in the form of freight forwarders. Many freight forwarders provide a door-to-door service, covering all arrangements for transport, insurance, customs, packing, and even finance if required; others simply arrange transport and documentation. By combining consignments from various sources (known as consolidation and groupage) they can often offer advantageous prices for small consignments.

COUNTERTRADE

Countertrade has again become a feature of international transactions. It harks back to what must have been the earliest form of international trade, the barter transaction. This was adopted to solve payment problems when deals were done between countries belonging to different currency blocs, for instance if Russia bought coca-cola from the United States and paid in vodka. It has also been used by governments to force countries wishing to export to them to accept imports in return, not just because they were short of foreign exchange but also to increase their export trade. Purchase departments and marketing departments thus found themselves involved in selling furs, caviare, and other items that were not in their organization's normal product range.

CHECKLIST FOR BUYING ABROAD

Some of the points to check before sourcing abroad are listed below.

(1) Legal system: is the contract subject to English law or to some other legal system? Should legal advice be taken on contract terms? Is the relationship with the supplier such that difficulties can be sorted out without lawsuits? If the relationship deteriorates, have we recourse against the suppliers? Is there an arbitration clause?

(2) Language: if the contract is not written in English, have we a certified translation?

(3) Mode of payment: is payment to be made on normal domestic terms, such as 30 days after date of invoice or satisfactory receipt of

goods, whichever is later; or is it to be by letter of credit (revocable or irrevocable), or by bill of exchange, or by cash against documents? Several modes of payment are used for international trade, some more advantageous to the seller, some less so.

(4) Currency: in what currency is payment to be made? In what currency is price stated? Is the rate of exchange likely to change appreciably, and if so which party will lose by it, and should any special arrangements be made to reduce or share the loss? Is any action required to ensure that currency will be available when needed to meet the obligation?

(5) Tax and other regulations: many transactions are subject to import or export tax, duty or tariff, to exchange control regulations, to customs, to licensing or other quantitative restrictions. Are the goods subject to quota? Are they liable to duty/tariff? Is an import license required? Are there any special regulations which apply?

(6) Transport: how are the goods to be moved from the supplier's premises to ours? Have we considered air freight? Have we consulted several forwarding agents?

(7) Price: in comparing delivered price with quotations from local sources have we taken account of transport, insurance, shipping, unusual payment terms, currency exchange risk, tax, and incidental expenses?

(8) Lead time: have we fully allowed for possible late delivery due to frontier delays through incorrect documentation, incorrect description or other breach of regulation, as well as loss or damage in transit, strike, bad weather, and delays in port or customs where applicable? Do we need special buffer stocks as insurance?

(9) Terms: it is important to establish who is liable for insurance, freight, and loss or damage at various stages, and also when the buyer becomes the legal owner of the goods. A number of standard terms have been in use for many years, such as FOB, FAS, CIF, C and F., together with their variations such as FOC (free on container). Although these terms are widely used there are local differences in their interpretation, which can be avoided by the adoption of the standard definitions published by the International Chamber of Commerce in Paris as Incoterms 1953.

16

Buying
commodities

The primary commodities are the natural products of the earth, which usually enter into trade in a partly processed condition. They include minerals such as copper and tin; vegetable products such as coffee, cocoa and wheat; and animal products such as wool, bristle and hides. In their country of origin they are traded in various ways, but they often enter into world trade through the international commodity markets.

These provide three important services. First, they enable the producers and the consumers of commodities to make contact, often through intermediaries, and arrange contracts for physical supply. Second, they provide a means to determine the world price, as distinct from local prices. Third, many of them provide a form of price insurance by means of futures contracts.

Organized commodity markets exist in many countries. In Britain, the London Metal Exchange provides all three of the services mentioned above for copper, lead, zinc and silver. Silver is also traded on the London Bullion Exchange, and the New York Commodity Exchange (COMEX) is another important market for silver and copper. 'Soft' commodities traded in London include coffee, cocoa, rubber, sugar, soya bean meal, vegetable oil and wool, for all of which futures markets are provided by the Terminal Market Associations using the London Commodity Exchange; cotton, tea, furs, jute and grain. The Chicago Board of Trade is the largest and oldest of the many American commodity markets and its rules and procedures have provided a model which several other exchanges have followed.

Typically official trading occurs in short bouts of 'open outcry' in a 'ring', supplemented by unofficial or 'kerb' trading. The London Metal Exchange 'ring' was originally a chalk circle, later replaced by an arrangement of curved benches at which the dealers sit with their assistants behind them. Official prices arrived at during the day's trading are published widely by the news media. Transactions are typically for multiples of a standard quantity, of goods of a specific description, for delivery either immediately ('spot', 'cash', 'physicals') or at a specified future date, in accordance with the rules of the exchange.

The most striking difference between these commodity markets and the markets for manufactured products (apart from the actual procedure for striking a bargain on the floor of the exchange) is the variability of price. Commodity prices often, though not invariably, fluctuate from deal to deal, and from day to day; they can move up or down by large amounts from year to year.

Coffee prices for instance almost doubled between 1985 and 1986. The international Coffee Organization, with 75 exporting and importing members, had been trying to keep the price below 150 cents a pound, but it stopped trying when fears of an exceptionally low crop made it impossible to hold the price at previous low levels. Drought in Brazil during the flowering period of the coffee trees made a much lower crop of coffee berries likely, and frost was feared later in the year, during the southern hemisphere winter, which would further reduce the crop. Earthquake and floods in South America and wars in parts of Africa were further threats to the coffee crop, which all comes from trees grown in tropical regions on well-drained hillsides in areas of high rainfall.

What actually happened in the next six months is shown in Fig. 16.1. Prices fell instead of rising.

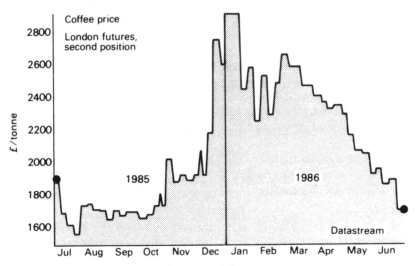

Fig. 16.1 Commodity prices change rapidly.

Prices vary in this way mainly because of variations in worldwide supply and demand. On the supply side, crop failure can be caused by flood, drought, frost or the incidence of fungus and other diseases. Strikes, war and political troubles can also affect supply. Demand is affected by the state of industrial activity in the industrial countries which are the principal customers. In some years all the industrial economies are very busy at the same time, driving up prices because of the high world demand. The increasing use of substitutes and the gradual depletion of natural resources can also affect the situation.

In theory, both shortages and surpluses are self-correcting: shortages attract new supplies through high prices, surpluses drive out marginal producers through low prices and thus reduce supply. But there is a considerable timelag with most primary commodities. Minor increases in the output of a plantation can be achieved by more intensive cultivation, but to achieve major increases, new trees must be planted. It takes three years for the Arabica coffee tree to produce a crop and five years for the Robusta variety. Rubber trees are normally tapped in their sixth or seventh year. Cocoa trees yield their first crop three to five years after planting, but take ten years to come to full bearing.

High metal prices can bring more supplies on the market, but it takes time to reopen old marginal mines and even more time to discover and exploit new ore bodies. In the same way low prices lead eventually to a reduction in supply, but there is always a delay before decisions are taken to close the marginal mines, root out old trees, cut back production. During this delay low prices persist, and the result is larger swings in price than are required to adjust supply to demand, followed by swings in the reverse direction.

A further complication is that many of the main exporters of primary commodities are developing countries which rely on the revenue from them to yield foreign exchange, support paid employment, and provide disposable government revenue to finance development schemes. A fall in price tends to lead to demands to increase the quantity sold in order to maintain export revenues, which would lead naturally to a further fall in price.

The markets themselves can be overresponsive to expected changes in supply or demand, and when supplies are scarce the prudent make them scarcer by stockpiling and the speculators by trying to corner them.

These large price variations are not liked by either the producers or the users of commodities. Industrial users prefer price stability because it suits their planning and budgeting systems, and have often said they would be willing to pay a little more in return for a stable and predictable price. Commodity producers prefer higher prices but they too are often willing to make some sacrifice to avoid periodic swings from high to low.

Consequently there have been many attempts to regulate world prices in the interest either of one or of both sides of the market. Methods used include producer cartels, bilateral contracts, multilateral contracts, compensatory finance arrangements and international buffer stocks supplemented by export quotas. Several of these have been successful in the short term, but long term price stabilization has proved difficult to achieve.

A typical arrangement is to appoint a buffer stock manager and provide him with funds and warehouses so that he can support a falling price by buying for stock or attack a rising price by selling from stock. The finance for this may be provided by a producer cartel, or by an international council with representatives both of buyers and sellers who are allocated votes in proportion to their market share subject to a minimum. The controlling body usually sets floor and ceiling prices for the buffer stock manager to work to, and as long as he is successful in keeping market price between the limits all goes well. But buffer stocks are unlikely to be large enough to prevent the price from going through the ceiling when there is a world deficit of a commodity. Nor is a buffer stock manager likely to have a long enough purse to keep prices from falling through the floor when there is a world surplus. Action must then be taken by the cartel or the council to adjust production. Apart from the time delays in implementing an agreement to do this, which have already been mentioned, it may be difficult even to achieve agreement if individual members find that failure to agree would better suit their individual interest.

The International Tin Agreement, after some 30 years of successful operation, collapsed towards the end of 1985. The agreement authorized the Tin Council, with 22 member countries, to intervene in the market, buying or selling to stabilize price. Over 30 years price had moved steadily upwards; from the £1400 to £1600 range of the early 1970s, to the £6000 price of the late 1970s under the fifth Tin Agreement, to over £8000 a tonne in the middle 1980s under the sixth Tin Agreement. In October 1985 the buffer stock manager ran out of money and suspended operations, with about 60 000 tonnes of tin in stock, forward commitments to buy a similar amount, and enormous debts of at least £300 million. World consumption was about 150 000 tonnes a year and it was thought that if producer stocks were included with the Tin Council's stock a whole year's supply was probably available from world stock.

When production increases faster than consumption, price tends to fall. Buffer stock operations can stop this happening for a while, but holding price at a high level keeps marginal producers profitable and thus adds to the surplus of supply. When the London Metal Exchange, badly hit by the collapse, suspended tin trading, the big tin consumers, producers of solder or tinplate, soon began to deal direct with producers, at prices of around £6000, about 25% below the level which the Tin Council had tried to maintain, and before long price fell even further.

Futures markets exist for many commodities. They started in the 19th century, when shipping delays for commodities which fluctuated in price put traders at considerable risk. They can exist only when price fluctuates, and there is a large volume of trade between many buyers and sellers, and the commodity is capable of being stored and is sold in standard grades or specifications. The main purpose of futures markets is to enable firms to hedge against adverse price changes. Hedging is a process of balancing a position by making compensating transactions in futures. Two examples will be given.

The first is an example of a selling hedge. Coply Wiredrawers Ltd is in business to buy copper wirebars and convert them to copper wire and strip by drawing down. The selling price of their wire products is based on LME spot price on the day of sale, plus a £25 margin to cover processing cost and profit. Quite a small fluctuation in copper price between the date they purchase material for conversion and the date they sell the wire products could wipe out their small operating margin, although it could also produce windfall profits. To reduce this risk, they hedge by making compensating future transactions whenever they buy material or sell product.

For instance, on one occasion 50 tonnes of spot copper were bought for £800 a tonne. On the same day 50 tonnes of three month futures were sold for £780 a tonne. A month later the resulting wirecoils were sold for £775 a tonne, the spot price of copper having declined to £750. On the same day they bought back the futures contract for £740 a tonne. The result was that the loss on material account of £2500 was partially offset by the gain on futures account of £2000. Overall they were not out of pocket.

The second example is a buying hedge. A flour mill receives in July an order for 100 tonnes of milled flour for October delivery at a fixed price based on the current spot price for wheat, £50.75. The wheat is required in mid-September for processing, and meanwhile the flour mill hedges the risk that wheat prices will rise by purchasing 100 tonnes of September wheat at £50 a tonne. Price does in fact rise and in mid-September

Table 16.1 Effect of hedging. Based on a diagram by Bauer and Yamey (1968)

If price movement is that		Then result will be			
		If long in spot and –		If short in spot and –	
spot price	future price	unhedged	hedged	unhedged	hedged
falls	falls same	loss	breakeven	profit	breakeven
falls	falls more	loss	profit	profit	loss
falls	falls less	loss	smaller loss	profit	smaller profit
falls	rises	loss	greater loss	profit	greater profit
rises	rises same	profit	breakeven	loss	breakeven
rises	rises more	profit	loss	loss	profit
rises	rises less	profit	smaller profit	loss	smaller loss
rises	falls	profit	greater profit	loss	greater loss

100 tonnes for immediate delivery are bought at £61 a tonne. On the same day the futures contract for September wheat is sold for £60 a tonne. The result is that the hedging profit of £1000 almost covers the £1075 loss on materials account.

How effective the hedge is depends on the relative movement of spot price and futures price, as shown in Table 16.1. A perfect hedge occurs only in the two cases where the price changes in both spot and futures are in the same direction and of the same amount. In the second example given above, the buying hedge, this was approximately so; this example corresponds to the fifth line in the table, where the firm is 'short in spot' and thus breaks even. In the first example, the selling hedge, spot price fell by more than futures. This corresponds to the third line in the diagram; the firm is 'long in spot' and its hedging operation, although not perfect, results in a smaller loss.

Spot and futures prices often move in parallel for long periods, although the one is dependent on current supply and demand, and the other on expected future supply and demand; and hedging then works reasonably well. Futures price is normally higher than spot price, the difference being known as the contango on some exchanges. The contango is limited in amount; if it rose above a certain figure it would pay merchants to buy spot and simultaneously sell futures, warehousing the material until the future contract matured. Sometimes the futures price is below the spot price if there is little interest, or if the price is likely to fall. There is no theoretical limit to a backwardation, as the gap between the two prices is then called; at the time of writing there is a £385 backwardation on coffee.

The form of price insurance provided by hedging is clearly less certain and calls for more skill and market knowledge than fire insurance or other forms provided by insurance firms, but it is the only form available. In practice, as analysis of exchange statistics has shown, futures are bought and sold, partly indeed for price insurance, partly for speculative purposes, and partly to exploit favourable relationships between spot and future prices in order to procure materials at the lowest prices.

MARKET POLICY FOR FLUCTUATING PRICES

Manufacturing organizations, some of whose raw materials vary in price by substantial amounts in short periods of time, have to adopt some policy for the supply of such materials. They may not trade on the commodity markets but they are still affected by the fluctuation. For instance copper fabricators generally buy raw copper direct from the producers. Contracts are normally placed in the fourth quarter of the year (known to the trade as the mating season) and include upper and lower quantity limits and calloff arrangements. The purchase price, however, is based on the London Metal Exchange price and varies as deliveries are made. Selling price for the copper (in various fabricated forms) which is their product, is also based on London Metal Exchange prices, but they are at risk during the period between receiving material and supplying product (at least; buyers and sellers have various kinds of agreement relating date of order and date of delivery to date of exchange price). Another example is the carpet manufacturer requiring large quantities of wool; this can be bought at the auctions direct, or it can be bought through a wool broker, but prices will still vary in the same way.

The classical policy for substantial purchases is to employ an expert commodity buyer. Within trading limits set by management, he adjusts the time and size of orders and the time coverage of stocks according to the trend of prices. When the trend is down, stocks are used up and small orders only are placed. When the market trend is up, large orders are placed to stock up. If for instance the firm uses 100 000 lb a month of a commodity whose price has just increased by 5p a lb, sooner or later material cost will increase by £5000 a month. With six months supply in stock the firm can operate for six months at the old cost basis, saving £30 000 in comparison to another firm with no stock. If on the other hand the price change is a reduction of 5p a lb, it would take six months to bring material costs into line with replacement price, and the firm with no stock would be £5000 a month better off than competitors. If price changes of similar or greater magnitude occur not every six months but daily, it will be clear that considerable market knowledge and skill is required for successful buying.

Success is measured by comparing actual material cost with market price, over a period, offsetting losses against gains. (Nobody wins all the time, since what the buyer tries to do is to find out what other buyers are going to do and do it first; to anticipate which way the market will go, when what makes it go is not only changes in supply and demand but how these are anticipated by other commodity experts.)

Risk cannot be avoided. Hedging can reduce the risk, but this can go wrong too. An extreme example of this occurred when a major British food product manufacturer revealed that they had lost £32.5 million in transactions in the cocoa terminal market. The buyer concerned had exceeded his authority, but his objective had apparently been to reduce material cost by futures transactions.

At the other extreme is a safe and simple policy (known as 'hand-to-mouth' or 'averaging') which ensures that over a period the average cost of material used is the same as the average market price over the period, and consequently material cost must be as low as most other businesses using the material. This policy consists in buying just the quantity required at just the time it is required, carrying no stocks and paying the going market price. The buyer need give no thought to market trends and indeed to do so might tempt him to depart from the policy. He will not do better than the average, as the expert commodity buyer tries to do, but neither will he incur criticism by doing worse than the average.

This policy can be adopted for the purchase of commodities which have no significant effect on product cost. (For instance, a certain carpet production process requires the purchase four times a year of copper fabrications to replace beater blades. If the price of the fabrications doubled the cost of the carpets would hardly alter.)

If the cost of the commodity has a significant effect on the cost of the product, the policy can still be used if selling price can be based on the purchase cost of the material used rather than its replacement cost. (For instance, a small paint brush manufacturer used to buy Chinese bristle, make a batch of brushes and sell them at a price based on what he had paid for the bristle plus his margin.)

The averaging policy is less suitable when price fluctuations are large, and it is not applicable to firms which need to carry large base stocks, as for instance, when raw material has to be shipped halfway round the world from an area with political problems.

When prices fluctuate in a fairly narrow range about a predictable mean, there are formula approaches which are said to enable one to buy as well as the expert without actually having to become an expert. For example, if we use 100 tonnes a week, and if the average market price is £100 a tonne, we can beat the market by spending a fixed budget of £10 000 a week (hence the name 'budgeted buying'). When the price is below £100 this buys more than 100 tonnes and increases stocks. When the price is above £100 less than the week's requirement is bought, the balance being drawn from stock. This technique will indeed procure materials at below the average market price so long as the average is predicted correctly, and the market price fluctuates around the average and does not develop a trend.

Some years ago the Club of Rome sponsored a study carried out by people at MIT into the future of physical resources. The conclusions, published in *Limits to Growth* (1972), were extremely gloomy, and the book sold by the million. It is now regarded as fundamentally unsound. Materials expected to be in very short supply remain abundant. Demands predicted to rise steeply have fallen. Prices predicted to become much higher have become much lower. The future of physical resources remains unpredictable, and no long-term prediction is likely to have any practical value. Contrary to the conclusions of *Limits to Growth*, the consensus now is that there is no rational basis for pessimism about the future of physical resources.

17

Constructional contracts

Factories, hospitals, supermarkets, bridges, tunnels and motorways are built by contractors in the construction industry working to civil engineering or building contracts. These contracts range from enormous works such as the Channel Tunnel costing thousands of millions of pounds to minor works such as an ordinary house or garage.

The word contractor itself indicates that the contract and its clauses are more important in construction than in other industries such as batch production or retailing. Standard form contracts are normally used except for small jobs. The procedure for requesting and considering offers to supply is often very formal.

In addition to the purchaser, often referred to as the *client* or *employer*, and the seller, usually referred to as the *contractor*, an *engineer*, or in the case of buildings an *architect*, who may be an employee of the purchaser, or an independent consultant retained on a fee basis, may carry the main responsibility for designing and supervising the work. Consultant engineers may be structural, electrical or mechanical; a firm of quantity surveyors may also be involved.

TYPES OF CONTRACT

Many types of contract are used, including fixed price contracts, cost reimbursement contracts, and incentive contracts.

Incentive contracts, or target cost contracts as they are also called, were discussed in Chapter 5.

Cost reimbursement contracts are those in which the contractor is reimbursed for the cost of labour and materials actually used in the contract, plus a fee for supervision, head office expenses and profit. The fee may be a fixed amount or a percentage of total prime cost. Although cost plus contracts of this kind may have to be used when the work is very urgent or when it is hard to decide how much work is required, they have obvious drawbacks: for instance there is no risk to the contractor and no financial incentive to work efficiently or to seek ways to save money.

Fixed price contracts are of two main types: lump sum contracts and measured contracts. In lump sum contracts a single total price – the lump sum – covers the whole contract. This is considered suitable for major works if they can be specified precisely and described in detail in the contract documents, and also for minor works and alteration and repair jobs.

In measured contracts price is fixed in the sense that bidders quote itemized prices for doing work and supplying materials, using a bill of quantities, but the total price payable is determined by measuring the amount of work done and materials supplied, multiplying by the agreed price for each item, and totalling.

The bill of quantities is a list of all the items necessary to complete the work. Each item is fully described and the quantity as calculated by the quantity surveyor from the engineers' or architect's drawings and specification is stated. In preparing bills of quantities computers are often used, and this facilitates their presentation in several formats useful in tendering and contract planning and execution.

Bidders enter against each item their unit price, which when multiplied by the quantity gives the total price for the item. The sum of these item prices, plus other costs, is the bidder's tender for the contract.

The 'tender total' is not the same as the 'contract price'. The bill of quantities is an estimate. Subsequent changes and corrections, including price fluctuations and differences between the quantities of labour and materials actually used and those provided for in the tender, make the contract price different from the tender total used at the bidding stage for price comparison between bidders.

CONDITIONS OF CONTRACT

For constructional contracts it is important for the contracting parties to think of what might go wrong and who would be liable, and to try as far as possible to cover all eventualities in their agreement. This is why standard contract forms are used. These have been devised by professional associations with knowledge of the work, assisted by legal advisers with knowledge of the law. The best known are the ICE and the JCT forms of contract. As Brian Meopham puts it (Meopham, 1985), these conditions 'are for the practical man employed to move mountains. They have evolved over many years of negotiation between employer and contractor interests, from the traditions of the great Victorian engineers.'

The current ICE form is the fifth edition, issued 1973 and subsequently revised, of the Conditions of Contract, Forms of Tender, Agreement and Bond for use in connection with works of civil engineering construction. Available from the Institute of Civil Engineers (ICE), it is approved by the ICE, the Association of Consulting Engineers and the Federation of Civil Engineering Contractors.

The JCT standard form of building contract is issued by the Joint Contracts Tribunal, representing the Royal Institute of British Architects (RIBA), Building Employers Confederation, Royal Institute of Chartered Surveyors, and other bodies. Available from RIBA Publications Ltd, it includes several versions for use in different circumstances. Most major building work is carried out under the Joint Contracts Tribunal Standard Form of Building Contract, 1980, commonly referred to as JCT 80.

OPEN, SELECTIVE AND SINGLE TENDERING

Three methods are used to obtain tenders or offers to supply:

(1) Open tendering: an advertisement is published inviting anyone interested to submit tenders.
(2) Selective tendering: a few selected firms are invited to submit tenders.
(3) Single tendering: one firm is selected to submit a tender and the contract is negotiated with that firm.

Open tendering is used mainly by some local authorities, perhaps as a way of avoiding criticism. If anyone can bid and if the contract is awarded to the lowest bidder, how can the purchaser be called to account for discrimination, favouritism, or corruption?

However, open tendering has been strongly criticized by experts as wasteful and hazardous (see Banwell (1964) in particular). It is wasteful because many contractors incur the expense of submitting tenders and it is hazardous if it leads to the contract being awarded to a low bidder who is not in fact competent to undertake the work. Some protection for the client is obtained by requiring the contractor to provide a guarantee bond. The guarantor is normally a bank which undertakes to pay the client anything due as a result of non-performance or default by the contractor, up to the limit of the guarantee.

Selective tendering is the preferred method. This means that the buyer invites tenders from contractors selected for the purpose who are regarded as competent to do the work and financially sound. An *ad hoc* list may be drawn up specially, or names may be taken from a standing list of approved contractors.

Single tendering means that only one firm is invited to submit a tender. Tender documentation can be much reduced and price can be negotiated progressively as the design develops. This can save a lot of time and lead to earlier completion of the work.

Single tendering has to be used if for technical or management reasons only one firm is suitable. But it is also used to make the contractor part of the team from an early stage in the project and thus make full use of the contractor's expertise.

OTHER METHODS

Other methods such as turnkey contracts or package deals, serial contracting, continuation contracts, and two-stage selection are used. The two-stage procedure is used to get the contractor into the design team at an early stage. In the first stage outline proposals are sought from several firms. These are considered on their merits, and also with reference to the management ability, price, capacity, etc of the firm. In the second stage the selected contractor works as a member of the design team in the development of detailed designs and the preparation of bills of quantities, submitting a tender at the end of this period.

Continuation contracts are new contracts with existing suppliers on similar terms to existing contracts in order to benefit from continuity of work. Serial contracting is a form of standing offer, where a contractor states his willingness to undertake a series of contracts on the terms and conditions used previously at lump sum prices. These are different ways of handling the tendering stage.

Package deals or turnkey contracts are different ways of handling the contract stage. In these the contractor takes responsibility for the whole design and construction from beginning to end.

With selective tendering only those qualified to undertake the contract are invited to submit tenders. Checking which suppliers are qualified is known as prequalification, which may be done by sending a preliminary enquiry to potential contractors. The three factors that need to be considered are: the financial security of the contractor; its technical and management capability; and its performance record on work of a similar kind.

Preparing tenders for large projects is expensive. Preliminary enquiries give brief details of the requirement, state the closing date for tenders and the completion date for the work, and ask if the firm wishes to submit a tender. Any firm not wishing to tender will still be eligible to tender for future projects, when its commitments may be different.

At least four weeks are allowed for the preparation of tenders, eight weeks for large projects.

RECEIVING TENDERS

Formal procedures are often prescribed for receiving tenders. These procedures must be stated in the instructions to tenderers sent with the tender forms and documents. Tenders usually arrive by registered post or recorded delivery service. If they are delivered by hand a signed and dated receipt should be given to the person making the delivery.

Late submission of tenders is often not allowed. Buyers chase up preferred suppliers to make sure they get their bids in on time. Tenders received after the closing date are returned with a covering letter explaining why they have been excluded from consideration. Tenders may be withdrawn until they are accepted under English law, but under Scottish law they remain open for acceptance until the time stated in the offer.

Once the tenders have been opened and examined, it is good practice to notify within seven days both those whose tenders are being considered in detail and those whose tenders are not being considered further, so that unsuccessful bidders are released from the need to hold resources available in case they are awarded the contract.

MAKING THE CONTRACT

Detailed examination of tenders often involves meetings with the tenderers, not only to clarify matters but also to obtain further information about construction methods, organization aspects, resource availability, qualifications, etc. Changes in the detail of what is required may also be negotiated, although it is considered good practice in such post-tender negotiations to preserve the principle of parity of tender and not to give any bidder an unfair advantage over any other.

When it has been decided who gets the contract, the successful tenderer should be notified immediately. A common practice with civil engineering contracts is to write to all tenderers enclosing two lists: one showing the names of all tenderers in alphabetical order, the other showing the amounts of tenders in order of magnitude.

If the tender is accepted as submitted, a short letter of acceptance is sufficient to make a contract which binds both parties. If this is done, the standard purchase order form will follow, marked 'confirmation of our letter of acceptance dated . . .', in order to put the contract into the normal procedure for processing and recording purchase expenditure. Alternatively, and perhaps preferably, the purchase order form can itself be used to accept the offer made in the tender.

If the contractor has been decided on, but details of design or contract conditions are still being negotiated, it is sometimes useful to send a *letter of intent*, which states the intention of the purchaser to sign a contract with the addressee and may also authorize expenditure on work or materials up to a stated limit.

Contracts should be placed within two months of the closing date for tenders. Delay at this stage is most undesirable for fixed price tenders.

THE CONTRACT PERIOD

The contract period runs from start date to completion date. Start date for most contracts is the date of the contract. But for some construction contracts it has to be delayed until access to the site can be given. Start date must then be notified in writing to the contractor. It should be within a reasonable time after acceptance of the tender.

Completion date can be calculated by adding to the start date as notified the number of weeks stated in the tender plus any extension of time which has been approved. The contractor may be liable for liquidated or ascertained damages for late delivery if this completion date is not met. Contract price adjustment under variation clauses will also be calculated with reference to the contract period as defined above.

Actual completion is certified by issue of a certificate of completion by the engineer. This is done when the work is substantially complete and has passed any required tests, even if some relatively insignificant work still remains to be finished. In the case of building contracts under JCT 80, a certificate of 'practical completion' is issued by the architect.

THE CONTRACT PROGRAMME

The contractor provides a detailed programme showing when the various stages of the work will be completed. This may be in words or in bar chart form or may use network analysis techniques. For both the contractor and the customer, this document provides a basis for progressing and contract control.

'Within 21 days after the acceptance of his tender the contractor shall submit to the engineer for his approval a program showing the order of procedure in which he proposes to carry out the works,' according to clause 14 of the ICE conditions of contract. Building contracts under

JCT 80 also require the contractor to provide the architect with two copies of a master programme as soon as possible after the contract is signed (clause 5.3.1.2).

SUBCONTRACTING

The main contractor usually sublets parts of the work to specialist sub-contractors. Selection of subcontractors may be subject to the approval of the purchaser or client. Subcontractors may also be nominated by the purchaser, or by the engineer or architect, subject to the contractor's right to object to a nominated subcontractor for reasonable cause, including of course refusal to make a satisfactory agreement. The client or purchaser is not legally a party to a subcontract even if he takes part in deciding on the subcontractor and approving terms and conditions of the subcontract.

PAYMENT ARRANGEMENTS

Most contracts provide for monthly payments on account with a final payment after completion. Retention sums, that is, amounts retained for future payment, are normally deducted from both interim and final payments at rates of 3–5%. Half the retention sum becomes payable when the work is certified to be complete, and the other half at the end of the maintenance period stated in the tender form and when any defects have been put right. The maintenance period is normally 52 weeks.

Arrangements for varying contract price to cover increased costs are normally laid down in the contract. In building works a formula devised by the National Economic Development Office in 1975 is often used. It is a complicated formula, based on 48 work categories that follow the divisions used in the quantity surveyor's standby, the Standard Method of Measurement of Building Works. Indices published every month show the average national change in labour and material costs in each category.

PROJECT PURCHASING

Purchasing for a contractor whose business is to work on projects of this kind has much in common with purchasing for other kinds of producers. Very small projects are similar to jobbing production or, if undertaken regularly, to batch production, which accounts for about two-thirds of manufacturing output, with batch sizes ranging from six to 6000. Very large projects are different in that each one is rather like starting a business and winding it up when the project is complete – except that the contractor is still in business even if the project organization has been wound up.

Project purchasing has two main sections: buying parts and materials, and placing subcontracts. Closely associated with these buying activities are the related activities of progressing or expediting, to ensure delivery on time; inspection and quality control, to ensure delivery to specification; and stores management and stock control.

Project production is discontinuous, unlike batch and continuous production. Even when the company undertakes a series of similar projects, each project stands on its own and requires terms and conditions of contract which are to some extent individual to the project. Although standard form contracts aim to cover so far as possible all eventualities in standard terms and conditions, special conditions may need to be negotiated.

For large projects, the project manager may have a purchase manager and other staff seconded to him for years, as well as making use of purchasing staff attached to him for shorter periods. Some of the purchasing will be done by permanent staff not attached to the project as part of their normal work. Outside personnel may be hired on short contracts to cope with peak workloads.

The project purchasing manager normally answers to two bosses: the project manager and the purchasing director in the permanent organization structure. He has line responsibility to the project manager, and functional responsibility to the purchasing director. One is concerned more with what is done and when; the other is more concerned with how it is done. Matrix organization structures of this kind work, and are widely used; but conflict is inbuilt. Fluid situations, political pressure, uncertainty, conflict of interest and battles between bosses all add to the interest of jobs in matrix organizations, discussed further in Chapter 22.

Questions
on
part two

(1) Explain the steps which might be taken to ensure that purchased goods or components comply with detailed quality specifications, *either* in a large chain store selling clothing and food products, *or* in a mass-production manufacturer selling consumer durables.

(2) Discuss the merits and disadvantages of the following types of specification for purchases:
   (a) specification by sample,
   (b) specification by brand,
   (c) specification by British Standard.

(3) What part does the purchasing department play in specifying and controlling the quality of purchases, in any specific industry of your choice?

(4) Explain the difference between capital and non-capital expenditure, state what you understand by the terms first cost, total cost and life-cycle costing in this connection, and summarize the nature of the contribution which the purchasing department can make to capital expenditure decisions.

(5) Most countries have their national standardization bodies. Briefly describe the standardization organization for the United Kingdom (or for your own country), and explain why collaboration internationally between such organizations is both difficult and desirable.

(6) Distinguish between specification quality and conformance quality and discuss the part played by the purchase department in connection with each of them.

(7) Explain the main aim of purchase quality assurance and discuss the approach suggested in current British standards for the achievement of this aim.

(8) Explain three of the following terms used in commodity markets:
   (a) prompt date,
   (b) lending,
   (c) borrowing,
   (d) contango,
   (e) hedging.

(9) Some commodity markets regard their hedging services as important facilities which buyers would use more extensively if they knew about them. Explain what hedging means, what hedging services are offered by any market of your choice, and what help they could be to the buyer.

(10) 'Contangos favour the forward seller, while backwardation favours the forward buyer.' Explain this statement.

(11) In what circumstances is it important to weigh up supplier capability? Describe how this can be done.

(12) Some firms use a system of vendor rating which summarizes facts and judgments about supplier performance into a single numerical score. Briefly describe one such system and discuss the advantages and disadvantages of its use.

(13) What do you understand by an organized commodity market? What conditions must be satisfied before futures can be traded on such markets?

(14) 'Profitable suppliers are a better risk' for the purchaser. Does this in your view imply any duty on the purchaser's part to ensure that a supplier does not lose money on a particular order he has to place?

(15) The IPS has published an 'Ethical Code' setting forth some precepts and guidance on ethical matters, and some firms include similar guidance in their internal buyers' handbooks or departmental manuals. Describe one such code and argue the case for and against their use.

(16) Western economies seem to be increasingly dominated by large organizations. In view of this do you consider that the small supplier has much prospect of surviving?

(17) Define supplier development, describe when it is important to do this and explain some of the approaches adopted.

(18) Listed below are a number of tasks or decisions which may contribute to the specification and control of quality. Delete those which do not apply to your organization, and state for the rest which department carries the primary responsibility, and which department(s) have a secondary responsibility to contribute to the task or decision in some significant way. Briefly comment on your statement.

- Outline definition or design of requirements
- Detailed specification preparation
- Constructive criticism of specification if needed
- Suggested alternative specification if appropriate
- Survey supplier quality capability by visit
- Grade supplier for quality capability
- Approve new supplier/select supplier
- Negotiate price and terms
- Negotiate inspection and QC arrangements
- Communication with supplier:
    of order/contract requirements
    on test and inspection arrangements
    about defective goods delivered
- Inspection of incoming goods if needed
- Decision to accept rejects at reduced price
- Decision to rework rejects with price concession
- Grade supplier for quality performance
- Achieve better quality performance

(19) 'Level pricing can be the result either of keen competition or of collusion between suppliers.' Explain; and discuss any differences you consider likely in the level of the level pricing resulting from the two situations.

(20) Opinions sometimes differ as to whether it is in the buyer's interest for large contracts which require a year or more to complete to be on a fixed price basis. Outline the arguments on either side and explain the sort of price adjustment clause often considered a better alternative in times of cost inflation.

(21) 'When making decisions, price is rated as the most important factor, followed closely by technical specifications. Nevertheless, other factors are sufficiently important to ensure that approximately half of the persons involved in purchasing would not change from their best supplier to buy an identical product from a new supplier for a price reduction of less than 5%, i.e. an average

27% increase in profitability. Approximately one fifth would not change for less than 10% reduction in price.'

    (a) Explain what Hugh Buckner means by 'an average 27% increase in profitability' in this quotation from *How British Industry Buys*.

    (b) Account for the purchasing behaviour described in the quotation.

(22) 'Value analysis should not consist of a group of people sitting round a table muttering "Let's make it in plastic"', according to one writer. What in your view should value analysis consist of?

(23) Discuss the advantages of adopting special systems for small orders, and describe two or three of the systems which are used.

(24) Describe and distinguish between cost analysis and value analysis.

PART THREE

Supply
policy
and
organization

18

Supplying merchandise for resale

Manufacturers and other organizations buy articles for resale as well as for their own use and for production. For instance British Telecom buys telephones and computers for resale; and some manufacturers of consumer durables buy out part of their product range, as well as buying parts and materials for the manufacture of the rest of the range.

But it is the distributive industry which is mainly occupied with supplying merchandise for resale. Firms in this industry are in business to buy goods from producers such as farms or factories or from other distributors including importers and wholesalers and to make them available to their customers where and when they are wanted. The distributive trades thus include wholesalers and specialist agents which sell to farms, factories, mines and other producers, as well as agents and wholesalers which form part of the channels of distribution between these producers and their customers. The largest part of the distributive industry is the retail trade, as shown in Fig. 18.1.

Types of retail organization keep changing as consumer needs change, the constraints imposed by law, society and the economy alter, and new ideas are thought up. Department stores, chain stores, coops, supermarkets, hypermarkets and discount stores, as well as non-store retailing such as mail order, door-to-door selling and vendor machines, have appeared and flourished as needs and opportunities were perceived.

Purchasing and stock control are very important to distributors, whose whole business is to buy goods, hold them in stock, and sell them to customers. Perhaps 70% of sales turnover is spent on purchases, as shown in Fig. 18.2. 'Whether the firm is large or small, wholesale or retail, if it doesn't buy what it sells, or doesn't sell what it buys, it is heading for trouble,' it has been said. 'Two major ways of losing profit are to have unsold goods gathering dust on the shelves and to have unsatisfied customer demand.'

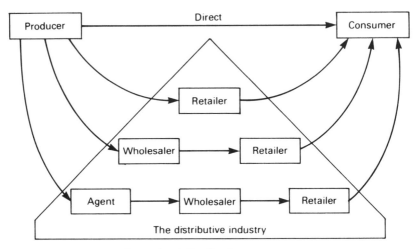

Fig. 18.1 Alternative channels of distribution.

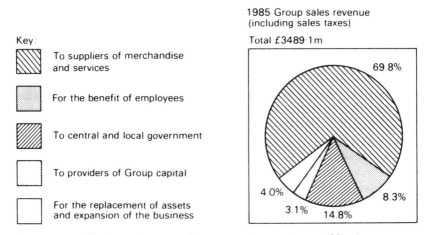

Fig. 18.2 Application of group sales revenue in a major retail business. (Source: Marks and Spencer PLC)

TYPES OF ORGANIZATION

Four common types of retail organization are:

(1) *Independents:* small shops usually, corner shops and husband-and-wife businesses; these traditional owner-managed establishments exist everywhere in the free world and have existed since civilization began.
(2) *Department stores:* include under one roof a number of different departments each specializing in some merchandise group, usually in pleasant surroundings with free delivery and credit facilities; did very well in the early part of the century but are less successful now.
(3) *Chain stores (or multiples):* their retail outlets usually have a uniform appearance all over the country and sell mostly the same lines which are purchased centrally. Some chains sell a single product group such as shoes or food, some sell a wide variety.
(4) *Superstores:* very large shops usually located out of town with ample parking facilities, aiming to offer one-stop shopping for the car-owner; usually part of a group, this is the fastest developing form of retailing at present.

Retailers can be divided into three groups: single outlet, small multiple, and large multiple. In 1984 there were about 237 000 retail businesses in the United Kingdom, controlling 342 000 shops. The average was 1.48 outlets per retail business, with an average turnover of £240 000 per outlet; but there were big variations in size between these outlets, so the averages do not tell us much.

Or they could be grouped by the type of goods they sell. Three main types of shop when they are divided up in this way are, those which:

(1) specialize mainly in food;
(2) specialize in other things such as clothes or electrical goods;
(3) do not specialize, but sell mixed goods, such as department stores and variety chains.

The largest number of shops are small independent businesses, in which buying decisions are taken by the managing proprietors, who usually buy from wholesalers. But the largest part of sales are accounted for by the big retail businesses, which are also expanding faster. Less than a 1000 organizations handle 60% of UK retail sales. In 1985 large operators sold 61% more than in 1980, an annual growth rate of 10%, while small operators sold only 30% more, a growth rate of 5.4% per annum. Consequently the market share of the large retailers improved

by about 5% over this period while the market share of the small operators fell by a similar amount (Economist Intelligence Unit, 1986).

The large retailers also employ most of the people working in the
trade. Their buying decisions may be taken by department heads or
shop managers, but are most often taken by central purchasing specialists.

The usual arrangement in department stores is for each department to
be managed by a buyer whose responsibilities include sales and staff
supervision as well as buying. This arrangement is said to provide high
job satisfaction as well as motivation to perform well.

Buying in chain stores is normally centralized, and the economy of
scale which this facilitates has been one main reason why chain stores
grew so fast in the middle part of the century. Despite this, when a
multiple operates establishments which differ in character as well as in
size and location, it is sometimes considered good marketing policy to
give the stores manager some discretion in the selection, pricing and
sourcing of merchandise even though the normal policy is central
buying.

This growth in central buying has been partly at the expense of
wholesalers. Retailers bought most of their merchandise from wholesalers in the early part of the century. Wholesalers bought large lots
from manufacturers and supplied small lots to retailers, often on credit
– 'breaking bulk' it was called. Now the chain stores place large
contracts directly with manufacturers. Some wholesalers still do well as
special middlemen for small retailers, with new developments such as
voluntary buying chains and cash-and-carry warehouses.

BUYING FOR RESALE

The basic difference between buying for manufacturing and related
industries, and buying for the distributive trades, is that in the first case
one is buying for requirements defined by other departments, and in
the second case one is buying for requirements defined by the buyer. In
the first case the buyer has to arrange for parts and material which have
usually been specified already to arrive at times defined by other
departments in order that products can be made available to meet
customer requirements. In the second case the buyer has to decide what
customer requirements will be and arrange for articles to be in stock to
satisfy them.

The retail buyer may thus be involved directly both in purchasing and
in marketing. Some organizations allocate the marketing part of the
occupation to merchandise controllers and merchandisers, whose

Table 18.1 Open-to-buy (OTB) calculations

Month	1	2	3	4	5
Sales estimate	5000	6000	7000	6000	5000
less Opening stock	3000	5000	6000	5000	3000
	2000	1000	1000	1000	2000
plus Closing stock	5000	6000	5000	3000	
Net requirement	7000	7000	6000	4000	
less Gross margin (25%)	1750	1750	1500	1000	
Net requirement at buying price	5250	5250	4500	3000	
less Already on order	1250	750	250		
OTB	4000	4500	4250	3000	

responsibilities may include range planning; achieving sales, stock and profit targets; controlling open-to-buy and taking appropriate action; monitoring product availability from suppliers in the United Kingdom and abroad; and liaising closely with central and local management.

Range planning refers to planning the range or assortment of articles that are offered for sale. The stock assortment or range and the market the company aims to serve are matters of company policy. The detailed merchandise list with the brands and styles stocked, deletions and additions is under continuous review in a profitable business, which is also aware of what direct competitors are doing.

Open-to-buy (OTB) is a version of budget planning and control used by many retailers. The simple calculations involved are shown in Table 18.1. Sales estimates for each month are adjusted by adding on closing stock and deducting opening stock to arrive at the planned net requirement for the month. This is reduced by deducting gross margin to convert net requirement at selling prices to net requirements at buying prices. The figure is further reduced by deducting outstanding orders due for delivery that month, leaving a net purchase requirement at buying prices, known as the OTB, which is the buyer's expenditure budget for the month.

The closing stock for any month is the same as the opening stock for the next month, and average stock is a major determinant of stock turn rate. Buyers do not aim at the same figure each month, because monthly sales vary. They increase closing stock for one month if next month's sales are expected to be higher, and vice versa.

Despite obvious differences between the work of the retail buyer and that of the industrial buyer, there is also much in common between these occupations, as considered later in Chapter 21. One common area is the importance of suppliers as the external manufacturing base of the business.

For many years industry and the public sector have taken a particular interest in the way Marks and Spencer plc do their buying. One of the world's most successful retailers which pioneered a new approach to supplier relationships, Marks and Spencer have been called a 'manufacturer without factories'. In one annual report the company said:

The unique relationship we enjoy with our manufacturers has been built up over many years of joint effort to extend and improve the range of St Michael merchandise. Our partnership is based on commercial and technical collaboration between independent companies with a common interest and approach to production, management and human relations. We are working together on a range of problems from technology, engineering and administration to staff management and welfare.

Most of the goods sold are made to detailed specifications by carefully selected suppliers. Production and quality control advisory services are offered on a consultancy basis to assist suppliers to meet the standards required.

In the words of the firm's official history (Rees, 1969):

through its technical services and its merchandising departments, Marks & Spencer undertook to ensure that at every stage of production back to the primary producer of the raw fibre the needs of the consumer were represented, and at each stage of production its specialists and technologists collaborated with the firm responsible.

These specialists and technologists were not 'backroom boys who operated in mysterious isolation. They were fully integrated into the commercial organization of the business, so that they were active and indispensable members of its buying department.'

PRICING RETAIL MERCHANDISE

Markup pricing is widely used by retailers. The buying cost of goods is marked up by adding a percentage to arrive at the selling price. Thus the mark-up is the difference between buying and selling price, expressed as a percentage of buying price. The gross margin, out of which the retailer has to meet expenses and make profit, is also the difference between buying and selling prices, but expressed as a percentage of selling prices. Gross margin averaged 27.4% for the trade as a whole in a

recent year. Markup and margin are affected by several factors, including stores policy and competition, and also stock turn rate achieved.
Goods with relatively low stock turn rates such as furniture typically
carry much higher markups than goods that turn over quickly such as
newspapers and fresh grocery.

Stock turn rate is the ratio of average stock over a period to demand
for stock in that period. For instance if a business carried an average
stock at selling prices of £0.5 million for a year in which it sold £4 million
from stock, the stock turn rate would be given by 4/0.5 and would thus
be 8. This is close to the average stock turn rate of the retail trade as a
whole, although some do much better, for instance multiples such as
Sainsburys and Marks and Spencer. The reciprocal of the stock turn rate
shows how much stock is held in relation to demand; a stock turn rate
of 8 indicates that average stocks amount to one-eighth of a year's
supply, or a month and a half's supply on the average.

Markdown is the term used when previously decided selling prices
are reduced, for instance when perishable commodities reach their sell-
by date.

INFORMATION TECHNOLOGY

Small shops as well as big stores are making use of new electronic
equipment sometimes known as information technology. One chain
(W. H. Smith) sells 100 000 product lines.

Every year, more than a million orders are placed with around 2000 different
suppliers. So keeping the shelves stocked at precisely the right level is an exact-
ing task. Hence the new till. It's not just a cash register, it's also one of the most
advanced stock control systems in the retail industry. By feeding sales
information directly into a computer, it enables stock to be replenished automatically and quickly – and frees staff to help customers and increase sales.
(Quoted from an October 1986 advertisement)

Point-of-sale terminals have scanners which identify articles by preprinted bar codes, look up the price, show it on a screen and calculate
the amount due. They also can check credit rating for charge accounts,
give change for cash transactions, and adjust stock records and accounts
through links with the instore computer or the main computer at headquarters.

19

Supplying
the
public
sector

The public sector comprises:

(1) the national government;
(2) local governments and other local authorities;
(3) a variety of state-owned services, businesses and quangos.

The various departments of the national government procure a great range of items from major construction projects to copy paper, from battle-cruisers to carpets. Local governments and other local authorities provide public services in all parts of the country.

In addition to these government activities, the public sector includes for instance the National Health Service, and an extraordinary variety of other businesses and services which have been taken into state ownership, for one reason or another, good or bad.

In socialist countries dedicated to the nationalization of the means of production, distribution and exchange, the public sector tends to engulf the whole of industry. Even in capitalist countries such as the United States it can include major enterprises such as the National Aeronautics and Space Administration (NASA). In Britain at present many manufacturing, processing, extractive and service organizations are for one reason or another in the public sector, although many of them are currently being privatized. From Paris to Singapore, privatization seems to be the fashionable cure for the ills of nationalized industries.

NATIONAL GOVERNMENTS

National governments rank high among the big spenders of the world. The federal government of the United States for instance is probably the largest single purchaser of goods and services in existence, if indeed when so many departments and individuals are involved it is meaningful to speak of a single purchaser. The British government buys about 10% of the entire output of British manufacturing industry. The range of purchases is very large, from things in common supply such as paint and cleaning materials to complex specially designed products such as weapon systems or satellites.

The basic aim of those buying for the government is 'to obtain what is needed at the right time and in such a way as to ensure the best value for money spent', according to a White Paper on Public Purchasing (CMND 3291, 1967). This does not differ from the basic aim of those buying for the private sector, yet considerable differences in procedure have developed between government buying and industrial buying. Some of these procedural differences are the result of the need for public accountability, in spending money which belongs to the public. Some result from differences in the way government employees see their responsibilities, their opportunities for promotion, and indeed the whole nature of their work, based on a long tradition of government service which is in many ways admirable.

Successive governments have striven to make government buying more cost-effective, bringing in top-level advisers from commerce. Both in Britain and the United States, every few months the newspapers carry stories such as 'the taxpayer is overcharged for most government supplies and £400 million could be saved, according to . . .'. Some ridiculous but verifiably true story usually accompanies this, about some gross waste of public money, amounting perhaps to thousands of pounds. When total expenditure is in billions it cannot be very difficult to find isolated examples of this kind. Nevertheless, taxpayers are right to ask if better buying by the public sector could reduce their tax bill.

LOCAL GOVERNMENT

According to an official report (Audit Commission, 1984), local authorities excluding utilities spend nearly £3 billion a year on purchases. Considerable scope for cost savings by better buying was said to exist: probably amounting to as much as five to ten per cent of total expenditure.

Each local authority needs to procure goods and services for a heterogeneous collection of departments such as libraries, parks, highways and schools. Collaboration between buyers in different authorities enables the requirements of similar departments to be pooled, and two advantages are claimed for this.

Table 19.1 A successful county supply organization

Vision	Provide a central purchasing organization that will enable clients to achieve delivered costs 10% lower than they could secure by themselves		
Strategy	*Structure*	*Systems/style*	*Skills/staffing*
Use available scale to negotiate better terms and achieve economics in ordering, storage and distribution:	Organized by product groups	Run it like a wholesale distribution business:	Lean, professional staffing with close understanding of suppliers' economics as well as users' needs:
Large range (100 000 catalogue items, 10 000 in stock)	Clearly defined levels of authority and responsibility for buyers	Item-by-item costing, to cover administration, warehousing, stockholding and distribution	Total staff 275*, 4.5 per £1 million supplied
Wide coverage – 5400 dropping points, districts and health authorities	£5k Buyer	Mark-up, to cover costs (only)	30 buyers, all with relevant professional qualifications
	£5–20k Senior buyer		
	£20–30k Buying manager		
Mix of channels:	£30–50k Assistant director	Online computers, linked to suppliers and users for ordering and payment	20 buyers with suppliers' or private sector experience
weekly delivery, ex stock (14%)	over £50k Director		
direct order, supplier delivers (45%)	Close links with trading standards on contracts and supplier's performance	Batching of deliveries to smaller users	
cash off contracts (37%)	Separate cost/contribution centres for buying groups, reprographics, maintenance	Monthly statements of costs/contribution *vs* budget for all responsible managers	
in-house production (4%)			
Enforceable contracts – rejects under 1%			
High share: over 95% of county orders for bought-in goods and services			
High service levels: 98% availability on stock items			

* Administration, purchasing, warehousing and distribution

Firstly, lower prices can often be obtained when larger quantities are purchased on a single contract. Operating costs can also be reduced if authorities share storage and distribution facilities.

Secondly, a larger scale of operation can justify the employment of specialist staff with professional skills in purchasing and perhaps with special knowledge of catering, office furniture, printing and stationery or other types of purchase.

'Whether individually small or large, local authorities collectively are big business and it is up to local authorities to see that either individually or by acting together they purchase as supermarkets and not as cornershops', it has been stated (JACLAP, 1972). 'Central purchasing is too often associated, in the minds of elected members and officers, with the provision of unsuitable goods, in inappropriate quantities and in unappealing plain packs, from the quartermaster's stores; and reservations are rightly expressed about imposing patterns of consumption on children's homes and other local authority services having a high degree of involvement with individuals. But the aim of central purchasing is not to impose a uniform pattern. Variety reduction does not mean reduction to a single variety. The aim of central purchasing is to allow local authorities to provide the best possible services to ratepayers and inhabitants for their money, through buying what in their own estimation is the most suitable product at the best possible price.'

Table 19.1 depicts a successful county supply organization, aiming to provide its clients with what they need at a delivered cost 10% below what they could get for themselves and with high service levels. The detailed contents, organized under the six Ss of current management theory, are worth careful study, and may be found applicable to purchasing and supply organizations outside the local government area.

A number of local authorities have banded together in consortia or purchasing groups. These include the Yorkshire Purchasing Organization, the Welsh Purchasing Consortium, the Consortium of Purchasing and Distribution based in the west country.

Although some local authorities have antiquated purchasing and supply organizations, hidebound by obsolete regulations, there are others with clear value-for-money and customer service objectives, in which purchasing and supply can provide challenging roles – as indicated in Fig. 19.1.

OTHER PUBLIC OR NATIONALIZED ORGANIZATIONS

The public sector also includes some public services provided by the state, for instance the National Health Service, comprising hospitals

---

**Handling £20 million turnover, 1300 suppliers
and 6000 delivery points**

County
Supplies Officer

Up to £23,988
A Challenging Role in a Major Local Authority

Our Supplies Department provides a comprehensive service on a self financing basis to all departments of the County Council as well as to District Councils, District Health Authorities and other public bodies within the County. Such is our level of success and reputation that we also serve a number of adjoining local authorities.

As County Supplies Officer you will have overall responsibility for all areas of the procurement operation – everything from food to furniture, computers to cleaning materials, trucks to textiles – as well as tendering for contracted services. The emphasis is very much on 'value for money' and providing a first class service to our customers in a free market situation. It is a role calling for someone with an appropriate professional qualification and a sound background in both administration and management as well as the technical aspects of purchasing and distribution. Particularly important is the ability to direct and organize the department to ensure that operational objectives are met through a well motivated workforce and within budgets.

A very pleasant environment in which to work and live. Largely rural but within easy reach of London it has excellent communications by road and rail and first-class social, recreational, shopping and educational facilities.

Benefits include car loan / car leasing scheme and where appropriate removal expenses, disturbance allowance and temporary accommodation.

Fig. 19.1 New attitudes in local authority supplies.

and other health care institutions all over the country, whose combined purchase expenditure is equivalent to that of a major industry. It is the biggest customer for the pharmaceutical and related manufacturing industries.

A number of manufacturing and service industries, from coal-mining to the BBC, happen for a variety of reasons to be in state ownership and are known loosely as the nationalized industries. Because they are public property, a high standard of propriety is required in the allocation of purchase contracts. They have to be careful what they do, because the Audit Commission may be looking over their shoulders, questions could be asked in Parliament, commissions could be set up to haul them over the coals, and of course the media are looking for good stories.

PUBLIC ACCOUNTABILITY

The basic difference between public sector organizations and other organizations is that the public sector can draw on public funds. This access to public funds entails a responsibility to the public to account for the expenditure incurred on its behalf. Some strange things are done in the cause of public accountability, but the need for it is unquestionable. If we do not have public accountability, we do not have a free society.

GOVERNMENT INTERVENTION

Those public sector organizations which draw heavily on government funds to pay their debts and keep their employees in work are even more subject to government intervention in their purchasing policies and decisions than others, on the principle that the one who pays the piper calls the tune. But all public sector organizations get pressures of this kind from national government.

Governments have many objectives and priorities, which may include providing more work for industries in their catchment area, protecting such industries against foreign competition, providing more jobs for voters, national prestige, military strategy and foreign policy, balance of payments and international currency exchange considerations, supporting small business, favouring ethnic minorities, and helping to develop business in distressed areas.

In the hope of furthering such objectives they may lean heavily on their airlines to equip their fleets with aircraft A, which is made in the country, instead of aircraft B, which is probably made in America. They may insist on their civil servants buying computer X instead of computer Y even though both are made in the country, if they are subsidizing the manufacturer of computer X while the manufacturer of computer Y is a multinational in no need of propping up with subsidies. It has even been suggested that some government decisions of this kind are taken by politicians in order to ingratiate themselves with their constituents, rather than in the national interest, whatever that may be.

These are complicated questions. It could be argued that the government

should simply act as a hard-bargaining customer in buying its defence needs, and encourage the airline corporations to do the same with their purchases. If this policy causes the domestic aircraft industry to prosper, well and good; if the result is that most British orders go abroad so that the British industry withers away, it is a pity but nevertheless the best thing for the nation in the long run.

And perhaps a government which decided to buy defence needs abroad could negotiate something of a quid pro quo with the suppliers.

It could also be argued that in some markets

an injunction to act simply as a competitive buyer is ambiguous and impossible to formulate as a clearcut policy. . . . Where relatively few big producers are making extremely complicated products to the detailed specifications of a handful of big buyers, buying and selling must necessarily involve complex judgments. There is the difficulty of making useful cost comparisons between products which often differ greatly. There will be elements of monopoly power on both sides; sellers will try to undercut rivals and drive them out of business with the aim of securing the advantages of monopoly or near-monopoly in the long run, and the buyers will seek to prevent this. In situations such as these, a purchaser has to do much more than merely apply simple market-place tests to particular transactions.

These quotations from the Plowden report on the aircraft industry (Cmnd 2853) illustrate the difficulty of finding the right answer to questions of this kind.

PUBLIC SECTOR PROCUREMENT IN THE EEC

Since 1978 public supply contracts worth more than 200 000 ECU (£138 000) have to be advertised in the official journal of the EEC, with certain specified exceptions. Tenders from the lowest or best bidder, of whatever nationality within the Community, should be accepted, subject to proof of competence.

Similar rules apply to public works contracts if they are estimated to cost a million ECU (£690 000) or more, again with certain specified exceptions. Contracts must be awarded to the lowest or most economic bidder, taking into account price, period of completion, technical merit, etc., and subject to proof of competence.

A 1986 background report from the EEC states that neither the letter nor the spirit of these rules has been generally respected. The main abuses were project splitting, failure to harmonize technical standards, calling for bids by dates which effectively exclude foreign bidders by not giving them enough time, and non-competitive tendering. The report also criticizes the official rules themselves for allowing exceptions which include some attractive markets, and for weak enforcement procedures. Changes in the rules and in the enforcement procedures are proposed, both for supplies and works contracts, as well as for service contracts, which will effectively open up public sector procurement within the EEC and require public sector purchasers to buy from the best source and to accept the best offer from anywhere in the EEC.

20

Cost reduction in purchasing and supply

Cost reduction is often considered an important objective for purchasing and supply personnel. Most textbooks include an illustration of the cost reduction potential of purchasing similar to that shown in Fig. 20.1. If an organization is making £2 million profit on a sales turnover of £20 million, and if it spends £10 million on purchases, then the effect of a 5% reduction in the cost of purchases (£0.5 million) is to increase profit by 25% (£0.5 million).

Although this is a theoretical illustration, it is not unrealistic; 50% of sales turnover is quite a typical figure for a manufacturer's purchase expenditure, with some organizations spending much higher proportions, and some spending lower proportions.

An actual example taken from an internal memo in a particular organization is shown in Fig. 20.2. Here a target has been set of a £63 million reduction in the cost of purchases, currently £563 million. If this is achieved, profit will go up from 10% of turnover to 13%. This is a big increase, over 30% on the figures before rounding off.

Cost reductions of this order are sometimes thought to be possible only by substituting inferior goods or patronizing inadequate suppliers. There is a common misapprehension among those who do not have much understanding of purchasing, including a lot of people with a great deal of knowledge and understanding of other matters, good engineers and competent managers who make a big contribution to the success of their organization, that 'you only get what you pay for'. Of course we have to pay for what we get, but paying more does not always get us something better.

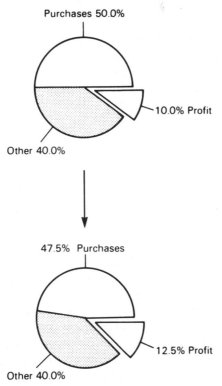

Cost reduction potential of purchasing

Purchases 50.0%

10.0% Profit

Other 40.0%

47.5% Purchases

12.5% Profit

Other 40.0%

Fig. 20.1 How 5% reduction in cost of purchases can increase profit by 25%.

For such people, a convincing example has been given by the Audit Commission (1984). The Commission obtained information from 490 local authorities about the quantity purchased, the prices paid and the type of contract used for a sample of 47 items on which about £500 million a year was spent, about a fifth of total purchase expenditure by local authorities.

Analysis of the results revealed that significant cost reduction opportunities were available, amounting perhaps to as much as £200 million nationwide, if all authorities bought at prices as low as those obtained by the most successful 25% of them.

For a certain specification of buff envelopes, price paid varied from less than 40p per 100 to about £1.40 per 100. For heating oil, price paid varied from under 15p to 20p a litre. These differences in price could not be attributed to differences in specification. Also, they could not all be

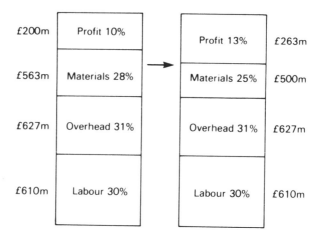

Fig. 20.2 Example of profit impact of purchase cost reduction in one organization.

attributed to differences in the size of the order, although perhaps some could. There was no clear relationship between quantity and price; many authorities with relatively low annual volumes obtained prices at least as keen as those buying much greater volumes. How could this be?

The Audit Commission was in no doubt about the answer. 'The key to successful purchasing is not simply high volume but rather the level of professional attention devoted to this function.' Good buyers make good buys.

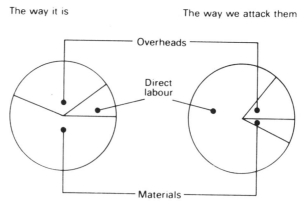

Fig. 20.3 Cost breakdown as it is, and as it is sometimes seen. (After Little and Barclay, 1986)

OTHER ASPECTS OF COST

Price paid is not the only thing to look at in cost reduction. As Little and Barclay (1986) put it, with 'common sense, experience, costing data, and technological skill, a program can be drawn up which will examine the effectiveness of material usage at every stage from supplier evaluation prior to purchase right through to the packing and despatch of finished goods'. In manufacturing, direct labour costs are usually only a fifth of direct material costs. That is the way it is; but cost reduction often concentrates on direct labour costs instead of materials and overheads, as shown in Fig. 20.3.

In advising local authorities how to cut the cost of their supplies, the Audit Commission gave the summary of possible initiatives and benefits shown in Fig. 20.4. With modifications where appropriate, this could be used by many organizations outside the public sector in planning a cost reduction programme.

Value analysis is one technique that has long been used to improve value for money in the products a company offers to the market. Since it is to a large extent a review of the specification, it has been considered in Chapter 11 on purchase specifications.

MATERIALS ANALYSIS

A planning and research technique which has a lot in common with value analysis is materials analysis. It is intended to improve purchasing performance or stock control performance by systematic investigation, fact-finding and the generation of testing of creative proposals.

Six steps are taken in the application of materials analysis:

(1) Decide whether to aim at lower purchase cost or reduced inventory.
(2) Set up materials analysis team.
(3) Select target items after analysis of range of purchases or stocks.
(4) Collect data on target items.
(5) Analyse and evaluate data, formulate and present recommendations.
(6) Follow up and review.

In taking the first step, the number and seriousness of problems perceived in purchasing and in stock control will be relevant. Both areas make substantial demands on financial resources. Materials analysis concentrates on the stock items which tie up a lot of money, or on the purchase items which cost a lot of money, aiming to reduce costs on these.

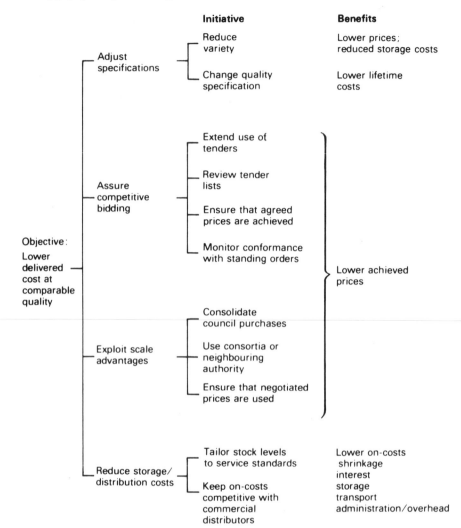

Fig. 20.4 Summary of possible initiatives and benefits. (Source: Audit Commission)

The materials analysis team is a group of representatives of various departments, at middle management level, selected from people whose knowledge, skills and attitude enable them to make a contribution, and who are motivated to do so by reason of their interests or the effect proposals will have on their work. In a manufacturing firm the materials analysis team normally includes people from purchasing, production control, inspection and quality control, receiving, stores and handling.

There may also be representatives from engineering design, marketing, operations research, etc.

The third step is to pick the targets. Pareto analysis or ABC analysis is the normal starting point. This has been previously discussed (p. 114). It turns out, apparently by a law of nature, that most of the annual expenditure on stock replenishment goes on replenishing less than 10% of the stock range – group A. ABC analysis is often used as the basis of stock control policies such as, for instance: order C items once a year, B items four times a year, and A items once a month unless it is possible to cover them by a contract for several months supply with monthly, or weekly, or even in the case of very high volume items daily, deliveries. Such policies imply a caretaker role for the C item stock controllers and an executive role for the A item stock controllers. Materials analysis is intended to provide guidance for the executive role.

ABC analysis can also be applied to *average inventory value* rather than to annual usage value, and this sometimes has advantages. Apart from high inventory value and high annual expenditure, other criteria may justify inclusion of certain items on the materials analysis hit list. There may be a policy decision that certain items must never be out of stock – life-or-death drugs in a hospital for instance. There may be policy decisions that large stocks or special reserve stocks of certain items will be held, for instance:

(1) those imported from a country halfway round the world with political problems;
(2) those with an exceptionally long lead time;
(3) those where the risk of supplies being interrupted by strikes is acute.

Such policy decisions can be reconsidered. It may be possible to devise some more economic way to achieve the end in view.

The same sort of analysis can be made of purchase expenditure to see where the money goes, and many organizations extend the ABC classification which has become well established for stock, to all purchases. Both invoice price and quantity required affect this. Hospitals use costly nitrous oxide as well as inexpensive X-ray film; but they tend to use a lot of X-ray film, making it an A item in spend analysis, and not very much nitrous oxide, making this a B item. They also use paper clips, but it is difficult to see how they could use enough of this low cost item to get it out of class C.

A preliminary list derived by spend analysis will be amended by crossing off items where there seems little chance of effecting any worthwhile saving, and adding on items which while not perhaps among the most expensive, do for one reason or another offer opportunities or challenges for cost reduction.

Having decided the main priority, nominated the materials team, and selected a short list of target items, the next step is to collect information.

What information do we need, is a question which the team should tackle at an early stage. Organizations in similar lines of business often have considerable commonality in their C items (for instance all engineering manufacturers use lubricating and cutting oils, bar steel and machine screws), while having little or no commonality in the A items which are the main targets for materials analysis. Consequently, reference can be made to textbooks or consultants for advice on how to economize on C items, while for A items recommendations have to be specially devised for specific organizations. Consultants can help to structure the process of reaching a solution, or to professionalize the presentation of a recommendation, but the solutions and the recommendations themselves should be developed by the organization's own staff.

Each target item can be allocated a filing pocket or folder. In this, data are collected for subsequent circulation to the materials analysis team under such headings as the following:

(1) detailed specification;
(2) applications: what do we use it for?
(3) usage: what quantity was used last year, this year? Future usage?
(4) source: where do we buy it? Where else could it be bought, and why not?
(5) conformance: what is the rejection percentage or scrap rate?
(6) inventory: how much do we hold in stock, what stockholding costs are incurred, how frequent are shortages, how were policies determined?
(7) transport: how does it reach us, what transport alternatives are available?

The next stage, after collecting the data, is for the materials analysis team to get down to detailed work on the target items and to come up with some constructive recommendations.

If the first priority is purchase cost reduction, factors to look at include:

(1) value analysis;
(2) alternate sources of supply;

(3) alternate materials;
(4) transport;
(5) ordering practice and payment method;
(6) in-process loss and other losses.

One shipbuilder found that the major cause of trouble in the purchase of A items (defined in this organization as equipment items costing £5000 apiece or more, and constituting 60–70% of material cost per ship), was delays in the drawing office. It could take as long as nine months after signature of the ship contract for requisitions to reach Purchasing complete with full drawings. The original quotations from suppliers which had been used in Estimating would be out of date by the time purchase orders could be sent to them, and new quotations would invariably be at a higher price and often at a longer delivery time.

One line of attack would be to ask the drawing office why these long delays occurred. Some delays might be avoidable. Another line would be a look at the ordering practices. Some kind of letter of intent or provisional order could be used to book capacity or indicate requirements to the supplier, although of course the official order should follow as soon as possible.

If reduced inventory is the aim, experience suggests a different selection of areas for examination:

(1) operational effectiveness;
(2) safety stock and reorder level policy;
(3) work-in-progress rules;
(4) order quantities;
(5) stock location;
(6) special factors.

As the folk-saying goes in Cambridge, Mass.: optimizing subsystems can mean suboptimizing the system. For instance, one chief inspector optimized his subsystem by keeping a 16 day backlog of work at the inspection bay. He could plan work in advance, his inspectors had a steady workload. But he had not realized that inventory is normally shown in the accounts either from invoice date or from delivery date, rather than from date of clearing inspection. The materials team got the backlog reduced from 16 days to seven. Inventory was reduced by £120 000. The chief inspector was amazed.

Safety stock and reorder levels are affected by lead times, both their length and their reliability. At least a third of the average stock holding of production parts and materials is normally attributable to safety or buffer stock, so substantial inventory reductions can be achieved if shorter and more reliable lead times can be arranged. Three lines of attack here are to:

(1) Look for new suppliers with shorter and more reliable delivery periods.
(2) Exert pressure on existing suppliers to improve their performance, for instance by complaining to representatives, and sending a quarterly letter comparing their actual delivery performance with that of other suppliers, and taking the matter up with them if their performance gets worse.
(3) Explore with suppliers the reasons for their unsatisfactory performance and work with them to improve matters.

For instance, suppliers could be advised to prepare a monthly internal report showing date goods were despatched against date originally promised. In many firms executives simply do not know how bad their performance is. The BIM Survey Report 35, published in December 1976, found that 40% of the respondent plants did not measure delivery performance against delivery promise. This simple step could lead to much better performance. Frequent change of schedule by customer is another cause of poor delivery performance, and if we are the offending customer the remedy is in our own hands.

What tends to happen when deliveries are perceived as unreliable is that all along the line people set up private emergency stocks, from exaggerated estimates of usage rates to a physical emergency supply under a foreman's desk, so stock location may be worth looking into – actual, as opposed to planned, location!

Group interaction by the members of the materials team needs time to develop; the group needs to play itself in. It is a good idea to start with some known problem area where there is a widely felt need for a better solution and a good chance of finding a better solution. Friendly, non-critical consideration of various alternatives – the 'What if we tried x' approach – should help to stop representatives of the various functional areas being defensive about the possible discovery of skeletons in their closets. It should constantly be stressed that this is a fact-finding, not a fault-finding, exercise. The aim is not to unearth old mistakes but to invent new solutions.

SIMPLIFYING PAPERWORK

The purpose of paperwork is to provide a compact and convenient means of communication and semipermanent record. This blameless object has a splendid aspect, for it is after all on paper that our present civilization is founded. Few of the age's great achievements would have been possible without the written or printed word. Yet paperwork has a fault.

The vice of paper is a tendency to breed. Forms and records and reports unless firmly checked can multiply like rabbits. Many purchasing people handle 50 or more standard forms; a large concern has hundreds. One major aircraft manufacturer in the United States once stated that the tonnage of paper consumed by his factories was greater than the tonnage of aeroplanes they produced. How can this deplorable tendency be reversed?

Textbooks are not always free from blame; they sometimes present as if for general use elaborate routines, records and forms which only special circumstances could justify. In practice too, forms are often designed in haste, to be repented at leisure; or become so consecrated by the customs and traditions of the organization that no one in a position of authority would dream of tampering with the design and only the baffled tyro is fully aware of its faults.

'Every form,' Peter Drucker has written, 'should stand trial for its life every five years.' Regular reports too should be stood in the dock; the trouble here is that report receivers can usually recall some occasion when the report proved useful and may therefore oppose any move to simplify or abolish even though nine times out of ten they have no time to read the thing and have to 'file and forget'. Those who prepare the reports may resent reform as an attack on the value of their work. Personal pride and the force of tradition may make a major effort necessary before any improvement can be effected. It is sometimes possible to put trainees on the job of tracking information flows down to their source and suggesting improvements. At worst this will further a trainee's training; at best, it will lead to worthwhile improvements.

Common sense and careful thought are the main requirements in this sort of task. Most paperwork can be considered from three aspects:

(1) as a document;
(2) as a flow of information;
(3) as a sequence of operations or piece of work.

Considered as a document, some useful questions are these:

Has it got its name at the top? Can its function be understood without a lot of information given verbally? Is it clearly printed on suitable paper? Is the layout clean, uncluttered, logical, such that data can be entered in natural sequence? Does it use abbreviations where there is room for full names? Is there enough room to write in data; if it is typed is the spacing typewriting spacing; is it easy to read when completed?

Is it on the right weight of paper – flimsy for temporary forms like advice notes, durable for forms like invoices which are kept longer, impressive for letterheads? Is it too big, or too little for what has to go on it? The size should be consistent with average rather than exceptional use. Does the size cut without waste from standard printers' sheets? Does it comply with published standards?

Can we cut it out altogether? Simplify it? Combine it with some other forms? Does it need all its features?

Having made a preliminary examination on these lines, the next stage might be to study the form in its native habitat, trace its life-cycle, interview people who use it or make it out. A useful visual aid is the flowchart, which maps out on paper where the data come from, where it goes to, and how it gets there. Some questions are these:

Is all the information which is given, needed? (for example, on a goods received note, do we need supplier's address as well as his name?) Is more needed? Do all who get the form need it? Do all who need it get it? Is it in the most suitable form (would a list of items needing reordering be better or worse than a batch of separate requisitions?), are codes used, what sort of codes, why are they used, do they make more work than they save? If codes are not used, do they make more work than they save? Should they be used? How long is the record filed, and how often is it referred to? Who refers to it, what for, is there any other way of getting the facts, is it worth the trouble and cost of keeping?

Many departments keep on file a lot of information which really ought to be thrown out or shifted to low-cost bulk storage. Less than three file drawers per employee should be enough. Most purchase departments keep many more old records on file than they are ever likely to require. New computer filing methods, which can accommodate twelve books the size of this one on a single disk, do not solve the problem of what documents to keep. High density document storage just makes it possible to keep them in less space.

Microfilming requisitions, orders, goods received notes, invoices, catalogues, correspondence and engineering drawings enables them to be stored in very little space – about 2% of the space required by filing cabinets and plan chests. Some microform systems identify documents by a coded blip for fast location. A microphotograph is a photograph of a document much reduced in size. Rolls of film bearing microphotographs are called microfilms; pieces of film bearing microphotographs are called microfiche; microform is a name sometimes used for both of them. Microform readers project the small photograph on a large screen so that it can be read, and if required printed out.

Many organizations have specialist work study, method study or O and M people. If you have them, use them!

Other chapters refer to specific techniques useful in cost reduction such as learning curves, breakeven analysis, price analysis, cost analysis, etc. Reference may be made to the index.

21

Personnel for purchasing and supply

Better purchasing and supply performance is achieved by recruiting, training and developing people who have the capability and the motivation to do good work. ('Have better people – and try harder!' – an old prescription for success.)

We could begin by defining the jobs to be carried out and then drawing up job descriptions. Job specifications are more precise, and can lead to person specifications which list the characteristics thought likely to qualify someone to perform well in the jobs specified. Staff recruitment and training can be based on these.

A *job description* is a broad statement of the purpose, scope, duties and responsibilities of a particular job. Job descriptions usually include: job title, name of department, the job title of the person to whom the job holder is responsible, and where appropriate limits of authority (for example, for expenditure). They also state the main activities and responsibilities assigned to the job.

A *job specification* is a detailed statement of the physical and mental activities involved in a particular job. As such it is more appropriate for those jobs for which precise performance standards or tests can be prescribed, such as shorthand or typing speeds in error-free words per minute, absence of colour blindness, manual dexterity, etc.

Typical job descriptions for a number of jobs in purchasing and supply are given in this chapter, which makes use of a general guide published under Crown copyright in 1972 under the title *Classification of Occupations and Directory of Occupational Titles* (CODOT). This was based on 20 000 detailed job studies throughout the country, supplemented by background research and consultation with a large number of organizations. It provides a system for defining and classifying occupations, generally compatible with other national and international classifications. An occupation is defined as a collection of jobs which are sufficiently similar in their main tasks to be grouped under a common occupational title for classification purposes. Many thousands of different jobs were identified, and they were brought together in CODOT under 3500 occupational titles.

PURCHASING AND BUYING

Those jobs which involve buying materials, plant and equipment for use within an organization rather than for resale, whether the organization itself is a manufacturing or a resale organization, are referred to in CODOT by the occupational title of *purchasing officer*, and the main features are shown in Fig. 21.1.

Buying merchandise for resale is the job of the *retail distribution buyer* who buys goods from manufacturers, importers, wholesalers and other sources for resale through retail distribution outlets. In doing this job retail distribution buyers attend trade shows, fairs, displays, etc. to look over new lines. They interview trade representatives who call. They decide on the range, type, quantity and quality of the merchandise to be bought, bearing in mind store policy, budget limitations, customer demand and fashion trends – one difference between this job and that of the 'purchasing officer'.

Another difference is that retail buyers decide on selling prices for merchandise. They watch stock movement, order more of fast-selling lines and arrange special sales promotions or price reductions for slow-selling lines. They arrange 'sales', marking down surplus, discontinued or end-of-range stock and buying in special sales lines. They keep records and prepare reports as required – for instance sales forecasts and budget estimates.

Like 'purchasing officers', retail distribution buyers place orders with appropriate suppliers, trying to obtain the best terms they can; check that goods delivered comply with orders; return any unsatisfactory goods to suppliers; and authorize invoices for payment.

Some specialize in particular types of merchandise – household goods, food, sports equipment. Some are in charge of other buyers, or buy centrally for a group of shops; they may be called group buyers, or merchandise controllers.

essential characteristics of the occupation:
Buys raw materials, plant, equipment and other items from manufacturers, wholesalers and other suppliers on behalf of an industrial, commercial or public undertaking.

important tasks normally carried out in the occupation:
Ascertains the type, quality, quantity and cost-ceiling of items required and the dates by which they must be available;
determines whether orders, or part orders, can be met from current supply contracts, whether new or renewal contracts should be negotiated with suppliers whether orders should be put out to tender and whether it would be more economical for the organization to manufacture certain items themselves; examines suppliers' literature, price lists, samples, etc and as necessary obtains price, quality and delivery quotations from one or more suppliers; evaluates terms and selects most suitable suppliers; negotiates new or renewal contracts with suppliers, endeavouring to obtain the most advantageous terms possible; draws up orders and contract documents specifying type of items, quantities, qualities, delivery requirements and other relevant factors;
finalizes orders and contracts within his authority or submits them to a finance committee, board of directors, or other authority for finalization; arranges for incoming suppliers to be checked for quantity and quality and for items which fall below specifications to be returned to suppliers; arranges for, or undertakes, the expediting of orders when delivery delays occur; interviews suppliers' representatives and visits trade fairs, exhibitions, etc.; notes any change in standards likely to affect future purchases; keeps appropriate records and prepares reports as required, for example expenditure analyses.

specializations within the occupation and additional tasks frequently associated with it:

May (01) recommended stock levels to be held
(02) negotiate contracts for the production of items on sub-contract
(03) undertake centralized buying for a group of factories, works, etc.
(04) specialize in raw materials
(05) specialize in production equipment
(06) specialize in components
(07) specialize in castings
(08) specialize in office supplies

Fig. 21.1 Job description: purchasing officer.

PURCHASING MANAGERS AND SUPPLY MANAGERS

Differences are fewer at management level.

The purchasing manager's job is to plan, organize, direct and coordinate the work of buyers, purchasing officers and others, and the resources appropriate to purchasing and procurement activities. He/she performs the normal functions of any manager, but he/she does this in relation to buying or procuring merchandise, materials, equipment, services etc. He/she may be involved in preparing estimates, financial statements, and reports on the department's work, but usually specializes in retail, wholesale or production buying. Purchasing managers differ in the number of staff they control, and in the extent of their authority in financial, staff and organizational matters. Some negotiate with worker's representatives.

Many purchasing managers are in charge of stock control staff. Some are in charge of stores staff and perhaps transport staff and production planning and control staff. They may then be known as supply managers or materials managers.

Large purchase departments include specialist support staff of various kinds, as well as buyers, typists and clerks. One such department had 156 purchase engineers, purchase cost estimators, and purchase analysts in its total work force of 550. This was high in relation to 190 buyers.

Purchase engineers 'get out in the field ensuring that suppliers have tooling adequate for our needs and that it will be ready in time. They also act as consultants to suppliers with serious production difficulties,' it was said.

The purchasing cost estimators were recruited from people with formal qualifications in mechanical engineering and at least five years' experience in manufacturing, preferably gained in work study and estimating. Their main task was to study and evaluate suppliers' manufacturing methods in order to advise buyers and assist them in negotiations. They also prepared cost estimates for the external manufacture of complex components and assemblies, established price objectives for negotiators, surveyed technical publications and kept in touch with costs and production methods by factory visits.

Purchase analysts were recruited from economics graduates or persons with accountancy qualifications. Their main task was to evaluate price trends and economic changes, and they were required to have experience in estimating and in industrial engineering. They also compared costs, reviewed delivery performance, and consulted suppliers; developed methods for compiling price indexes; prepared, presented, interpreted and evaluated statistical data; computed purchasing savings and attended meetings of purchasing staff to discuss savings; assisted buyers in price negotiations, especially where complex analysis was required.

STORES STAFF

The relationship between the purchasing and stores departments is close, since one buys what the other keeps, one originates requests the other meets. Common practice in most non-manufacturing organizations and in many manufacturing organizations, is to make the stores part of a unified supply department which also includes buying. As well as widening promotion opportunities for stores personnel, this enables the many activities which involve both stores and purchasing staff to be performed efficiently without interdepartmental delays.

Admittedly at the lowest level, stores work is labouring and handling work with some clerical element, perhaps the least skilled work in the supply structure. If stores workers are engaged, dismissed and paid, often by the hour, on a similar basis to factory workers and on a different basis to office and administrative workers; if the stores premises are part of the main factory and if it accommodates numbers of made-in parts and work-in-progress with which purchasing is not concerned directly, then the simplest option may be to manage the stores as part of the factory. The purchasing manager may however, retain a considerable degree of functional control, especially when he is responsible for stock control.

Stores operation, or storekeeping, means the physical handling and housing of material and parts before and after processing. It includes the provision of suitable places – warehouses, stockyards – and equipment – cranes, fork trucks, pallets, racks; the employment of suitable staff; and the operation of suitable procedures to receive, store and issue goods securely and economically. The CODOT occupational descriptions for industrial storekeeper and stores manager give a clear picture of the work involved.

Stores managers for instance, plan, organize, direct and coordinate, usually through or with the assistance of foremen, the receipt, issue and storage of raw materials, components, finished products and other items in an organization's stores.

They perform the appropriate functions of any manager, and in addition are normally responsible for the following important tasks:

(1) Decides on optimum stores layout, ensuring as far as possible that

items are kept in good condition and that accessibility relates to demand.

(2) Arranges for the recording of items in and out, the maintenance of inventories of items held and the regular inspection of stock for deterioration and damage.

(3) Controls the issue of required materials, components, tools, etc., to production departments.

(4) Notifies purchasing department of items to be reordered.

(5) Constantly reviews stock levels and suggests to stock control manager any changes in levels considered necessary.

(6) Implements security procedures against theft and damage by fire, flood or other cause.

(7) Prepares reports on expenditure and storekeeping activities and advises on future storekeeping policies.

They may also control internal transport; undertake quality control inspection of incoming goods; arrange for sale of obsolete, used or damaged goods; negotiate with employee representatives; and undertake some or all of the functions of the purchasing officer.

Other factors affecting the job include the number of foremen and other workers controlled; the extent to which computers and other forms of information technology are applied in storekeeping procedures; and the amount of authority delegated on finance, staff and organizational matters.

STOCK CONTROL

Buyers, purchasing officers, production planning and control personnel, accountants, storekeepers, stock checkers, stock control clerks and stock control managers may all take part in stock control. Academically it is a somewhat anomalous area. The theory is very learned and mathematical. The practice often ignores the theory.

A clear distinction between stock control at clerical level, and at managerial level, may be found in CODOT. The stock control clerk checks and records details of stock movements and maintains records of stock held. His/her main tasks are typically to examine delivery documents for incoming goods, prepare record cards and/or enter details in stock records, check requisitions and receive vouchers for goods despatched and adjust stock records accordingly, prepare requisitions for stock replenishment, report on damaged goods and stock deficiencies. He/she may also carry out physical checks of stock against stock records for audit or stocktaking purposes; handle enquiries or routine correspondence from suppliers or customers; and collect samples for laboratory test for quality control purposes. Other titles for this occupation include: docking clerk (warehouse); kitchen clerk (hotel); goods inward clerk; stock records clerk; stores clerk; warehouse clerk.

Many organizations do not appoint a stock control manager, his/her functions being performed by the purchasing, stores, or other manager, or in some instances not being performed at all. If there is a stock control manager, his/her job is to plan, direct, organize and coordinate, usually through or with the assistance of other managers or foremen, procedures and resources for maintaining stocks of raw materials, components, finished products and other items at optimum level, and for ensuring their availability when required.

In addition to the functions appropriate to any manager, he/she also normally:

(1) Ascertains, by discussion with production, sales, maintenance and other managers the materials, parts, finished products and other items required for current and future production programmes, sales commitments, and other activities, and the dates by which they will be required.
(2) Makes allowance for possible contingencies which could affect requirements.
(3) Develops stockholding policies to ensure minimum investment of money, space, labour and other resources while achieving maximum satisfaction of requirements.
(4) Advises purchasing department on type, quantity and quality of supplies required and dates by which they must be available.
(5) Ensures that adequate records are kept of all items held in stock.
(6) If there are several stockholding centres, decides on optimum distribution of items among those centres.
(7) Develops and implements systems for automatic reordering of standard items.
(8) Advises on parts and material standardization.
(9) Prepares reports on expenditure, draws up department budget for approval, and advises on future stock control policies.

He/she may also undertake some or all of the functions of the purchasing officer or the stores manager and arrange for the expediting of supplies when suppliers do not deliver on time. Stock control managers differ in the number of foremen and other workers they control, the extent of their authority on financial, staff and organizational matters, and their computer experience. Alternative titles for the stock control manager include: inventory control manager, inventory controller, materials control manager, materials controller, stock controller.

RECRUITMENT OF STAFF

Purchasing and supply departments recruit staff from several sources: school leavers, recent graduates, other departments in the organization, other organizations. Most responsible purchasing jobs are at present held by men, but an increasing number of women are entering purchasing, and some of the top jobs (especially in retail distribution) are held by women.

In selecting staff for senior positions one needs to decide, not only what the job is, but also what personal characteristics are likely to lead to effective performance.

Most purchasing jobs are strongly commercial and should appeal to people who enjoy being in the thick of things, can cope with desk work but prefer not to be tied to the desk, and like the cut-and-thrust of the marketplace; but there is also scope for the planner, the investigator, the thinker. Buyers deal with people all the time, inside and outside their organization; like salesmen they need to communicate, persuade and convince. They work with facts and figures, like accountants and engineers. They are expected to deal honestly, fairly and courteously with colleagues and with representatives of other organizations. In senior positions, particularly, they need to take a long view and plan ahead. Some jobs require specialist knowledge of a commodity or product group and its supply market.

As specified by purchasing people, the buyer seems to be a paragon of all virtues, with just that dash of vice that makes him/her business-like. As RGA Hadnam told the IPS National Conference in 1985, 'a buyer must be a super person. I say "person" deliberately because we now have, I am delighted to say, women buyers entering the profession in increasing numbers. Buyers will need to be in future economists, currency speculation clairvoyants, linguists, engineers and diplomats. The high flyers should also have the capability to walk on water.'

As described by salesmen, a less attractive figure appears. 'Someone who knows that 99 pence is less than a pound, and that's the only damn thing he does know' – well, they exist. 'A person past middle life, spare, wrinkled, bald, passive, intelligent, cold, non-committal. With eyes like a codfish. Polite in contact but at the same time unresponsive; cool, calm and as damnably composed as a concrete post or plaster of Paris cast; minus bowels, passions or sense of humour. Happily they never reproduce and all of them finally go to hell.' This has been attributed to Elbert Hubbard in America and perhaps it refers to the auditor rather than the buyer. In either case of course it is not true

Talent, character and experience are the three things to check in appointing someone to a post. It is difficult to check character in an interview – except character-in-interview, which is largely irrelevant – and it is almost impossible to check talent. Experience is easier to check, although neither what the applicant says nor what one is told by referees in firms he has worked for can be regarded as completely reliable.

Ability to work under pressure, a firm character, a clear conscience and an open mind are desirable characteristics. A keen interest in the job is most desirable. Arithmetic reasoning ability and numeracy should be above average, though not necessarily to the same extent as market researchers or accountants. Communication skills, persuasiveness, persistence and a resilient temperament are required; salesmen probably require these characteristics even more than buyers, and some firms rotate people between sales and purchasing as a form of staff development. The buyer should not be so introverted as to be incapable of teamwork, nor so extroverted as to be incapable of sticking to principle.

Kostishack and South (1973) published a list of performance criteria which might be useful to personnel recruiters and purchasing managers in reviewing an applicant's qualifications, as well as in designing performance appraisal and training and development programmes. They developed a list of 35 descriptive statements, such as:

(1) Properly applies company purchasing policy in the performance of his job.
(2) Works effectively with members of other departments.
(3) Keeps his office and/or desk neat and orderly.
(35) Keeps abreast of current academic developments by attending evening classes, seminars, etc.

This was sent to managers of multiple-buyer purchase departments in service, distribution, and manufacturing organizations. The managers were asked to rate each statement on a scale from: 5 – highly descriptive, to 1 – not descriptive, and to do this three times: once for an outstanding buyer, once for an average buyer, and once for a below average buyer.

Cluster analysis techniques were used to group together those statements that had a high degree of correlation. Fig. 21.2 shows the first-order cluster analysis result. Respondents' judgements were also tested for consistency. The Kuder and Richardson (K–R) 20 test was used, and the figures obtained are shown in brackets; complete consistency would give a K–R score of 1.00 and complete inconsistency would score 0.00.

Neatness, getting to work on time, and being good at detail work did not correlate well with any cluster and did not differentiate between outstanding buyers, average buyers, and below average buyers.

(1) Personal Appearance (K-R 20 = 0.99)
　　9　Is well groomed
　27　Dresses well
(2) Interpersonal Relations (K-R 20 = 0.95)
　　4　Is well liked by members of other departments
　12　Has the ability to get along well with people
　31　Is well liked by fellow purchasing employees
(3) Independence and Resistance to Work Pressures (K-R 20 = 0.92)
　　8　Can initiate and proceed with project without continued direct
　　　supervision
　15　Makes sound decisions under conditions of stress or pressure
　28　Readily accepts additional responsibility
(4) Innovativeness (K-R 20 = 0.90)
　13　Is inquisitive as to the reasons for, or the end use of, the products he/she
　　　purchases
　17　Suggests new or improved purchasing methods or procedures
　23　Develops new sources of supply
(5) Personal Insight — People (K-R 20 = 0.90)
　30　Is a good judge of character
　33　Is well liked by supervisor
(6) Work Follow-up (K-R 20 = 0.88)
　26　Follows up work and reacts to feedback
　32　Follows supervisor's orders well with little need for continuous checking
(7) Communications — Speaking and Writing (K-R 20 = 0.92)
　10　Communicates well by writing
　11　Communicates well by speaking
(8) Product — Market — Price Knowledge (K-R 20 = 0.89)
　　7　Adequately communicates the company's requirements of price, quality,
　　　and service to vendors
　20　Has a good knowledge of the characteristics of the market of products
　　　for which he/she has the responsibility of purchasing
　29　Gives assistance or advice to fellow purchasing employees
(9) Ethics and Morals (K-R 20 = 0.94)
　18　Has high moral standards
　24　Exhibits ethical behaviour in his job performance
(10) Rules and Policy Adherence (K-R 20 = 0.86)
　　1　Properly applies company purchasing policy in the purchasing area
　　5　Keeps work current
　22　Shows savings achieved in purchasing as measured against previous
　　　costs, standard costs, or market costs
(11) High Work Output (K-R 20 = 0.80)
　14　Has high work output based on the number of purchase orders issued
　16　Has high work output based on the dollar value of purchase orders
　　　issued
(12) Knowledgeable Interdepartmental Communication (K-R 20 = 0.81)
　　2　Works effectively with members of other departments
　19　Has a good knowledge of the legal aspects of purchasing
(13) Professional Development (K-R 20 = 0.72)
　34　Attends Purchasing Management Association or other trade association
　　　meetings frequently
　35　Keeps abreast of current academic developments by attending evening
　　　classes, seminars etc.

Fig. 21.2 Performance criteria for industrial buyers
(Source: Kostishack and South, 1973)

22

Organizing
the
department

There are several problems in deciding how to organize a purchasing and supply department.

(1) How should work be allocated to the people in the department?
(2) If the organization operates more than one establishment, should purchasing and supply work be done centrally, at headquarters; or locally, in the establishments; or should there be an arrangement where some is done centrally and some locally?
(3) Which functions should be included in the department: purchasing, obviously, but should stock control, order progressing, invoice processing, stores administration, also be included? What about production planning and control, transport, goods inwards inspection, certain aspects of quality control?

SMALL FIRMS

Small firms have the more basic question of whether or not to set up a purchasing and supply department at all, or even designate someone as a buyer. The answer really depends on how much work of this kind has to be done.

Small manufacturing firms employ less than 200 people. They comprise 94% of UK manufacturers, and account for 20% of employment in manufacturing. A small construction firm might have 25 employees or less, a small road transport firm have five vehicles or less, and there are many small retailers and wholesalers. Most small firms do not employ full-time purchasing staff because the amount of purchasing they do does not constitute a full-time job.

There are millions of organizations managing without either full-time purchasing staff or supply departments, purchasing work being done by management. It is only when people spend at least half of their time on purchasing work that they can be described as purchasing staff.

Medium-size firms have from one to six purchasing staff. Large firms may have hundreds. The work can be planned, organized and allocated to people in many ways.

Allocating buying work

For instance, some manufacturers have specialist raw material buyers as well as general buyers. These are all buyers: they all arrange with outside organizations for the supply of goods and services in return for a price. But there are differences in what they do.

The raw material buyer is usually an expert in the narrow range of commodities he or she buys, is directly involved with preparing specifications, and may be personally responsible for specifying what is bought. The general buyer cannot have expert knowledge of everything bought and other people generally draw up the specifications. The raw materials buyer may spend huge sums in price variable markets where wrong decisions could cost the company tens of millions of pounds and right decisions could save them a lot of money, as discussed in Chapter 16 in connection with commodity buying. If his/her performance materially affects the trading results of the firm, the raw material buyer will be part of senior management. The general buyer becomes conspicuous to management mainly when something goes wrong: late delivery or inferior quality causes manufacturing stoppages for instance.

Some firms consider the differences more important than the similarities and set up separate departments for raw material buying and for general buying. Other firms have a single buying department that buys everything including raw materials.

A similar problem occurs in large chain stores. Should the people who take the initial merchandising and sourcing decisions be in the same department as those who handle the more routine work of reordering and replenishing stocks?

Progressing purchase orders is normally done by the purchase department, although some mass production manufacturers take this activity out of purchasing and combine it with progressing works orders for internal manufacture, normally a production control activity.

Processing purchase invoices and approving them for payment may be carried out in purchasing or in accounting.

When there are several buyers in a department, the buying work can be allocated to them in several ways, for instance:

(1) by value of order, with one buyer specializing in quick service on small orders, and another dealing only with big orders such as machine tools or construction;
(2) by type of material bought, with one buyer specializing in packaging, for instance, another in castings and forgings, another in electronics or subcontracts;
(3) by end-product, with one buyer specializing in all requirements for product A, another in product B, and so on – project purchasing is a large-scale version of this.

Project purchasing

Some firms undertake large contracts for the construction of oil rigs, hospitals, bridges or tunnels, etc. For each contract a project manager may be appointed. For very large contracts matrix organization structures may be used, as shown in Fig. 22.1, with purchasing and other staff seconded for various periods to work full-time on the project. The project manager is the line manager, with direct authority over what they do; but corporate purchasing management have functional authority over the way they do it. Matrix organizations mean that senior people have at least two bosses, contrary to traditional organization theory.

We see in the organization chart shown in Fig. 22.1 that the project manager has a project procurement manager directly responsible to him/her (along no doubt with other section managers). However the project procurement manager is also functionally responsible (that is, responsible for the way he/she carries out his function) to the divisional procurement director.

At the next level down, the senior project expediter and the senior project inspector are both functionally responsible to the expediting and inspection manager in divisional procurement; line authority over what they do is exerted by the project procurement manager.

LARGE ORGANIZATIONS

Well over half of the firms employing at least 500 people employ them at more than one establishment. Some of these establishments may be branch offices or local distribution centres, that can buy minor consumables out of petty cash and put everything else through central purchasing. Some of them may be factories or other large establishments, as in

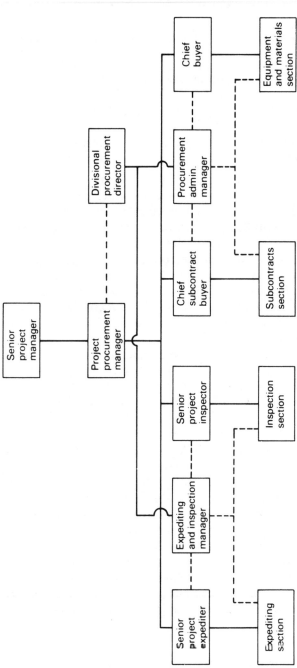

Fig. 22.1 Project procurement organization. Solid lines show authority; dotted lines indicate how project staff were functionally responsible to corporate management.

the gas industry or the health service, which require large numbers of purchased items.

In principle, three approaches to organizing the purchasing can be used:

(1) Centralization: everything is bought centrally except for petty cash items.
(2) Decentralization: everything is bought locally, at branches or divisions.
(3) A combination approach, with some purchases made locally and some made centrally; this can take many forms.

Complete centralization is used by some retail chains selling the same merchandise (or, in the case of smaller outlets, a selection from the same range of merchandise) everywhere in the country.

Complete decentralization may occur in a few manufacturing groups comprising several divisions each with its own product range and purchase department, but even then buyers tend to get together periodically to agree on group contracts for common use items. It tends to shade into a combination approach, without a head office purchase group, but with informal cooperation between divisional purchasing heads who meet officially every few months. This is not uncommon in medium-size organizations.

Larger organizations usually have some full-time staff in central purchasing, although the number considered appropriate is now very much smaller than it used to be.

The basic objective of the purchasing departments is to supply the factories with what they need when they need it. The men on the spot, the divisional buyers, are best placed to attend to this. Central or corporate purchasing may be able to assist, advise and encourage them. A further objective is to buy economically, and here the headquarters staff may be able to do better than divisional staff. Indeed, if they cannot, it is hard to see how their existence can be justified.

Headquarters staff can only do better than divisional staff when they are able to aggregate requirements from several divisions for the purpose of negotiating contracts. They may then be able to employ a specialist whose exhaustive knowledge of a particular market and skill in dealing in it get better results than a general buyer could. They are also often in a position to negotiate group contracts at lower prices or at better terms than the divisions could arrange separately.

Group contracts

Normally the group contract covers a large part of the group's requirements, or even the entire requirements of all the divisions in the group.

It is negotiated centrally and covers a longish period of time: 12 month contracts are by far the most common. Group contracts can be arranged at lower prices because:

(1) the supplier's costs are reduced;
(2) the supplier, threatened with the loss of substantial orders, may be willing to make do with a lower profit margin;
(3) the several divisions of the purchasing firm are not pushing up price or delivery by bidding against each other, as it were.

Group contracts can reduce the supplier's costs by guaranteeing him a substantial volume of business that he does not need to go out and drum up and can plan and provide for; it may well reduce the variety of products he needs to offer and the amount of selling he has to do, and it probably means a bigger order than he would otherwise be able to get from the purchasing firm even though it may be for delivery at various times to various places. (For instance, explaining Marks and Spencer methods at a conference, one M and S speaker said: 'suppliers need no advertising, no salesmen, little office space and equipment and only one invoice a week to cover deliveries to 246 stores' (*Modern Purchasing* March/April 1971 p. 50)).

Direct savings through bulk buying and specialist talent are the main reason for having a central office, but indirect savings should result from various assignments a central office may undertake in order to improve service or efficiency. Useful studies could be made of organization and methods for the benefit of the whole concern; of paperwork procedures and the design of forms, work routines and filing requirements. It could obtain and supply expert help on legal matters, special contract conditions for particular circumstances, import and export questions requiring special knowledge.

The central purchasing office can spread word of new products, processes, techniques. On the personnel side, it can help to devise a comprehensive scheme for recruiting and training staff. Training may include sponsored attendance at colleges and outside courses, planned job rotation within the firm, and in-company seminars and conferences – often with contributions by outside purchasing training consultants. Group-wide promotion opportunities and common salary structures and job descriptions are often devised.

Best use of scarce materials in difficult times could be a task to be done centrally – the efficient use of dispersed stocks in the interest of the company as a whole, preventing one factory going short of something of which another has more than it needs, perhaps, and a joint attack on suppliers rather than separate approaches by which branches compete with others for available supplies.

One danger with group contracting is that branch buyers may lose heart if they are not left enough freedom of action. Individual buyers should be able to feel that their own contribution to the prosperity of the group can be identified and rewarded. Some groups allow branch buyers to opt out of group contracts wherever they can give sound reasons for so doing; such as the need for quick delivery in emergency, or finding a better buy – which ought to lead to a better group contract. Most groups allow branch buyers full discretion for purchases below certain figures, unless there is a group contract for the item. More than one contract is drawn up whenever this is economically practicable, so that the factory buyer has some choice.

Like every specialist service in the large enterprise, the purchasing department has to steer between the reefs of too much responsibility and the whirlpool of not enough. Many arts and studies can be pursued for their own sake, but purchasing is not one of them; it is well done only inasmuch as it contributes to the good of the business. Too much authority can result in specialist departments getting obsessed with their specialism, losing sight of the real objects and their proper part in achieving those objects for the sake of flourishing their professionalism. Too little authority is just as bad; a purchase department hamstrung by excessive subordination and lack of recognition is unlikely to turn in a superior performance. This applies not only to the amount of authority entrusted to purchasing relative to other functions, but also to the amount of authority branch buyers have relative to head office. Making decisions centrally enables the best advising and deciding talent to be used. But those who have to implement plans should be involved as much as possible in formulating them. This produces better plans. Its main advantage however is in the better communication and motivation which in turn makes the plans work better. Branch purchasing staff should be consulted before plans are decided centrally, and so far as possible they should be actively involved in making the plans.

MULTINATIONALS

A business which produces, as well as sells, products in several countries is described as a *multinational*, as distinct from a firm which just sells in several countries and is thus operating *internationally*.

Multinationals employ people who are nationals of several countries and decisions may be affected by intervention from several national governments. Purchasing decisions are complicated by political considerations about how the various governments within whose patches they operate will react. They are also complicated by the need to take account of local variations, for instance in tax, subsidy, exchange rates, wages, salaries and living costs. Multinationals can shift their manufacturing operations around the world, perhaps to get near the customer, perhaps to go where labour is cheap and governments cooperate.

NOT SO SMALL

Some firms have grown to a considerable size while still behaving and being managed like small firms. The classic example is Henry Ford in the 1930s. British Rail also in its early days of nationalization provided a remarkable instance of how not to buy, which was discussed in Parliament. Said one member:

It appears, 'that on occasions certain experienced firms which have been contracting with . . . (the railways) for long periods are employed without alternative tenders being invited. I can understand the reason for that. Engineers and technicians with long experience know what their requirements are, and they may have been dealing with one firm for a long time, and it may be far easier for them to continue dealing with that firm because they know that if they do they will obtain the quality that they require. But that is not good business.

He went on to say that the system of making technical staff responsible for placing contracts had been inherited from prenationalization railway companies which had 'no supply or services organization with the qualifications for buying the goods or placing the contracts'.

Another member pointed out the dangers of a situation, in which very large sums of money had to be spent with few suppliers in an overloaded industry. He illustrated this by relating that an order had been placed with a well-known firm which had supplied the railways with equipment for years to their satisfaction. The order was for about a million parts used in connection with a new vacuum braking system. 'The quotation of £30 per unit was accepted in the first place, but before it was confirmed . . . competitive tenders were sought. It was then found that other firms of equal standing were prepared to quote between £20 and £24 for that article. Hearing of that, the original firm reduced its price to £23 (Hansard, 1957). This was a £7 reduction per part, and a million parts were to be ordered.

Seven million pounds is a staggering amount of money to save, at the last minute, simply by obtaining a few quotations. Replying, the government spokesman said things were being reorganized on the basis that 'purchasing should be regarded as a special technique, that it should be in the hands of specially experienced men, that it is the business of the technical staff to define or design what is wanted and that they should be relieved of the commercial dealings involved in its procuring'.

ANTIPURCHASING

When organizations, whether small or large, are restructured in a way such that the organizational role of the purchasing department is stepped up, a considerable antipurchasing feeling may be generated. Some reasons for this are pride, a feeling that any change implies a criticism of the way things have been done in the past; inertia, the tendency to continue in a state of rest or uniform motion in a straight line until force is applied; fear, that price-chiselling and substitution of inferior materials will interfere with the flow of materials or otherwise hamper operations. There is nothing more annoying for an executive than to back the appointment of a purchasing clerk to take some of the tedious paperwork off his desk, only to find later that the man is insisting on procedures which are even more tedious than the original paperwork, and is getting the backing of top management because of some trifling savings he has been able to make. Such savings are soon converted to losses when customers with defective products insist on having their faulty cut-price components put right at your expense. In his book *Up the Organization*, Robert Townsend sums up the antipurchasing case in the swingeing style which made the work a bestseller: 'Fire the whole purchasing department! They cost ten dollars in zeal for every dollar they save through purchasing acumen. And that doesn't count the massive unrecorded disasters they cause.' Rueful amusement at a recognizable caricature of certain purchase departments is a common reaction of purchasing staff to this.

Relations with other departments

The purchase department works with almost every other department in the business, either daily or occasionally. Everyone in the firm should look to purchasing for advice and assistance on such matters as what to purchase, when, from whom, and at what price. Many purchase departments maintain up-to-date indexed libraries of catalogues and standards, and perhaps also sample rooms, for the convenience of their colleagues. Other services apart from actually purchasing include circulating data on new developments, price changes, market trends, new products or processes; arranging for technical experts from suppliers to call for discussions with design or operating or maintenance personnel; participating constructively and analytically in discussions at the early stages of projects and designs. Even at the time of purchase most buyers are encouraged to review requisitions and suggest any alterations that will be for the good of the company – though they should not alter requisitions without consulting the requisitioner.

Purchasing managers give a good deal of thought to coordinating activities with other departments. This sometimes presents problems. User department may requisition parts too late for purchasing to do a proper buying job, too late even for the fastest supplier to deliver them on time. Specifiers may commit the company to accept particular offers or deal with particular suppliers. Buyers may be blamed for troubles not of their making but caused by inadequate planning and consultation by colleagues in other departments. There is little you can do to make others cooperate with you, but a whole-hearted willingness to co-operate with them is a long first step in the right direction. Walter E. Willett, in *Purchasing Magazine* wrote:

We've found two ways to get co-operation. 'First, prove that you can get what they want when they want it. And quit crying about every rush job. Other people have problems too. Get the goods – that's purchasing's job. Nothing builds confidence like performance. And second, give credit where credit is due. It's rare to be complimented, isn't it? Well, try it on the other fellow. When we make a saving, we send a note to the person concerned with a copy to his boss. This note usually includes a sentence like this: ''Thank you for enabling us to make a cost reduction of. . . .

Obviously it is no use just sitting in an office waiting for requisitions to come in and then complaining that they do not allow enough time. Clear explanations of what lead time to allow and what data are required should be given. If this does not work, further thought should be applied. A fast-growing firm in a fast-changing, rapidly evolving industry, which purchases vast quantities of made-to-order components of considerable complexity, cannot use the wait-for-the-requisition approach. Often such firms attach to the purchase department several 'procurement liaison engineers'. These people work with technical groups on preliminary pricing, on investigation of standard components to determine which will best perform the desired function at lowest cost for its value, on the formulation of specifications, and in arranging close working relationships between engineering design and suitable suppliers. They keep buyers posted with advance information about forthcoming purchases, so that thanks to this early warning buyers can go ahead immediately the project is approved – or even make tentative commitments before then, subject to confirmation, if this is necessary to get a place in the queue. The job of purchasing is to help, not to hinder, others in their work; and effective purchase departments lean over backwards to give the best service possible, consistent with their duty to buy well and control expenditure.

LATERAL RELATIONSHIP TACTICS

Considerable frustration is experienced by purchasing staff who feel that they are not allowed to give of their best because of the attitudes and expectations of top management, line management, and in some instances departmental management. Individuals work of course for their private ends as well as for the official objectives of the organization. These private schedules of objectives typically include the achievement of more status, recognition, security, pay and promotion. Good management is partly concerned with producing congruence between the organization's schedule of objectives (survival, growth, profitability, etc.) and the private objectives of its staff. When the organization recognizes the importance of skilled and economic purchasing by appropriate rewards to purchasing staff, this supports and reinforces their efforts to buy well. The purchasing manager is able to achieve his private objectives of recognition, advancement, etc., by working for the organization's objectives, by seeking out value for money and giving a superior service to other departments. When this is not the case, when buyers do not get this organizational support, their behaviour could be described as dysfunctional, although George Strauss managed to avoid this dreadful word in his research into this situation (Strauss, 1962).

It appears that the saintlier buyers may do good by stealth, as it were, slipping in a superior bit of performance whenever allowed to. But this is unusual. When purchasing staff are treated as order-placers, tightly restricted by detailed instructions as to what to buy and where to buy it, denied a voice in the relevant decisions and the chance to use or develop skill and judgement in buying, they have been observed to bend most of their energies to gaining some kind of recognition within the organization. They could adopt, for this purpose, the patient and humble tactic of doing the best they can in the hope that someday someone will notice. But the research showed that a touch of vindictiveness tended to creep in.

Rigid formal procedures are prescribed for initiating purchases. By manipulating these procedures buyers are able to exert power of a kind over their colleagues. They may even punish executives or departments who bypass them, by delaying order processing. Such buying departments do not buy particularly well; they are preoccupied with internal politics, and much too busy to develop and apply buying ability. Nor do they give a particularly good service to the rest of the organization; but they can hardly be called to account for this, since they stick rigidly to the approved rule-book or purchasing manual.

They are trapped in a vicious circle. Managements that believe their buyers are capable of nothing but clerical routines will not allow them to do more. Frustrated buyers then tend to perform the routines in an aggressive and restrictionist fashion, leading management to conclude that the buyers they have cannot even do clerical work very well. Stewart Lauer (1967) has written:

I think that the relatively low level of expectation on the part of general management, of their purchasing operation, is one of the most significant problems we have to face. Unfortunately many of our purchasing people are satisfied to meet this low level of expectation despite the fact that major opportunities are available to them to contribute to the profitability of the business. There is little chance that significant changes will occur in a purchasing operation until management becomes aware of and defines the impact that purchasing can have on product costs, and sets objectives for purchasing to meet.

THE PURCHASING MANUAL

Some large companies issue purchasing manuals which lay down rules for purchasing's relations with suppliers and with other departments and prescribe the procedures to follow. The foreword is usually written by top management, without whose backing the whole project is a waste of time. Subsequent contents can be classified under the headings: purpose, principles and procedure. That is, for each activity the purpose, or scope and object, is stated; under 'principles' the rules for making decisions are set out, and often the persons entitled to take the decisions are named; under 'procedures', details of how things are done – though not too many details – are given.

The readership for a purchasing manual comprises, first, supply department employees; second, employees outside the department; and third, suppliers. Within the department, the manual's main purpose is to standardize work, save time in handling jurisdictional conflicts and in dealing with problems that come up rarely but regularly. A subsidiary purpose may be to help train newcomers. Of course the risk in this is that instead of clarifying procedures the handbook may consecrate them into rituals; if it is to remain a reliable guide, regular revision is a must.

As well as telling people inside the department who does what and how, the manual will tell colleagues outside the department what services are available from the supply department and how to get them. This is especially useful in fast-growing firms whose annual intake of senior staff is high. One manual comprises a set of two-page leaflets, each a general description of some aspect of procurement, followed by a two-part procedure guide: 'What You Do' side by side with 'What Procurement Does'.

Finally, the manual may tell suppliers how to deal with the company and who to contact. Visitors to a large concern find it a convenience to get a booklet telling them what the company makes, what it buys, which people are responsible for which purchases, where the establishments are sited, and what rules must be followed in calling on the company.

Writing such a manual demands skills that are less widely available than is sometimes supposed. It also demands a deal of hard work and hard thought, and a lot of cooperation with other departments.

Although the effort may be justifiable when changes are being instituted, to let everyone know where they stand, Robert Townsend's advice (in *Up the Organization*) is worth considering: 'If you have to have a policy manual, publish the ten commandments.'

PURCHASING RESEARCH

Purchasing research is defined by Fearon (1961) as: 'systematic investigation and fact-finding to improve purchasing performance'. A certain amount of systematic investigation is done as a normal part of the buying process. Before dealing with a new supplier, or selecting a contractor for a major project, or taking the final decision on costly capital expenditure or on the adoption of some novel material, a competent purchase department would be expected to undertake a 'course of critical investigation; endeavour to discover new or collate old facts' – which is a dictionary definition of research.

Emergency investigations are also undertaken to solve problems, such as a sudden shortage or an unacceptable price increase; or in response to other exceptional situations, such as a change in the law.

But there is a problem for purchasing management in organizing research which goes beyond what is a prerequisite of some complex new purchase decision, or a crisis response. Rapid developments in technology, changes in the structure of the economy and continual evolution in the complex environment in which purchase decisions are made have made this problem more urgent. How can purchasing management make available to the buyer information which will improve purchasing performance now? How can future purchasing performance be improved by looking ahead, studying trends, exploring options, when buyers are fully occupied with the problems of today? The development of new systems, techniques and methods is another area which is difficult to handle on a part-time basis.

Consequently, some larger purchase departments include, alongside the buying staff, people who are employed full-time on 'systematic investigation and fact-finding to improve purchase performance'.

Full-time research workers of this kind go by a variety of names, including: purchase analyst, cost analyst, systems analyst, value analyst, commodity specialist, cost estimator, supply market analyst, purchasing research, purchasing services.

They are often grouped together in a separate section known as: purchase planning and research, purchasing research, purchasing services. Such a section may provide other information services such as a catalogue library or the preparation of management reports or expenditure budgets.

The technical qualifications of such personnel vary considerably and will depend on the nature of their work; see, for instance, the jobs considered towards the end of Chapter 21. Their personal qualifications are just as important. In providing a useful and appreciated service to buyers and to purchasing management, their technical qualifications should be adequate to ensure that the service is useful; but to make it appreciated they need social or interpersonal skills. If buyers get the impression that research personnel are going to interfere with the way they buy, criticize their buying decisions and generally act as backseat drivers instead of helping them, then the back-up service provided by the section is not going to be fully used.

Personnel in other departments may contribute to research in the purchasing department. For instance, quality control engineers often assist in supplier evaluation, marketing research personnel sometimes help with supply market investigation, and systems or O and M people may be called in on systems and methods. Outside consultants are also used.

In organizations not employing full-time purchasing research staff, two methods are used by purchasing management to ensure that purchasing research is not confined to *ad hoc* or emergency investigations. The first is an individual approach, and the second is a collective approach.

The individual approach is to agree with individual buyers special projects. By an agreed date they must each complete an investigation and put forward recommendations, for instance on revised conditions of contract, on acceptance of hospitality, or on new sources. These projects arise from or are related to the normal work of the people concerned but are additional to it. In management by objectives, staff development schemes, and graduate training programmes such special projects are common.

Collective approaches usually attempt to focus the attention of all the buyers on one problem at a time. One purchasing manager refers to this as the 'roving spotlight'. Each month he turns the spotlight onto a new problem area. Particular aspects may be assigned to individuals but the whole department is expected to concentrate on the general problem.

The best way to keep interest alive may be to have a number of different approaches operating simultaneously. One large organization had one group looking at supplier appraisal methods while another group worked on system development with the computer specialists and a third group discussed long-term prospects with the corporate planning staff. Meanwhile all buyers were encouraged to read trade and commercial publications, attend exhibitions, visit suppliers, and contribute to planning and policy formation. Graduate trainees spent at least six months in purchasing research, and often did work which was of noticeably high standard but was not seen by the buyers as a threat to their prerogatives or an attack on their status.

Having organized a purchase research effort, either full-time or part-time, topics for research are selected. Table 22.1 shows some which have been suggested.

A thought-provoking definition of research was provided by C. F. Kettering: 'an organised process of finding out what you are going to do when you can't keep on doing what you're doing now'.

PURCHASES FOR EMPLOYEES

How far should the purchase department extend itself in making purchases for the private use of employees? Some companies encourage this; some prohibit it; most restrict its use to senior executives. It is a matter which company policy must regulate.

The typical employee purchase takes longer, and therefore costs more to handle, then the typical regular purchase. It is outside the usual routine, an isolated transaction rather than one of a series. The buyer will probably make a special effort to oblige a colleague who asks for something to be got for him wholesale. The accounting will probably be more complicated than for regular purchases.

However, most companies provide a whole range of fringe benefits for staff. These include subsidized sports facilities, subsidized canteens, legal assistance, help with tax problems, loans for house purchase, group life assurance, cash wedding presents, retirement pensions. Why should not a company add discount purchasing to the range if it chooses? But the purchasing time and processing associated paperwork ought to be charged to personnel or welfare rather than purchasing

Table 22.1 Some targets for purchasing research

RESEARCH AREA ONE: *FUTURE CHANGES WHICH COULD AFFECT OPERATIONS*

Market structures: monopoly, oligopoly; supplier development
Developments abroad and market trends
Legislation: likely trends
Shortages: where they are likely to develop
Prices: probable future trends for major purchases
Exchange rates: the future buying power of the £
New product development – purchasing engineering; relative cost of alternative
    materials and availability
Long-term forecasting and planning

RESEARCH AREA TWO: *PRESENT FACTS USEFUL IN BUYING DECISIONS*

Current legal position
Current position on taxes, tariffs, import licences and duties, etc.
Economics of procurement: make-or-buy studies, lease, rent or buy studies
Financial information about suppliers ⎫
Other information about suppliers ⎬ Source databank
Alternative sources   ⎭
Alternative materials
Cost analysis of purchased parts: target buy prices
Buying patterns: how many sources to use
Economic statistics and cost indexes

RESEARCH AREA THREE: *TECHNIQUES AND METHODS*

Developing more efficient purchasing and supply techniques
Reducing paperwork: cash-with-order, small order methods, etc.
Value analysis, materials analysis
Standardization and variety reduction
Computer development and applications: systems analysis
Capital expenditure appraisal: DCF, NPV, IRR, life-cycle costing
Contract price adjustment (CPA)
Technical vendor support
Supplier vendor support
Supplier appraisal techniques
Measurement of purchasing performance
Cost-effectiveness of purchasing research
Communications: management reports, relations with users, specifiers, suppliers

AREA FOUR: *PURCHASING SERVICES*

Purchasing library
Training, staff development
Preparation of departmental budget
Preparation of management reports
Expenditure audit and preparation of performance appraisals
Miscellaneous. A wide range of services from low level such as typing and filing,
    through expediting, to high level such as working with operations research or
    systems analysis is currently provided under this heading

overheads. And it may turn out that the cost of providing the service is more than it is worth. Making a small charge for each transaction usually simplifies the situation considerably.

DISPOSAL OF SCRAP AND SURPLUS

Every manufacturer, unwillingly but unavoidably, manufactures scrap. Getting this off the premises for what it will fetch is a chore usually undertaken by the purchase department. Scrap and byproduct can even in certain cases generate sufficient income to rank as an appreciable secondary source of revenue.

Apart from the scrap and byproduct which is inevitably produced by manufacturing processes, any buying operation that caters for changing requirements will gradually, through failure to foresee changes, or simply through buyers' blunders, accumulate a stock of goods surplus to requirements. Often the buyers are the best people to dispose of this stock, for the following reasons:

(1) Buyers know the sources from which the goods were acquired. Suppliers might be interested in buying back the goods, perhaps for recycling.
(2) Buyers know the prices they paid for goods and consequently have some notion of the resale value of what is being disposed of. For instance, the sales department of a diesel engine manufacturer would not be likely to know the market value of a lot of scrap bronze bushes, while the buyer who bought the bar stock they were made from should have a very good idea of what the bushes were worth.
(3) Potential customers for scrap and redundant items are not the same as potential customers for the end-product; rather, they are like other raw material customers. They are members of the markets in which the buyers operate, rather than the markets in which the sales department operates.

Regular bulk scrap, such as steel and iron turnings and borings in a metalworking plant, is usually sold on period contracts awarded quarterly or annually and providing for frequent collection. Non-recurring or unusually valuable scrap is sold to the highest bidder after asking a few dealers and merchants to inspect and quote. There are also specialist firms who are in business to buy and sell surplus industrial equipment such as bearings, fastenings, machinery and office equipment.

The realization that the earth's resources are finite has led to an increased interest in recycling and reclamation; scrap is the one raw material which is increasing in supply.

MATERIALS MANAGEMENT

The term materials management is often used to denote the broad range of activities concerned with procuring, moving, storing and handling materials from the supplier to the end of the production line, considered as a functional group to be managed as a whole.

The term *physical distribution management* is often used to denote the broad range of activities concerned with supplying, moving, storing and handling products from the end of the production line to the customer, considered as a functional group to be managed as a whole.

Some firms have both materials managers on the input side and physical distribution managers on the output side of their operations. Others make do with only one, who may well be responsible for some of the activities of the missing opposite number.

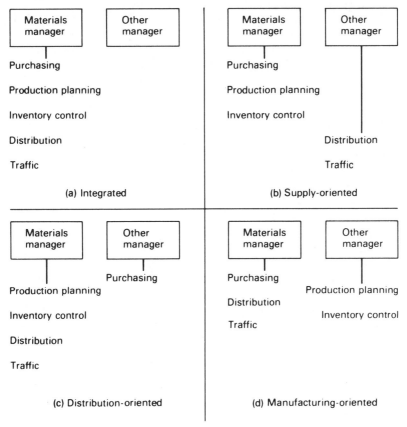

Fig. 22.2   Four types of materials management structure.
(Source: Baily and Farmer, 1982)

Figure 22.2 shows how some companies have reorganized for materials management by grouping together under a materials manager people carrying out various activities who were previously responsible to other managers.

Materials management is sometimes seen as the wave of the future, but it is not always appropriate. There may well be advantages in grouping together under a single head those people who plan, organize, control and actually implement the flow of material from source to user or consumer. But there may also be advantages in separating out the externally directed, market-oriented people who do the deals and sign the contracts. They may have entrepreneurial gifts and talents for commercial innovation that are different from the gifts and talents required in physical supply and distribution.

23

Control

Any system of control will:

(1) set standards of performance;
(2) measure deviations from standard;
(3) identify reasons for these deviations;
(4) take corrective action.

Budgetary control is a typical example of this. Other control devices such as savings reports and cost ratios are used in the management of purchasing and supply.

Planning and control are closely connected. Plans are sometimes made far ahead, as in corporate planning; although here as the saying goes, 'plans are nothing – planning is everything'.

CORPORATE PLANNING

Corporate planning is a systematic attempt to plan the future of a corporation as a whole. It is an attempt to foresee the threats and promises which the future holds in store, on various assumptions as to the form the future might take, and to devise strategies to ensure that the organization is advantageously placed whatever happens. The larger organizations have most need to look further ahead. Small organizations can adapt more quickly to change. It is also when the environment is changing rapidly that forward planning is needed; if the future is going to be much like the present, forward planning can still be useful but will carry a lower priority.

THE NEED FOR CONTROL

The measurement and control of the effectiveness and efficiency of an organization – how far it succeeds in achieving its objectives and how economically it uses its resources to do this – is of great interest to managers. It could be argued that the usefulness of purchasing to the organization it serves is to some extent a function of the authority vested in it and the confidence which management has in it. This is affected by the way its performance is controlled and measured, which partly depends on data that can only be supplied by the buying department.

It has been suggested that the job of the purchasing department could be summed up briefly as:

(1) to get the goods required; to ensure they appear on time, with as little fuss and inconvenience to those who require them as possible, and without spending too much time and money on getting them;
(2) and in getting the goods, to buy wisely and well.

Success or failure in achieving the first of these objectives is not too hard to assess, and a variety of measures are used. The second objective is very hard to assess, but it should not be ignored. Good buyers make good buys. If their performance is assessed on the basis of what it costs to employ them, how much they spend, how many requisitions they process and how many orders they place, and what proportion of goods arrive on time and are accepted by inspection, without taking note of their ability to make good buys, then something important is left out of the picture of buyer performance. What is not covered is an important aspect of the competent buyer's contribution to the company's survival and prosperity in competitive conditions.

SAVINGS REPORTS

Many organizations try to correct this by calling for savings reports. It has to be laid down what is, and what is not, a 'saving'. If three quotes come in, how much is saved by accepting the lowest? Nothing, of course, if we never intended to accept the highest. If the bottom drops out of the market, how much credit can the buyer claim for lower prices? If we are honest, none: we cannot take credit for the sun shining in summer.

Many people do not like savings reports, regarding them as easy to fake, likely to lead to price chiselling, and perhaps also as boastful. This came out in a cartoon: Jackson was hitting a huge gong marked 'Another Jackson Cost Reduction!', while one colleague told another: 'Jackson likes management recognition'.

Savings reports do not provide data useful in running the business. They are about past history. But they may help management to identify and encourage the specific contribution made by the buyer. They may also produce better performance. If you have to report on how well you have carried out an activity, you will probably try harder to do it well.

Often targets are set for cost reduction, and the savings report will then be related to targets set. Targets may be set by cost reduction committees including people from design, manufacturing, purchasing, accounting, etc.

Many manufacturers have a range of products each of which may start in a small way, building up later to big sales if it is successful, only to be superseded eventually. Purchase departments that buy parts and material for the whole portfolio of products could well be set savings targets of 2% of purchase expenditure every year. (Bear in mind that every year some products will sell in much larger quantities than in the year before, with obvious cost reduction opportunities.) Another savings target is four times what it costs to run the department: savings of £1 million a year, compared with last year, if the operating expenses in salaries etc. come to £250 000 a year. These targets (proposed by the head of purchasing at Westinghouse Electric in America) are quite realistic in some businesses, but would be extremely difficult to achieve in others.

Some firms negotiate savings targets individually with each buyer, on the basis of past performance and what is thought likely to happen in particular markets. One large company set an average savings target between 1–1.5% and 1.5% of spend: each buyer was expected to aim for savings of that order.

COST RATIOS

Cost ratios are used in controlling the operating costs of supply departments. These costs include wages and salaries, stationery and supplies, phone bills, telex and fax, travel and entertainment, and so on. It is always useful to compare this year's costs with last year's costs. The purpose of cost ratios is to relate operating cost to the work done.

The two ratios in common use are:

(1) the average cost of placing an order; and
(2) the average cost of spending £100.

The average cost of placing an order is obtained by adding up the total cost of operating the buying department for a year and dividing this by the number of orders placed in a year. Thus if it costs £500 000 to run the department for a year in which it places 50 000 orders, the average cost of placing an order is £10.

The average cost of spending £100 is obtained in a similar way, by relating operating cost to expenditure. Thus if it costs £500 000 to run the department for a year in which it spent £50 million, the cost of spending £100 is £1.

Both ratios have to be used with caution. Department operating costs will be low in departments that do not employ properly qualified buyers. But this does not mean that the buying is done efficiently. Most of it is done in other departments. So the figures for the buying department do not really tell us what our buying costs us in relation to expenditure. If we employ qualified buyers and pay them the rate for the job, buying department operating costs of course go up; but for the company as a whole, costs would well come down.

And in principle we could get a very favourable figure for the cost of spending £100, simply by paying twice as much as the normal price. That would halve our cost ratio. On the other hand, we could adopt more efficient procedures for handling small orders, so that we do not place so many orders. Result? Our cost per order goes up; so does our cost per £100 spent.

These examples show that cost ratios can give you useful indications that something has changed. They do not tell you if things have changed for the better or for the worse; you have to check up on that separately.

HEAD-COUNT

The number of people employed in the department – the 'head-count' – is also something to watch. It can be related to the total number of employees, but not very precisely. We cannot assume that if the labour force doubles, the number of people employed in purchasing should double too. Nor can we assume that if the amount of money we spend on purchases doubles, we should employ twice as many people to spend it.

In one firm 50% of the total sales revenue was spent by the 0.5% of employees in the purchasing department, but this cannot be used as a guideline. Economies of scale apply. One survey found that in small firms purchasing employees numbered over 1% of the labour force, and in large firms they were less than 0.5% of the labour force. But differences between industries were greater than differences between big firms and small firms. In military electronics, 6% of the workforce were in buying; in computer manufacturers, 5%; in cutlery, 0.2%.

VENDOR RATING

If the buying job is to arrange for goods of the right quality to arrive at the right time and at the right price, then a simple control on how well the job is done is to check if goods were of acceptable quality, and did arrive on time, and if the price was right. This has been considered in a previous chapter under the heading of vendor rating. Vendor rating is a way of measuring supplier performance, but since it is the buyer who selects the supplier and handles contacts with the supplier, it can also be used as a control on buyer performance.

GENERAL APPRAISALS

A good driver will be aware of what information is displayed on the instruments, but will also be conscious of the fact that a lot can go wrong with the car or the way it is driven which will not show up on the instruments. Managers of large departments, however little or much they require in the way of regular performance checks and ratios and trend charts, know that these indicators, useful as they may be, cannot tell the whole story.

Very occasionally it may be necessary to attempt a full qualitative appraisal of the whole structure and performance of a supply department. The only qualification for making such an appraisal is exceptionally good judgement based on thorough knowledge of supply work. Making the appraisal objectively – that is, so that several assessors would arrive independently at the same verdict – is not easy. Some of the many facets of departmental work which would have to be considered are: the state of long-term supplier relationships; the extent and quality of interdepartmental cooperation; whether the department is adequately staffed with people of sufficient ability who are adequately trained in the details of their work; whether duties are sensibly allocated and clearly defined; whether forms are well designed, systems and work routines efficient and sound and go with a swing, that is, flow instead of by turns slipping and sticking; whether the department is achieving the results required, making a real contribution to efficient operation of the company, and improving its performance over the years.

BUDGETARY CONTROL

Under budgetary control a manager within an undertaking is given financial limits within which he plans the activities under his command in accordance with the policy of the undertaking. Results are accounted for in such a way that continuous comparison is possible between actual and forecast results. If remedial action is necessary it can be taken at an early stage. Alternatively the budget objectives can be reviewed.

A budget is a financial and/or quantitative statement of the policy to be pursued during a defined period of time for the purpose of attaining a given objective. A manpower budget may be expressed in hours of work or number of men; an output budget may be expressed in product quantities, yards, or weight. Most budgets are in money terms because this is the simplest common unit. Despite this a budget is basically a programme of work to do and resources required to do it, even though it may be convenient to express it in money terms.

The budget is really a master-plan for the allotment of scarce resources. There seem always to be more things worth doing than money and other resources permit. Those in authority must decide between the claims of more hospitals or more schools, better roads or bigger universities, guns or butter. Their decisions are incorporated in the budgets that authorize expenditure by spending departments during the ensuing year.

Budget procedure in local authorities and in central government departments entails three successive stages. First, requirements for the period are estimated: how much money it wants to spend and what it wants to spend it on. Second, the appropriate body considers the budget proposal and either accepts or amends it. The Treasury, the Cabinet (and Parliament) are the appropriate body for central government; the Finance Committee and the Council are the appropriate body for local government. Third, the budget as approved becomes the department's authorization to spend, and it becomes possible to check that the department does work to its budget.

All three stages involve much detail and many decisions. For the first stage all the department's activities must be costed out in detail. New projects must be weighed carefully; they have to be approved in competition with similar requests from other departments; they will not be judged solely on whether they will increase the service offered by the department. After preparation, and often in the course of preparation, experts outside the department who are employed as the public's watchdogs will subject it to detailed scrutiny. The final scrutiny of expenditure and the initial work of preparing the budget have turned out to be valuable aids in managing a big department, quite apart from their original purpose of enabling those who pay the piper to have some say in calling the tune.

The business budget

But while government budgets normally begin with proposals to spend money, business budgets normally begin with proposals to earn money.

The plans of a trading organization are usually limited by demand – how much of its products it can sell and what the customer will pay for them – and the sales estimate is therefore the foundation of the whole budget. Profitability is a simple criterion for assessing alternative proposals, and it could be wished that some similar criterion could be applied to government budgets. Profitability is less simple than it may seem; it is long-term survival and prosperity of the organization rather than the maximum short-term profit which is the aim. Maximizing income and minimizing outgoings are quite inadequate as guiding rules. In fact for such things as research, employee welfare, publicity, management must allot resources by judgment in the same way as a government allots national resources to alternative claims.

The sales budget, then, is an estimate of what will be sold in the period, and of what it will cost to sell it – in salesmen's time and expenses, in advertising and other sales promotion activities, and so on. Next comes the production budget, a detailed plan for producing the things shown in the sales budget, with costs of materials, labour and overheads. Cash budgets and capital budgets will also be prepared, and there will be a budgeted net profit.

Events during the year may not fall out exactly as forecast in the plan, but the merit of an exact plan is that the unexpected, the exceptional, the operation which is not going to plan, can be identified.

Fixed budgets are only applicable to operations whose input and output can be tightly controlled. They are suitable for many government applications but few business applications. Even fixed budgets need some procedure such as supplementary estimates by which they can be adjusted if the occasion arises. But trading budgets must be flexible rather than fixed. An airline for instance made their budgets flexible by basing them on a standard variable cost per flight. They are adjusted to changing market conditions by leaving standing charges and overheads at the same gross figure as shown originally, but adjusting variable costs to the number of flights flown. Manufacturers' budgets need similar provision for adjusting to actual sales if these differ from the estimate.

Supply performance and standard costs

The materials budget is part of the production budget in a manufacturing firm. Often standard costs for materials are calculated for each product, and the monthly materials budget is worked out by multiplying the quantity of each product which is to be made in the month by the standard materials cost for that product. Each month actual expenditure is compared with the budget, and if there is a variance the purchase department may be called upon to explain it. It has been suggested that: 'Material price standards can be used to control purchasing and even influence the Purchase Department to introduce new materials so that standard prices can be obtained.' A material variance might appear in the budget statement like this:

Month: April Product: Widgets	Budget	Actual	Variance
Material consumption:	£52 500	£51 700	−£800

This is small enough. But there are two components in a material variance; either the quantity used may differ from the quantity budgeted, or the price paid may differ from the standard price. In this particular case we might find that the materials budget is based on a budgeted widget output of 100 000 with a standard usage of 0.2 kg (0.5 lb) of material per widget at a standard price of £1.05 per 0.5 kg. We might find that in April actual usage was 47 000 lb of material at an actual cost of £51 700. The material variance would then be made up of both a price variance and a usage variance.

The price variance is the difference between actual and standard price multiplied by actual usage. Since we have found that actual price multiplied by actual usage is £51 700; and since actual usage of 47 000 lb of standard price of £1.05 per lb comes to £49 350; the material price variance must be the difference between these figures, that is £2350.

The usage variance is the difference between actual and budgeted usage at standard price. In this case, actual usage is 47 000 lb and budgeted is 50 000 lb. The difference is 3000 lb, and at the standard cost of £1.05 per lb gives a usage variance of £3150.

In summary, we now have:

	£
material price variance	+2350
material usage variance	−3150
net materials variance	−800

These figures disclose a 5% price rise, which is large enough to be looked into. Its effect on material costs has been masked by a 6% drop in consumption of material, in itself a discrepancy big enough to call for investigation.

As a purchasing yardstick, the price variance is incomplete. But it does measure how the materials cost of the product compares with what at some time in the past it was expected to be; and this is a most important fact, since company planning, in particular of prices, is based on it.

The budget helps to focus purchasing effort where it will do most good. If steel bar contributes 40% of a product's factory cost, then a 10% price rise for steel adds 4% to product cost. Doing something about that matters far more than shaving another twopence a ream off typing copy paper cost. Costs can often be reduced even though prices are inflexible. In the case of steel we could ask if the right quality is being bought; could a different specification meet requirements and reduce costs; are there too many specifications, so that variety reduction could bring visible savings? Are the right sizes used and stocked? Is bright bar bought when cheaper black bar would do as well; or black bar where bright would more than save its extra cost through reductions in machining time? Can something be saved in price, terms, or carriage costs by switching from manufacturer to stockholder or vice versa? Since steel comes cheaper in large lots, are quantity discounts fully exploited? Can the buyer negotiate special terms of some kind? Can the product be modified to use less steel, or some other material be substituted?

By drawing the buyer's attention to price changes which affect product costs significantly, budget variances enable the major purchasing effort to be directed at the right targets. By showing management how material costs are varying from expectations, they provide a means of encouraging good buying performance. But they should be regarded as a means of encouraging good performance and not as a measure of the performance achieved. Otherwise buyers will get more credit than they deserve when prices are falling, and less than they have earned when prices are rising. In the latter case the variance may well remain unfavourable even though alert buyers have succeeded in keeping price rises below those suffered by competitors. On the other hand unfavourable variances may well be a sharp spur to alert and effective buying.

Departmental operating budgets cover departmental expenses such as salaries and wages, travelling expenses, postage and stationery, telephones and telex, furniture and equipment, etc. They provide an accounting check on the cost of operating the department, not of course on the performance given by the department.

MANAGEMENT BY OBJECTIVES

Management by objectives (MbO) has been a popular technique. In consultation and agreement with his manager, the buyer develops a plan of operation in which a number of specific tasks or objectives are defined and timetabled.

MbO has also been applied to stock control. In one example, 'the conceptual weaknesses, system deficiencies and operational shortcomings of the system of stock management were analysed to a limited extent using consultant specialists in operations research and data processing, and then a strong multidiscipline project team was established to investigate requirements and to devise the next-generation system'.

The targets or specific objectives agreed between the person concerned and his manager should be related to his normal work but should be something extra or something new or something which had been neglected in the past. Discussion with other departments will often be necessary since there are nearly always interface problems in supply improvement plans: for instance in changing specifications, materials, suppliers, procedures and paperwork, working capital requirements, etc.

These targets act as incentives and provide yardsticks against which performance can be measured objectively. Properly administered, MbO can provide the individual with an environment in which he can grow, achieve high job motivation, and monitor his own performance instead of being policed by cost ratios and supervisors.

MATERIALS DEPARTMENT AS A PROFIT CENTRE

The purchasing department as such does not make profits. Nor does the sales department or the manufacturing department. It is the organization as a whole that makes profits. But some qualification of this is needed in large organizations.

For measurement and motivational purposes it may be desirable to attribute portions of the profits earned to those departments primarily responsible for earning them. A multinational organization would normally treat each of its national 'departments' or subsidiaries in this way. A multiproduct organization may be organized in product divisions treated in this way, as quasi-firms with their own profit figures.

It is not possible to treat a buying department in this way, but supply departments and materials departments can be treated as quasi-wholesalers. The buying department often has considerable opportunities to reduce material costs. A net cost reduction constitutes a contribution to profits, other things being equal (Fig. 23.1); but it is misleading simply to equate cost reduction with profit increase. Buying personnel who favour the 'profitmaking' view of their work often stress the positive and creative side of it – seeking out new sources or new specifications, commercial innovation by new types of supply arrangement, etc. These factors can indeed lead to a more profitable operation.

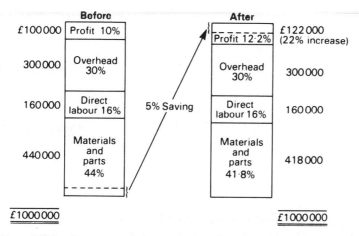

Fig. 23.1 Effect of cost reduction; a 5% saving on the cost of purchased parts and materials can increase profits by 22%.

When the buying department is combined with storage, stock control and transport, to form a materials department or supply department, it becomes possible to treat it as a quasi-firm which can earn profits or make losses, like a captive wholesaler. The purpose of doing this is to motivate supply people to behave like profit-minded businessmen instead of cost-minded service personnel.

(1) You are a student on industrial placement. You have been given the job of suggesting ways in which the performance of the purchasing and supply department could be measured. You will have to give a talk about this. Prepare a set of notes to be used as a short handout at the end of your talk.

(2) Explain the following terms: range planning, markup, markdown, OTB.

(3) You have been asked to give a talk to the local branch of a professional body under the title: 'Materials management, a challenge for the 1990s'. Indicate the content and structure of your talk.

(4) Discuss the concept of public accountability and its application to purchasing and supply in the public sector.

(5) It has been said that the chief executive of a large organization is personally responsible for corporate planning. To what extent can he delegate this responsibility? To what extent can purchasing and supply contribute to corporate planning?

(6) Explain the terms: physical supply, physical distribution, and materials management.

(7) Compare and contrast the work of the retail distribution buyer with that of the industrial purchasing officer.

(8) What does the job of a purchasing manager involve?

(9) A manufacturing organization with 5000 employees at two factories is in the process of adopting a materials management type organization structure, and preliminary studies have shown up considerable weaknesses in planning and control of stock. As a result of this it has been decided to appoint a stock control manager. This is an entirely new post. Write: (a) a description of the job

responsibilities and of the qualifications you consider desirable and/or essential; and (b) a short advertisement of the post to appear in the *Observer* and in professional journals.

(10) What qualifications and personal characteristics do you consider important for buyers working for large organizations, whether in the manufacturing, service or distribution industry?

(11)(a) Mr Green rents a greengrocers shop. The only asset he has in the business is his stock-in-trade which he turns over 50 times a year. What is his return on assets if his profit margin is 5% on selling price?

  (b) Mr Brown rents a furniture shop. His stock turn rate is five times a year. What profit margin would he require to get the same return on assets as Mr Green (on the same assumption: no other assets)?

  (c) Comment briefly on the advantages and disadvantages of stock turn rate as a performance measure.

(12) Define purchasing research, explain how it can be organized either on a full-time or a part-time basis, and list some important areas for investigation.

(13) Write a description of the duties and responsibilities of a stores manager in a medium-size manufacturing organization in which three production substores and one non-production substore are supplied from a main stores with 5000 stock items.

(14) What is a profit centre? In what circumstances is it possible for a supply department to be treated as a profit centre?

(15) In a large multiproduct multidivision manufacturing organization, to what extent is it: (a) a practical possibility, and (b) of economic advantage, to centralize purchasing?

(16) In a large multioutlet retail chain, to what extent is it: (a) a practical possibility, and (b) of economic advantage, to centralize buying?

References

Ammer, D. (1974) *Materials Management*, 3rd edition. Irwin, Homewood, Illinois.

Audit Commission (1984) *Reducing the Cost of Local Government Purchases*. HMSO, London.

Baily, P. (1983) *Purchasing Systems and Records*. Gower Publishing, Aldershot.

Baily, P. and Farmer, D. (1985) *Purchasing Principles and Management*. Pitman, London.

Bain, J. S. (1959) *Industrial Organisation*. Wiley, New York.

Banwell Report (1964) *The placing and management of contracts for building and civil engineering works*. HMSO, London.

Bauer, P. T. and Yamey, B. S. (1968) *Markets, Market Control and Market Reform*. Weidenfeld and Nicholson, London.

Bolton, J. F. (1972) *Small firms*, Cmnd 4811, HMSO, London.

Buckner, H. (1967) *How British Industry Buys*. Hutchinson, London.

Croell, R. C. (1977) Measuring purchasing effectiveness. *Journal of Purchasing and Materials Management*, **13** (1), 3–4.

Cyert, R. M. and March, J. G. (1963) *A Behavioral Theory of the Firm*. Prentice-Hall, Englewood Cliffs, New Jersey.

Dickie, H. F. (1951) ABC Analysis shoots for dollars not pennies. *Factory Management and Maintenance*, July.

Economist Intelligence Unit (1986) *Retail Business*, April, No. 338, London.

Edwards, R. S. and Townsend, H. (1958) *Business Enterprise, its Growth and Organization*. Macmillan, London.

Farmer, D. H. (1972) Source decision-making in the multinational company. *Journal of Purchasing*, **8** (1), 5–18.

Fearon, H. E. (1961) *Purchasing research in American business*, PhD thesis, Michigan State University.

Hansard, (1957), 10.7.57.

Heinritz, S. F. and Farrell, P. V. (1981) *Purchasing: Principles and applications*. Prentice-Hall, Englewood Cliffs, New Jersey.

JACLAP (1972) Report by the Joint Advisory Committee on Local Purchasing.

Kostishack, J. D. and South, J. C. (1973) The composition of industrial buyer performance. *Journal of Purchasing*, **9** (3), 50–63.

Kotler, P. and Balachandrian, V. (1975) Strategic remarketing, the preferred response to shortages and inflation. *Sloan Management Review*, August.

Kotler, P. and Levy, S. J. (1973) Buying is marketing too. *Journal of Marketing*, January.

Lauer, S. (1967) Westinghouse Plant X. In *Purchasing Problems* (eds Baily and Farmer) POA, London.

Lee, L. and Dobler, D. (1977) *Purchasing and Materials Management*, McGraw-Hill, New York.

Leenders, M. R. (1965) *Improving Purchasing Effectiveness through Supplier Development*, Harvard University Press, Cambridge, Mass.

Lewis, C. D. (1970) *Scientific Inventory Control*, Butterworth, London.

Little, D. and Barclay, I. (1986) Materials Management: the technologist's role in controlling materials costs. *Purchasing and Supply Management*, January.

Meopham, B. (1985) *ICE Conditions of Contract – a Commercial Manual*, Waterlow Publishers, London.

Moos, S. (1971) *Research Report 13*, Committee of Enquiry on Small Firms, HMSO, London.

Newman, R. G. (1985) Validation of Contract Compliance under Systems Contracting. *Journal of Purchasing and Materials Management*, Summer.

Porter, M. E. (1979) How competitive forces shape strategy. *Harvard Business Review*, March–April.

Rees, G. (1969) *St Michael, A History of Marks and Spencer*, Weidenfeld and Nicholson, London.

Rook, A. (1972) *Transfer Pricing*, British Institute of Management, London.

Rowe, D. and Alexander, I. (1968) *Selling Industrial Products*, Hutchinson, London.

Strauss, G. (1962) Tactics of lateral relationships: the purchasing agent. *Administrative Science Quarterly*, 7, Sept.

Tse, K. K. (1985) *Marks and Spencer*, Pergamon Press, Oxford.

Webster, F. E. and Wind, Y. (1972) *Organizational Buying Behavior*, Prentice-Hall, Englewood Cliffs, New Jersey.

Index